Some Comments from Readers

φ

I have found <u>Connection</u> a valuable resource for both my teaching and learning. Both newcomers and intermediate students of NVC find the explanations easily grasped and enticing. These exercises draw people into thoughtful consideration of nonviolent consciousness and how to apply this powerful way of thinking and speaking to their own lives. I have used many of the exercises in the NVC workshops that I teach and the practice groups I support. They are well received by teens and adults alike. Whether you are in an NVC practice group or doing individual study, I highly recommend this book for enlivening nonviolent thinking and communicating.

Peggy Smith, certified NVC trainer; co-founder of Maine NVC Network and principal writer for monthly newsletter, www. mainenvcnetwork.org; founder and principal trainer for Open Communications www.opencommunication.org

φ

The author clearly presents the basic concepts of Marshall Rosenberg's Nonviolent Communication, with examples and exercises that effectively facilitate understanding and skill development. She emphasizes throughout the importance of active self-care and self-awareness in order to improve our communication and conflict management. This text would serve well for group or individual study. I recommend it.

Jane P. Ives, Consultant and Reviewer of Resources for United Methodist Marriage and Family Ministries, www.marriagelovepower.net

φ

Here is an amazing resource filled with activities, which make learning NVC fun. <u>Connection</u> does not pull any punches. It is a wonderful self-learning tool for people of all ages. I heartily recommend it and have given it to friends.

Pan Vera, PSNCC certified NVC trainer, co -coordinator Vermont NVC, www.vermontnvc.org and workshop leader, www.compassionatecommunications.us/index.htm

φ

I loved this edition of <u>Connection: A Self-Care Approach to Conflict Management</u>. The first thing I noticed was the fifth component of the process: "An Attitude." As a long time practitioner and trainer I know that Intention, or Attitude, lies at the heart of successful communication. Bonnie captures this admirably. Another feature this book brings that is unique is the voice of the student. You see students struggling with concepts and incorporating these skills into their lives. I also enjoyed the change from Self Empathy to Self-Care. I see this as clearer communication and connection, especially with new students. All in all, a great revision to a very helpful tool.

Jim Hussey, Licensed Professional Counselor; Past Regional Coordinator for Oregon Network of Compassionate Communication; Moderator, http://groups.yahoo.com/group/nvccertificationcandidates

φ

Connection is a gentle introduction to NVC, with an abundance of inviting exercises to reinforce the communication skills the reader is learning. It sparkles with humor. The comfortable language was effective in engaging my college students and easily interested the adult learner, as well. I particularly enjoyed how the book encourages readers to become more aware of needs.

Jane Connor, Ph.D., certified NVC trainer; award-winning teacher of Compassionate Communication and of Multicultural Psychology, while at SUNY-Binghamton; co-author of Connecting Across Differences: A Guide to Compassionate, Nonviolent Communication

φ

I had high expectations for your book because of your use of self-care instead of the more abstract "self-empathy." My expectations were more than met. Your addition of "attitude" to the four steps is a crucial adjunct to the process. Then there is the accessibility of the material. It is so inviting that I am thinking of organizing a study group. You have done all the work.

Estill Putney, stone carver, dancer of Dances of Universal Peace, Blacksburg, Virginia

φ

What I loved about this book is that it allows for flaws and failures. While a regular communication book only provides the optimal solution, I have learned there are paths to be followed after making a mistake. If a conversation went badly, try again. If the solution that you and the other party came up with doesn't work out, don't lose heart, just start over. Look for problems before they arise, go and confront the person before they need to confront you, but if you don't, here's how to handle it when they complain.

Paul Duval, Norway

φ

Connection gave me words for where I am and where I want to go. I am launching myself into a world where people have honorable contributions to make, rather than stewing in a community where everyone else is "wrong" and "should be following rules." Looking over the Success Scripts, at the end of each chapter, I see my progression from perfectionism to more self-awareness, more self-acceptance. For me, this book has been life-changing. It has been exciting to see my kids starting to use these skills, too.

Emily Merrill, farmer, Burlington, Vermont

φ

While Bonnie anchors the book in a college setting, the group of professional adults we formed to teach ourselves NVC, found we could use the exercises with minimal revision. Bonnie captures the diversity of many voices as they learn, experiment with, and share Rosenberg's ideas. Building on his formula: "Observations, Feelings, Needs, Requests," Bonnie adds, "And an Attitude." An attitude of appreciation for self and others is a key component to success. To NVC, Bonnie adds years of counseling experiences to explain step by step how to get through conflict productively. I found it worth reading and re-reading.

Carolyn Stevens, real estate investor, Boston

CONNECTION

A Self-Care Approach to Conflict Management

Bonnie R. Fraser

Aging Tree Publishing Company
Scottsdale, Arizona

Aging Tree Publishing Company
601 N. Hayden Rd, #117
Scottsdale, Arizona 85257

ISBN 978-0-9836053-0-0

This book is based on the work of Marshall B. Rosenberg, PH.D., founder of the Center for Nonviolent Communication (www.cnvc.org) but reflects the understanding and opinions of the author and not necessarily that of Dr. Rosenberg or the Center for Nonviolent Communication. .

For additional information:

www.connectionselfcare.com

480-278-3702

e-mail author at bonnie@connectionselfcare.com

Thanks to my dear friend in Arizona, Patti Peplow, whose wisdom and editing abound in this book and in my life.

Thanks to my students who took on the challenge to become better communicators. This book would not exist without your courage to look at yourselves, make choices about your actions, and then share your experiences, successes, and struggles. You have taught me at least as much as I have taught you. I am deeply grateful for the honor of sharing in this part of your journey and for the gift you give to future readers of this book.

Contents in Brief

Contents in Detail

If you spend time on inner work,

many potential conflicts will
get settled before they begin

because your head is in
a different place.

Author's Dialogue with the Reader

What's this book about?

Connection: A Self-Care Approach to Conflict Management is about building connections with ourselves and with others—whether they have read this book or not. It teaches the reader, one step at a time, how to effectively resolve problems between people.

Marshall Rosenberg's Nonviolent Communication: A Language of Life inspired this book, which is based on his four steps for life-affirming communication. Actually, there is nothing new in either book. These skills have been around for centuries and are common in books on improving communication. Often we are only reminding you to apply skills you may already know.

Explain nonviolent communication. That is a weird combination of words.

We tend to define violence as a hurtful physical act, in which most of us seldom engage. Like Gandhi, Rosenberg reflects that outward violence always begins with a way of thinking and talking that alienates us from our inherent awareness of our connection with all beings. We often assign to others—or ourselves—criticism, blame, insults, and judgments that imply wrongness or badness or non-person-ness whenever we see actions that do not go along with our value system. This is the point where violence begins. Both Rosenberg's book and Connection explore ways to honor our values, notice our judgments, find more realistic ways to think and speak, and then to connect with others to resolve conflicts.

The common paradigm for conflict offers two options: we fight or we take flight; we win or we lose; we take power-over or we accept power-under. Many times we do not like either option, so we freeze and take no action. Connection invites us to construct a vibrant third option for thinking, acting, and communicating. It is to find solid footing in a place where we pay attention to both our needs and those of the other person. From that standpoint, we will likely be able to develop strategies that meet everyone's needs. As we gain in understanding of this viewpoint and in diligence in using it, we will find fewer conflicts emerging and will have more powerful skills in resolving them when they do arise.

Why is self-care so important?

One of the important features of this book is the emphasis on increasing our active self-care and our self-awareness as a starting point for communication and conflict management. If we are seriously committed to becoming familiar with our own needs and meeting them, we will clarify our values. Psychologists suggest that when we develop an internal frame of reference, we will have greater self-efficacy, self-confidence, and resilience. Because we are social beings, we cannot fully meet our needs until we take into consideration the needs of others. As we become more aware of the satisfaction of creating situations wherein everyone's needs are met, we are on the road to conflict management. Some call this enlightened self-interest.

You say Marshall Rosenberg's work inspired this book. Who is he?

If you are a college student, I especially hope you are asking, "Who is this Rosenberg guy? Does he have a degree? What life experience does he have to back up what he says? Who recommends him?" When you sit at your computer to check on all the authors of all your textbooks, go to www.cnvc.org to find out about the Center for Nonviolent Communication (CNVC).

Here are a few answers. Rosenberg earned a Ph.D. in clinical psychology from the University of Wisconsin in 1961, and he studied for a while with Carl Rogers, a noted humanist psychologist. Rosenberg developed a program to teach Nonviolent Communication. Some people call this NVC. Others prefer the term Compassionate Communication. NVC offers steps for moving into closer, more respectful relationships with others wherein we both are more likely to get our needs met and our conflicts resolved. He founded a center in 1984 to train people in these communication skills and conflict mediation. This center is currently located in Albuquerque, New Mexico.

Training in NVC is currently offered in 59 countries worldwide, by several hundred certified trainers who have learned this way of conflict resolution and by many others who have studied the NVC approach. Teams from CNVC have gone to trouble spots around the globe to build peaceful communication between previously warring parties. NVC is also taught in many schools, prisons, and businesses. Marshall Rosenberg lives in New Mexico, with his wife, Valentina.

How did this book come to be written?

Connection came out of my experience teaching Conflict Management at Champlain College in Burlington, Vermont. I saw the practical value of Nonviolent Communication and set out with my students to discover how this could be applied to our daily lives. I wanted to notice and celebrate the little steps one takes in learning any process. The students wrote weekly papers on their experiments. I found the questions, thoughts, and stories of my students so inspiring that I started collecting their quotes and getting their permission to share them with the class. Then I realized that other classes would find them inspiring too. With each semester, I collected more quotes, got more permissions, added more explanations and exercises, and repeatedly discussed the content with counseling and NVC friends. My retirement brought time to edit and produce this book.

As earlier versions of Connection were passed from person to person in ever-wider circles, I was gratified to hear how many had found it useful. Individuals and couples, wanting to work independently on their communication skills, reported finding this book easy to use and worth their time. Some people who are studying Nonviolent Communication have given Connection to a spouse or friend as a gentle introduction to ideas they themselves have found meaningful. This book has been used in several college classrooms by teachers exploring these ideas. I frequently return to Connection myself to remind myself of how I am aspiring to relate to others.

Many NVC practice groups have chosen to read and do the exercises in this book weekly before coming together to discuss and work on their improved ways of communicating. Some of these groups have used it in conjunction with Rosenberg's book, others as a follow-up book to study. Several church groups have formed study groups around this book—to strengthen both their internal communication and their efforts to bring more peace in the world. The authentic voices of the students have been a gift to many. I am eager to share them with you too.

Why did the students you've quoted take this class? Who were they?

My Conflict Management classes (Fall 2004 through Fall 2007) consisted of students majoring in Criminal Justice, Business, Social Work, Applied Psychology, and a smattering of other fields. A majority of the students were juniors and seniors and, for most, this was a required class. The students came from the U.S., France, Japan, Jordan, Nepal, Norway, and Sweden. Most were of traditional college age, but you will also notice the voices of older students. Some have chosen to use their real names; others have preferred a fictitious name. In a few instances different students have used the same name.

This book reflects thoughts of students at all levels of the process. Some arrived having already learned and incorporated many of these skills. Others have never noticed or thought about them. Here are some of the starting points for taking the class on conflict management:

Nicholas: *I hate feeling bad after the conflict. I find myself feeling bad about the things I said or the tone I used to defend myself. My problem with speaking before thinking has gotten me into a lot of trouble throughout my life. I have lost friendships, jobs and respect from many people. I want to learn to deal with conflict in a more mature manner.*

Abby: *I am so bad at settling fights, especially with my boyfriend. I need help with this.*

Tom: *Whenever I am subject to negative comments or criticism, I tend to get defensive almost automatically. I used to be a music major at my old college. My studies involved performing in front of various faculty members in order to be judged and criticized into the right direction. I wish I had learned to not take comments so personally, so I could have used the critiques of my performances in more positive ways. Instead of being caught up in inner anger at the teachers, I could have considered that maybe the teachers truly wanted me to improve my skills. Then I could have learned from their knowledge.*

Tiphaine: *I know I criticize people too much. I can be very aggressive against others to defend my opinions.*

Jay: *I can fly off the handle easily. It is hard for me to say, "Everything will be okay" when it isn't at the beginning. If I change the way I deal with conflict, my life will improve in that I will be a happier person. I will be able to have more free time with my mind to think about better ideas than how to escape the conflict at hand.*

Suzanne: *I am the biggest coward there is about conflict. I will do anything not to have to confront someone. My friends and family often get tired of hearing me complain about a person or a situation. They'll say, "Oh, my God, just say something about it or it will never change." I know they are right. I hope this class will help me find the courage to take better care of myself.*

Daphne: *I didn't want to take Public Speaking and I needed a replacement class. There is always conflict at hand, so it's good to know the correct way to deal with conflicts.*

Stevie: *I have lost relationships in my life due to the way I speak and deal with situations, and that is why I signed up for this class.*

Who are you and why did this project interest you?

Me? I have taught in high school and then college for many years. In 1983, I completed a Masters in Counseling from Arizona State University, and worked for twelve years as a family counselor. When I moved to Vermont in 1996, I gave my attention to teaching with Champlain College until I retired at the end of 2007. In 2003 someone gave me a copy of Rosenberg's book. It was electric to me, exactly what I was hungry for at the time. Learning NVC through books, trainings, and practice groups has been the most exciting, rewarding project I have undertaken for years.

Do you now do all this stuff yourself?

Absolutely not! One teaches what one needs to learn. I use many of these skills fairly consistently, but others only on good days. I like the outcome when I do remember to use them. Professional colleagues, friends, and students who had me before and after I started working with NVC have all observed my significant movement toward more authenticity and more patience with others. I still have many moments of sheer klutziness, as well as the regular joy of little successes which inspire my renewed commitment to keep working on getting better grounded in my own needs and developing stronger skills to share what is alive in me and to seek what is alive in others.

Students who complained about my assignment, a book, or a lesson, used to elicit from me a veneer of polite response covering an irritated attitude. Then I saw the honorable need under their complaint—usually a need for respect and a desire that their time be used in ways they see as helpful. It became easy for me to celebrate their hunger and respond in ways more likely to increase the learning that happens in our classroom. The students became more beautiful in my eyes and simultaneously more serious dialogue happened in the classroom. ¡Qué milagro!

A note on pronoun usage: In old English, the pronouns *you* and *they* were used to refer to both singular and plural numbers of people. If you think about it, you will notice that *you* is still used in that manner. I am reclaiming that usage for *they* to avoid the clunky use of *he or she*. I hope this works for you (you singular and you plural!)

A note on the NVC-ness of this book: Some Nonviolent Communication friends would like this book to be more "pure NVC." Other friends are grateful that I have included some additional info from my years of counseling and teaching. To all readers, I urge you to get Marshall Rosenberg's books for more depth in understanding of NVC. (See www.cnvc.org for more information.)

I am glad you are joining my students and me on this communication exploration. I am confident that you will experience improved relationships—personal and professional—by using these skills. I trust this will lead us, one person at a time, to a world where more people resolve conflict in a win-win manner. The need for connection between people has never been greater.

Bonnie R. Fraser, M.C.
See www.connectionselfcare.com for additional resources for teachers and students.

April 2012, 2nd edition. If your book has a blue back, don't bother buying this edition. Changes are mostly punctuation, a few word changes. If you are in a study group using both older blue back books and this edition (also blue back), please copy revised (re-arranged) pages 111-112 and share.

Part One: The Basic Tools = Four Steps and an Attitude

Amy: *I am excited to be a part of this class because I really, really want to make communication one of my strengths.*

So, here we are—about to begin the journey together. (I hope you did not skip the introductory dialogue with the reader. If you missed it, you might want to return and glance at the questions.)

So, if I read this book and do the exercises, will I become an expert in conflict management?

I wish I could say that becoming an expert was the work of one semester or one book. You could skim Connection, read the quotes, and find it mildly interesting or it could be exactly the challenge you are ready to really work on. You may just learn enough to lessen the number of arguments you have with your friends and to increase your ability to stay calm in stressful situations on the job. Or, you might find it so rewarding that you decide to keep on this path until you have walked yourself to a different vantage point on the ways you connect with others.

That depends on where you are on your life journey. When you consider the interactions you currently have with people, are you satisfied? Are you actively creating the kind of relationships you want? And even if you want to improve communication, is now the right time to address it?

Connection will teach you some ways to focus your attention on your own deep needs and those of people around you. This will likely shift the way you perceive yourself, others, and the world, even if you work on this in small increments. This book will ask you to study and take apart your patterns of communication, run some experiments, compare results, change the variables, and try again. This is a part of living an examined life. Any college hopes to inspire students to undertake this kind of examination with seriousness as young adults craft who they want to be in the world.

Many adults continue this practice of introspection, off and on, at all ages, as we consider ways to make more solid connections with ourselves and others in our lives.

On the other hand, this is your investigation. It will take some self-awareness, some willingness to be uncomfortable for a while, and some effort to disrupt habitual ways of thinking.

Perhaps your observations and experiences will tell you it is not worth your effort at this time. That is okay, too.

Only you know your next step.

What I can promise you is, that if you do the work, you can:

1. get yourself facing in a connecting direction.

2. take some concrete steps in that direction.

3. experience a few definite successes.

I glanced at this book. It looks like a lot of personal stuff. How is this going to help me in my professional life?

Most of these skills are ones that professional mediators and communication coaches teach to improve communication, to lessen the intensity of conflict, and to effectively resolve conflict when it arises at a personal level or a professional level. These skills are being used worldwide.

I believe that if you go through the book or the class and leave with only a workbook full of ideas, it will be of little value to you. Therefore, I will regularly offer you ways to practice these skills with the people currently in your life. If these communication skills work in real time, real life, for you, then you may choose to make them a part of your daily thinking and speech. That would be a more reliable place to carry them into the world than just talking about theoretical situations that may happen, filling the workbook with ink, and hoping you will remember to apply them.

I like the way I talk. I don't want to sound like a robot. People in the real world don't say, "Are you feeling x because you are needing y?"

I agree with you that your own language is important. <u>Please, do not read this book and then go about talking strangely.</u> I hope to invite you to a different way of viewing all interactions between people. This shift in perception is vital, and simple words are useful as one learns. The repeated words will help you focus on aspects you may be unaccustomed to looking for in yourself, and in conversations with others. When you get the ideas down, you will surely want to branch out into using a variety of words that work for you. Meanwhile, I will repeat the words frequently to help you remember. I will also use other words and images for the same ideas.

Sometimes it sounds like jargon to me, too. But I have personally met a number of people who have repositioned themselves in relation to others, who use nonviolent communication regularly, and they strike me as warm, alive, authentic individuals—not robotic at all. Hang in there!!

WHAT GOALS AND WHAT HUNGER DO YOU BRING TO WORKING ON YOUR CONFLICT RESOLUTION SKILLS AT THIS TIME?

WHAT ARE YOUR GOALS? What would you like to get out of this class / book?
HOW IMPORTANT ARE THESE GOALS TO YOU AT THIS TIME? What commitment, if any, are you willing to make to yourself to bring these goals into reality?

Ok. So if I decide this is important to me at this time, do you have suggestions on how I can proceed and not waste time?

We change slowly—learning to skateboard, to master a guitar, or to communicate more clearly. It will take time and patience to move from awkwardness to self-consciousness to integration of the new skills into a natural part of your repertoire. Here are some strategies I can identify:

- Get a vision of what you'd like to do

- Find the hunger / commitment to go for it

- Become aware of what you are doing now, your habitual patterns

- Let yourself become uncomfortable with what is

- Analyze past behavior with new insights

- Imagine speaking in a way that brings better connection with others

- Try this different way even though it will likely feel uncomfortable and phony for awhile

- Tolerate large amounts of klutziness in yourself and others

- Notice and celebrate little successes

- Laugh a lot

- And practice, practice, practice

Where did you get the model of four steps and an attitude?

This book is based on Marshall Rosenberg's Nonviolent Communication: A Language of Life. In the summer of 1943, when he was a child, his family moved to Detroit. Shortly after they arrived, an incident at a public park sparked race riots. More than forty people were killed. When he entered school that fall, he was beaten for being Jewish. This inspired his life quest—to understand what causes some people to disconnect while other people stay connected even in difficult situations, and how to help people return to their basic nature of connection and compassion.

Out of this concern, Rosenberg got a Ph.D. in Clinical Psychology and then worked and studied under noted psychologist, Carl Rogers. For years he has mediated with families, gangs, prisoners, businesses, and other organizations helping people find solutions to conflicts. Out of these experiences came a basic model on ways to increase understanding and cooperation, which is now called Nonviolent Communication or NVC. (Some call it Compassionate Communication.) In 1984, Rosenberg established the Center for Nonviolent Communication (www.cnvc.org) to teach the skills formally to others. Training workshops are offered today across the U.S. and in fifty-nine countries around the world. The Center has sent mediators to work in places of violent conflict within and between nations.

Part One of this workbook will introduce Rosenberg's four basic tools. Many students—old and young—find this outer practice much easier when they continually return to the underlying attitude that sustains this work. Therefore, I have added the section, entitled **And an Attitude**.

FOUR STEPS AND AN ATTITUDE

OBSERVATIONS
Increase the accuracy
of how you see, think, and talk about any situation.

FEELINGS
Notice the flow of your feelings
for additional information.

NEEDS
Identify which basic human needs
are most alive for you today.

Actively consider which basic needs
are priorities for others around you.

REQUESTS
Value yourself enough
to let others know what you would like.

Value others enough
to make requests, not demands.

AND AN ATTITUDE
Realize the deep satisfaction
of connecting with yourself and others.

Intentionally reach for that connection.

CHAPTER ONE

φ

Observations

Increase the accuracy of how you see, think, and talk about any situation.

> **Amber:** *I understand how much a judgment can alter my mindset. I can either think "that cashier was really rude" or "that cashier did not smile during the two minutes she cashed us out." Thinking she was rude makes me negative and irritated. When I focus on the facts, I remember I have no idea what is happening inside for her. Maybe she is having the worst day ever and she is doing the absolute best she can. If I do not label her as rude, I let it roll off my back instead of being rude myself.*

> **Marcus:** *In my whole life I have used evaluations in my communication. When I wanted my girlfriend to go to the gym and workout, and she didn't want to go, I just called her lazy. She might have known what I meant by lazy, but was she really lazy? She might have already done three workouts that week, and in that case turning down another would not make her lazy.*

In order to communicate effectively, the first fundamental skill is to sort out the difference between the facts and our personal opinion about the facts. This ability determines how accurately we can see what is really happening in our lives. Seeing reality apart from our evaluations is the beginning step toward making choices that will more fully meet our needs.

Our perceptions and our misperceptions inspire our responses to others. Sticking with the facts is vital in many professions. And making observations instead of judgments is an essential part in clear communication and in resolving conflict at all levels. Our judgments do hold useful information for us, but they must first be sorted out from our observations.

Here is a starting point for making clean observations. Imagine you have a camcorder with sound. What are you seeing and hearing that is catching your attention? This is your observation. If your observation is clear, it is likely that anyone involved would agree with it.

That sounds easy enough—what's the problem?

> **Meg:** *Observing without evaluation is being able to state a fact without throwing your own opinion in as well. This may sound easy, but—believe me—it's not. I have been trying real hard not to do these things this week. Every time I pass someone on the sidewalk, I quickly think something about them, even if I don't know them. Now the point of this is to see if the first thought in my head has any kind of label or insult or bad judgment. If it does, then I try to change it to a statement that doesn't.*

Let's consider for a moment some ways that observations slide into Faulty Language Usage and related common thinking errors. (Much of this info comes from the field of General Semantics.) First, according to scientists, we see, hear, touch, and smell, and from this acquire information about the world outside of ourselves. Some of us take in more information than others do, but all of us take in less information than is actually out there.

Joseph DeVito, a communications scholar, explains some of the ways we tend to distort what we do take in. His blog (cbdevito.blogspot) and his books on communication elaborate.

- Within four minutes at most, and usually within seconds, we habitually make judgments about other people. Clearly, these are over-simplistic and rely on few details.

- Our language and our culture make it easy to talk in extremes, black and white without shades of grey, while in real life the vast majority of people and ideas are in between. Our assigned extremes frequently include a moral judgment of rightness and wrongness.

- Finally, the categories and judgments so quickly assigned serve as rigid filters through which we perceive all future information. We have a strong tendency to discard any information that doesn't fit our models of reality. We create stories to explain behavior inconsistent with our models and attribute motives based on our initial judgments.

When we observe an event, mix in our judgments about it, and then store the whole thing under the category of FACTS, we do not have useful information. Computer programmers call these GIGO errors—garbage in, garbage out. We then view life through these stories instead of seeing living, moving, changing people who speak and act for a variety of reasons, in large part unrelated to us.

Some ask about hunches, intuitions, gut feelings. Perhaps these are a part of what scientists are referring to when they say there is more info out there than we perceive through our senses. If you find that these contain valuable info for you, do label them as POSSIBILITIES, not as FACTS.

Wait! Creating categories and making evaluations are just natural behavior. No?

We seem to be category-making creatures—either because of culture or biology. Apparently we seek the comfort of certainty. It is sometimes a stretch to stay open, wonder, and observe. Whether we want to or even can stop making categories, I leave to people more learned than I.

Faulty Language Usage is common in our society, but is culturally based and changeable. Until we notice, question, and make conscious decisions about our mental filing system, we tend to hold similar reality models with other people in our lives, just as we tend to wear similar clothes and live in similar houses. As we improve our filing system, we will become better at making observations.

I have a problem here. I do not have one word that summarizes stories, generalizations, labels, moralistic judgments, all or nothing thinking, and interpretations. These are all distortions of the facts. Nonviolent Communication (NVC) often uses the word "evaluation" for all of these. I will primarily follow that usage, and continue to remind you of other words for our distortions. I want to also call to your attention that the tools for recognizing or creating our value systems are much broader than our filters and evaluations. In upcoming chapters we will look a bit at value systems.

CHANGING OUR INTERPRETATIONS INTO OBSERVATIONS

Our inner dialogue about what is happening often focuses on making moralistic judgments, deciding who is right, wrong, smart, stupid, sketchy, or cool.
- Interpretation: *Benson is weird.*
- Observation: *Benson sings Russian opera as he walks across campus.*
- Observation: *Benson starts every day with yoga exercises.*
- Interpretation: *Jessica is awesome.*
- Observation: *Jessica took two hours to help me with my computer virus.*
- Observation: *Jessica starts every day with yoga exercises.*

We generalize from one or a few events and think that this behavior is ongoing across the board.
- Interpretation: *I am no good at math.*
- Observation: *I failed math in eighth grade and have avoided it ever since.*
- Observation: *I am getting low marks in my math class.*
- Observation: *I haven't yet figured out how to do the problems for the math homework.*

We exaggerate a bit to be more persuasive, to make a point.
- Interpretation: *Beth is always late.*
- Observation: *Last month Beth was late to five lessons, on time for two, and early once.*

We imagine we are mind readers and can tell the motives and thoughts of another person.
- Interpretation: *She thinks I am her mother, so she acts out all her mother issues on me.*
- Observation: *She walked away when I asked her if she had finished her homework.*
- Interpretation: *He is only polite to me because he wants to impress my sister.*
- Observation: *He always asks how I am doing. I do not know his reasons.*

If we want others to act in a certain way and they do not, we find the rule they have broken.
- Interpretation: *You need to act your age.*
- Observation: *The pizza boxes from your party last night are still on the coffee table.*
- Interpretation: *Friends go to each other's parties.*
- Observation: *I go to all of my friends' parties.*

We use variations of the verb *to be* about a person or group and imagine we have stated a fact.
- Interpretation: *Lonnie is a fool.*
- Observation: *Lonnie does things in class that seem foolish to me.*
- Interpretation: *Jordan is a great basketball player.*
- Observation: *Jordan made more baskets than anyone else on the team this season.*
- Interpretation: *Martians are lazy.*
- Observation: *The Martians who live near me mowed their lawn twice last summer.*

We use *it is* to imply that we are stating a fact and that everyone agrees with our opinion.
- Interpretation: *It is cold out.*
- Observation: *It is 50 degrees outside. (I plan to wear a jacket.)*
- Interpretation: *It is only fair that everyone share the cost equally.*
- Observation: *One strategy is to split the cost equally. (Does that fit for everyone?)*

IDENTIFYING INTERPRETATIONS: Anything you cannot hear or see on the camcorder is an interpretation. Note the part of the statement that is not observable; i.e. not an observation.

Evaluative Thoughts	Parts that are Interpretations / Evaluations
Jane is not cut out for school.	is not cut out for
Jake snarls at everyone.	snarls
Jill forgot to give me a ride because she is mad at me.	forgot, because she is mad at me
Jericho is a beautiful Vermont town.	
Jeepers is a real geek.	
Aunt Julie thinks she is hot stuff.	
It is time Joe started planning ahead.	
Japan produces the best video games.	
Johann S. Bach wrote inspiring music.	
Judd teaches juggling in order to make friends.	
Junior Lit bores all the students.	

CHANGING EVALUATIONS INTO OBSERVATIONS: Pick four evaluations from above. Make two sentences that could replace the evaluation with observations. Add details as needed.

Jane is not cut out for school →
Jane told me she hates reading. I notice that she already has more than the allowed absences in the English class we take together.

Hey! The juicy stuff is in the interpretation / evaluation column. The facts by themselves do not have much life or pizzazz. "I see you are wearing a blue shirt today." "True. I see you are in red." Sounds like a stupid conversation to me.

I hear you wanting more liveliness in your conversations. This would not be my idea of a lively conversation either. So hold the thought that the blue shirt is totally snazzy to you and hold your curiosity that your friend has been wearing only red shirts for weeks. We are not going to get rid of the life, just to express it in a different part of the sentence. Our opinions, feelings, and values are important—just not helpful when mixed into the observation.

Aren't evaluations useful—for example, in making decisions about who should be my friends?

> **Dorrie:** *My roommate considers himself "scene," wears tight pants and large plugs in his ears. He is my good friend, but when his girlfriend moved away, he started making new "scene" friends with lots of chains, tattoos, piercings and dyed hair in crazy styles. I have felt nervous around this new group, so I would just quickly say hello and leave.*
>
> *Recently they showed up and were waiting for my friend. I felt I had to entertain them. After talking together and really listening to them for an hour, I see them completely differently. They are interested in digital art, photography, and music and think their appearance is the best way to display their passion and to make a statement. I now hang out with them too, whenever they come over.*

We often use labels and categories as shortcuts. It does make life less complex. Unfortunately, these evaluations often distort our observations, giving us misleading information filed in our brain as FACTS. We easily forget and come to believe that our opinions are facts when indeed they are only stories we tell ourselves. When we let go of our distortions and moralistic judgments of people and try to see them without the habitual criticism and labels, we will have more accurate information.

Please remember that getting beyond evaluations does <u>not</u> mean that a person must now enjoy the company of all people. You are only asking yourself to observe with as few distortions as possible, to focus on seeing what is there. You will still want to apply your rational thought, values, intuition, awareness of current needs, and your sense of aliveness to decide in what way you wish to interact with this person. You can do this without negative judgments.

For example, you may decide you prefer to hang out with someone who shares your love of music. This does not make a non-musician bad or at fault, just not someone who interests you at the moment. Maybe you are currently hungry to increase your sensitivity to your own cultural biases, so you most want to spend time with people from other cultures. You may notice that you are frequently tense around someone, for no identifiable reason, and choose to withdraw at this time from them, without having to label them. You can even end a serious relationship without needing to blame and make wrong either person. If this seems like a strange idea to you, read on. We will return to this concept. Probably it will become clearer as we work with it.

You said something about observations being important in communication.

> **Brady:** *My parents went to Florida for a week and left my younger brother and sister home alone for the week. I went home on the weekend and found the house to be a disaster—dishes were piled high in the sink, things were left throughout the house and the carpets need vacuuming. I immediately thought how lazy my sister was.*
>
> *When we later got into a fight, I told her how I thought she was lazy. I came to find out that she had had to work after school the last couple nights and had to watch out for my little brother. She planned to clean on Sunday before my parents returned. I realized she was not lazy—she just had a lot to deal with.*
>
> **Kiki:** *One night just before elections, I got into a fight with someone who is a fierce Republican about Bush's tax cuts. I think the tax breaks are in place to aid the richest one percent of our country, so I decided this guy must be from a wealthy background. I got really angry with him. When I found out he came from a very poor family, but just believed that the "trickle down effect" would eventually help his family, I realized that I had not seen him as he really was nor talked to his concerns.*

Clear observations are a vital starting point in solving problems between two roommates, two partners, or two countries. A neutral ground is an observation of what is actually happening in clear enough terms that both sides can agree to the facts. If we have done well in focusing on actions, it is likely that anyone present (including the person described) will agree with our description.

This is an important first step before the two sides will be very productive in working together to find solutions that fully meet the needs of everyone involved. When we get tangled up in our judgments and enemy images of the other person, and do not take the time to get beyond them, our solutions will be limited and defensive instead of creative and inspired. Being judged generally does not inspire cooperation in meeting needs. Staying in our negative evaluations tends to weaken our current connections with people and to lessen the strength of our future connections—both in our hearts and in theirs. Positive evaluations create problems, too, but more subtle ones.

Sadly, in our culture, it is common to speak and think in a way that tends to increase difficulty between people, to separate them instead of encouraging connections. We focus on the differences. We exaggerate the differences. We make moralistic judgments about the differences—defining ourselves as right and others as wrong, when they see things in a way that is not the same as we see them or act in ways we would not. We have become quite fluent in using language in this way.

Rosenberg calls it a life-alienating language rather than a life-affirming language. It is life-alienating when we get angry and blameful at others for not giving us what we want, which increases the probability that they will distance further and still not give us what we want.

Reality is much broader and more fluid than evaluations. Therefore, a very empowering strategy in any situation is to notice when we use evaluations instead of observations and change our thoughts and language into more factual terms. This will strengthen both our communication with others and our ability to see clearly our own options.

Maybe making evaluations of others is not useful. What about making evaluations of my own actions? That keeps me in line.

We, of course, need to clarify our own values and needs, and then weigh our own actions to see if they are congruent with our needs and our values. It is difficult to find self-respect if we are doing behaviors that we would not respect when we see someone else doing the same thing. But, if by evaluations, you mean moralistic judgments involving blame or shame, I have concerns. I think we can notice our behaviors, decide whether we wish to continue them and make choices about our actions. Calling ourselves names is not a very effective way to inspire change.

Even the decision to "think positively about yourself" is an incident of Faulty Language Usage. Albert Ellis, a cognitive psychologist (www.rebtnetwork.org), challenges us to rethink such statements as, "I am a good person." Ellis explains you are never a good person—the term is not accurate. All of us are neither good nor bad. We all do some actions we find helpful and valuable. We all do some actions we find unfortunate and self-defeating. Pia Mellody, noted educator in the field of addictions and relationships (www.piamellody.com), defines us all as "mistake-making, precious human beings." Many find that a useful phrase for a description of every person. Also, you yesterday, you today, and you tomorrow are in some ways different.

Training ourselves to see, remember, and talk about actions, rather than labels—what a person does rather than who a person is—will move us closer to reality. Here is an exercise to stretch yourself a bit on this idea.

WHO AM I? (example)	
List one critical label you have given yourself	*airhead*
Describe two of your actions that inspired this criticism	*deleted an important e-mail before I answered it*
	went to the store to get milk and got other stuff I needed, but forgot the milk
Find one action you sometimes do that you like / admire when you do it	*work out at the gym some mornings*
Find one more action you sometimes do that you like / admire when you do it	*sometimes I can explain things in ways that help people understand a complex issue*

WHO AM I?	
List one critical label you have given yourself	
Describe two of your actions that inspired this criticism	
Find one action you sometimes do that you like / admire when you do it	
Find one more action you sometimes do that you like / admire when you do it	

How will this help me professionally?

> **Laurel:** *One of my values is a strong work ethic. I will do the job, even if there are tasks I don't particularly like, like filing. I work with someone who often leaves filing on her desk. I have called her "lazy." I could just have said, "We have different values." I recognize that my judgments are not the same as all our co-workers, so now I see her through different eyes. It is important not to waste time by getting stuck in these negative thoughts.*

> **Nesreen:** *Although I am not an expert at making observations, and I still have judgmental thoughts, my skills in this area have improved. Recently my manager switched the work schedule, scheduling me for work on a day I had requested off from two weeks ago. Instead of yelling and telling her she was responsible for the mistake, I calmly stated observations I had made. "I put in a request form for having a day off on this day. You and I discussed having the day off and you told me it was taken care of. I checked the schedule and I am working. I am a little confused as to why I was put on the schedule." By stating the facts in a manner that were objective and non-blaming, I was better able to discuss the situation with my manager and to resolve the problem.*

> **Sharaz:** *If police officers put labels on people that they apprehend on a day-to-day basis, they will be sued. As college graduates, we also need to treat people from neutral grounds.*

The Criminal Justice students shared with us the importance in their job of writing all reports in factual terms. They are reminded to ask the questions—who, what, where, why, when, and how. The police gather as many facts as possible that relate to the circumstances. This allows the judge and possibly a jury to later decide whether the action breaks the law.

Being "professional" means carefully excluding prejudice and judgments from our statements. Probably such thoughts will come into our head. Our task is to stay aware enough to stop, breathe, and choose to express our thoughts in non-judgmental terms. If we practice this often, we might notice that judgmental thoughts will come to us less frequently. One useful starting point is listening to our own words—both those spoken and those in our heads. Finding a neutral description helps us to increase our accuracy in perceiving situations. When we want to share this information with others, neutral words will be much easier for them to hear than evaluative words.

This sounds important. Do you do this stuff all the time?

No. I do not remember to. I return to doing it regularly. Forget. Remember. Forget. Remember.

Here is one General Semantics thinking error that still trips me up. They say, "The map is not the territory." "The menu is not the meal." I forget that just because I or someone else attaches a description to a person, does not mean it is accurate. Someone says, "I am a good communicator," and I get all excited. "Oh, lovely, I like hanging out with people who are good communicators." Then I may discover that what they mean by those words and what I mean are quite different.

Over time I have become much better in noticing and letting go of evaluations sooner. I am quicker to pick up my journal to explore what is happening inside. I fairly consistently value trying to find the reality of a situation over any of my stories about it. I can see concrete improvements.

⬇ ⬇ ⬇ DELVING DEEPER: EVALUATIONS & OBSERVATIONS ⬇ ⬇ ⬇

Here are five suggestions to help you capture and examine your evaluations. An exercise follows.

1. Notice your thinking more often.
Listen to your inner dialogue. Allow yourself some chunks of alone time with nothing happening. Take time to catch up with yourself the way you would with a friend you haven't seen for awhile. When you feel tense, let it remind you to sit with yourself for a while. Invite an awareness of whatever language seems to describe this particular occurrence of tension. Journaling, meditation, and talking openly with a listening friend will all help you slow down and become more aware of exactly what is going on in your head.

2. Stretch toward accepting all parts of your thinking.
Just sit with this listening to yourself, without judging or trying to change your thinking. This will sometimes include thoughts that you might be embarrassed to speak in public, such as racist or sexist comments, prejudiced insults, self-doubts, and other rantings and ravings. Congratulate yourself on hearing this hard-to-hear stuff. This brings light to the ways we are distorting, a first step in getting it untangled and making choices. It is also a gateway to finding our needs!

Judging yourself for having any of these thoughts will shut down and freeze the process. The more you can accept your many inner voices, the more accurately you will hear your thoughts. Learning to see yourself with honesty and with compassion is a solid start on your journey toward more accuracy in your observations, more aliveness, and more compassion for both yourself and others. The evaluations in your head cause the most problems to you when you do not know they are there. As you become familiar with them, you lessen their power to distort your thinking.

3. Find some evaluations. Insert the words "I am telling myself that" before each evaluation.
This will loosen your assumptions that the content of your evaluations is true. (Other phrases that can help you back off are: "It seems to me that . . ." or "One way of interpreting this is that. . .")

- *"I always mess up."* → *"I am telling myself that I always mess up."*
- *"That person is a total dip."* → *"I am telling myself that that person is a total dip."*
- *"Junior Lit is boring."* → *"I am telling myself that Junior Lit is boring."*

4. <u>After</u> you have gotten a clear hold on any evaluations you are thinking, change them to observations. (Your evaluations have useful information for you—we will return to them.)
Don't forget to do this step, but don't rush into it as your first step if you want to improve your ability to spontaneously make observations more often.

- *"I always mess up."* → *"I ordered chocolate cake instead of lemon cake last night."*
- *"That person is a total dip."* → *"He told Pat the wrong time for the committee meeting."*
- *"Junior Lit is boring."* → *"The class has been reading Faulkner. I don't like him."*

5. Create silence in your environment and then silence inside your head.
One unusual suggestion offered by the General Semantics folks is to take time for non-word experiences in your life. Cultivating times of silence outside and inside can loosen the grip of distorted thinking, and help you better sense reality. Meditation is a useful tool to clear your head.

PLAYING WITH YOUR EVALUATIONS: Consult the last page for details on each step.
Capture three of your own original evaluative thoughts or make up three evaluations.
a. *I always mess up.*
b.
c.
d.
Rewrite the original evaluation with the words "I am telling myself" in front of each.
a. *I am telling myself that I always mess up.*
b.
c.
d.
Describe the triggering event without any evaluations.
a. *I ordered chocolate cake instead of lemon cake last night.*
b.
c.
d.

**Reality
is much broader and more fluid
than evaluations.**

Success Script—Observations

Directions for Writing a Success Script: Practice the skills discussed in this chapter until you successfully use one new skill in some area of your life. As part of noticing and celebrating your learning, sit down and record the story of your success. Give it a title and a date. Of course, you could write more than one story about each skill and you will also see each chapter includes more than one skill. I invite you to fill your journal with many more stories. (This exercise came from Frances Delahanty, Ph.D., a college teacher who has written a book of Success Scripts.)

Title: On Earning Tips at Work
Name: Matt
Date: 9/14/06

Background: I work at a sandwich shop in Williston. This job actually requires a lot of work. We bake the rolls, prepare the meat, veggies, and bread each morning. Every sandwich is made to order. This hard work that is put into every sandwich makes me and my co-workers believe we should receive a tip for our efforts.

When co-workers and I do not receive a tip, I get annoyed. I think this person is cheap or a jerk. I always question why someone can't give another dollar to hard working college kids. The tips will buy my dinner that night. I feel angry at non-tippers. This also works in reverse. If someone leaves me a dollar or two in the tip jar, I become very appreciative. I think this is a better person. I put more meat on their sandwich. I also go out of my way to make their experience at the sandwich shop better, by creating a conversation or bringing sandwiches to the table with a smile.

New Behavior: Since learning about making observations instead of evaluations, I have taken a completely different approach to this situation. The first thing I do is to not judge the person because of what they leave me in the tip jar. Instead I think of reasons why they may have acted the way they did. Maybe they thought the sandwich was too expensive in the first place, or maybe they do not have any extra money themselves. Maybe they did not even see the tip jar. I mean, the list is endless. I have also been trying to treat everyone on the same level. I now make the sandwiches the same even whether this person usually leaves nothing or a $5 tip. I try not to think of them as "good" or "bad."

Why I Consider This a Success: My anger level at work has gone way down. I actually enjoy my days there. I also notice I get more pleasure out of getting a tip. I also like that I am being more fair to the customers in the quality of service they receive. And, I have been getting more tips, since I changed my attitude!!

Intention for the Future: I would like to continue to treat all people with respect, and not to label someone one way, just because of one action they took. This is hard to do because I have been taught to evaluate people instantly instead of observing. I plan to continue working on this technique.

Success Script—Observations

Title: Unfair Evaluations
Name: James
Date: 1/31/07

Background: *I have recently started a new job at [a nearby] Police Department and retain the title of Code Enforcement Officer. I wear a badge and a uniform just like the other officers but do not have nearly the amount of authority. I would say for the first week or two, it went to my head, but now I learned to accept what powers I have, i.e. writing parking tickets and towing cars, and try to have fun with it.*

After talking about evaluations in class I began to notice how many I make during a five hour shift. I was making them based on what kind of cars I was ticketing, for example, if I were to write a ticket on a BMW, I might evaluate the situation as "Oh, this guy drives a BMW—he doesn't care about a measly 20 dollar parking ticket." Another example is if a car is eligible to be towed I would look at how many unpaid parking tickets this person had, and think with sarcasm, "Wow, this person is a real genius for parking this many times illegally." For awhile I would write parking tickets left and right, 20 dollars here, 20 dollars there, and making the same evaluation that the driver of this car MUST be incompetent not to notice the signs and time limits.

New Behavior: *After seeing a person come to their car after I had just written a 35 dollar ticket on it, I saw tears coming down their face as if they were crying prior to receiving the ticket. It struck me that parking violators do have hearts and feelings. After that I tried to keep my evaluations to a minimum, and keep in mind that maybe people were parked here longer than the limit but they had important issues to tend to, maybe they didn't see the signs, maybe they are not from around this area and do not know about parking enforcement here. After talking about evaluations and observations in class, I began to realize how ignorant and unprofessional I was being, especially for a job of this nature.*

Why I Consider This a Success: *I consider this a success because my overall mood during a shift is positive and if for some reason I start to make evaluations based on how someone parked their car, I try to stay neutral and optimistic. I will continue to give tickets when violations occur, but I don't need to be a grouch about it. By keeping myself in a better mood it is much easier to handle confrontations when they arise unexpectedly. I want to handle myself in a respectable and professional manner, so issues can be settled peacefully and quickly.*

Intention for the Future: *I intend to keep this mindset forever because it has made me a better person and it also makes my job easier, safer, and more enjoyable. It is not something I can perfect, so I will always have to keep myself in check and aware of how I am reacting to a situation.*

Success Script—Observations

(Here is the space for your story. See directions on page 19.)

Title:
Date:

Optional: create a Mind Map above

Start with an idea from this chapter that caught your attention and place it in writing on the page. Play with it. You might want to use highliters or colored pens. Think of how this idea connects to some other idea(s) that you already find true. Be creative and show this connection visually with sketches, stick figures, patterns, etc. Consider one scene from a movie or line from a song that connects to this idea. Add this to your mind map. Identify situations in which this idea would be useful to apply and show that. Add any other connections that work for you to your map. Doodle a bit. For additional ideas, Google mind mapping, concept mapping, or visual thinking.

CHAPTER TWO

φ

Feelings

Notice the flow of your feelings for additional information.

Tucker: *In our class, every week you asked us to share with our neighbor or the class the highs and lows of our week, or what is alive for us. At first, I thought this exercise took too long and I could not see the meaning or importance. My outlook was that we were here to learn and not talk about ourselves—more or less like most classes. As time went on, this exercise became more meaningful to me. Taking a second to recognize what is alive for one, allows one to bring attention and to make choices that can fulfill oneself better.*

One class I talked about the great time I had at the Buddy Guy concert. I recognized how much I liked the concert and how it made me feel alive. As a result of recognizing this, I have made plans to go to two more shows this summer. Without paying attention to my experience of what live music does for me, I could have just said, "That was fun." and not gone to another concert for years. The exercise has made me more aware of my feelings and needs and more present to myself.

Some people let their feelings dictate their actions. Others prefer to have as little as possible to do with feelings. Neither approach is useful in acquiring self-management and solid communication skills. It is essential to notice our feelings because they invite us to pay attention to how our lives are going. Noticing our feelings is like keeping an eye on the speedometer or gas gauge.

Rosenberg reflects that when we feel stress / emotional pain, it is common in our culture to blame someone. NVC teaches the importance of connecting our pain to awareness of our needs instead. When resolving a conflict, it is vital to apply this awareness so that we can attach pain to needs rather than blame. When a person is having strong feelings, they will seldom be able to address the content of a conflict. In summary, to understand ourselves or others and to communicate effectively, we must include an awareness of feelings. We will look later at when and if we choose to share our feelings with others or to act in some way on them.

What are feelings?

Poets, psychologists, artists, religious leaders, and philosophers all attempt to define feelings and to prescribe how we might best react to them. Consequently, there are many definitions, and often not much agreement. Here are some a few observations about feelings. A feeling is an experience, which is inherently not definable. They are short-lived and will tend to pass within minutes if not reinforced by thoughts. Feelings are biochemical / neurological responses to stimuli. We aren't always cognitively aware of either the stimuli or the feelings. Feelings are highly responsive to the filtering system in our heads.

NVC calls feelings body sensations which are indicative of needs being met or not being met.

When our need for nourishment is not met, our bodies send us the feeling of hunger to let us know this need is not being met. If a basic human need is being met or appears it will be met, an energy is generated (feelings we enjoy) and if our needs are not being met, a different energy is generated (feelings we do not enjoy). Additionally, if we meet our needs such as sleep, recreation, exercise, friends, healthy food, and autonomy, we will be calmer and less easily distressed.

Psychologist Eugene Gendlin describes step by step how to listen to what he calls the body's wisdom. Paying attention to this body sense gives us information about our lives that he says does not arrive through our logical thought nor through our feelings. He says it is like the nagging uneasy sense that one is forgetting something before walking out the door. Gendlin defines this as more in the hunch, intuition category, perhaps even what some call "the gestalt of a situation."

I suspect people often gather data in this way and label this information "feelings." It might be related to "the sense of being in the flow" that one sometimes has while playing a sport or an instrument or even while teaching. Have you had that experience?

What is the difference between feelings and thoughts?

> **Jenny:** *In the first class this week, we discussed the differences between feelings and thoughts. I think I have an advantage over American students in understanding this because in Sweden, one might say, "I think my mom is angry at me" but not "I feel my mom is angry." Because my English is not so good (here I am comparing my English with other people), when I translate a Swedish sentence into English, I find that I say "I think" when an American might say "I feel."*

> **Sarah:** *Softened thought makes sense to me. If my mother asks me how something tastes when she is cooking, I'll respond by saying "I feel like it could use more salt" instead of saying "I think it could use more salt." I was trying to find a nice way of telling my mother without even realizing it.*

> **Phil:** *"I feel it is not right to play music all night" is a softened thought and a moralistic judgment, not a feeling.*

Our commonly used language interchanges feelings and thoughts regularly, which can cause problems. Complications come when we want to direct our attention to feelings so we can get some useful information. This is why it is so important to sort out our thoughts from our feelings. One way we use "I feel" is as a softened thought.

Consider the range of statements on the next page: from Arthur talking like he is the sole owner of absolute truth to Felix being more open to the opinions of others. Yes, you are right—it is valuable in communication to always speak in a way that leaves room for different opinions. However, these are all forms of thoughts and are not feelings in the way we are defining feelings as body sensations. The following examples are for the purpose of helping you notice the difference between hard thoughts and softened thoughts and to recognize that softened thoughts are something different from feelings, even if the wording says, "I feel . . ."

THINKING STATEMENTS WOULD BE:

Arthur: *The Florida Marlins are the best.*

Bart: *I know the Atlanta Braves are the best.*

Clyde: *I think the Minnesota Twins are the best.*

Don: *I believe the Detroit Tigers are the best.*

Elliot: *IMHO, the Oakland A's are the best.* [IMHO = in my humble opinion, in Internet slang]

Felix: *I feel the Toronto Blue Jays are the best.*

FEELING STATEMENTS WOULD BE:

Gabe: *I am so psyched that the San Diego Padres are winning.*

Harry: *I would hate to lose my bet that the Cincinnati Reds will win.*

Ira: *When I consider the Texas Rangers' record and my hunger for them to win, I am discouraged.*

Jeremiah: *When my roommate is rooting for the Yankees, I am irritated. I want him to join me in cheering for a Red Sox win.*

Ken: *When my roommate is rooting for the Red Sox, I am pleased because I like the Yankees, and I like having someone to argue with and insult. I, of course, will never tell him that.*

THINKING STATEMENTS WOULD BE:

I feel that	*I feel that my friend is right.*
I feel I	*I feel I should be given the award.*
I feel you	*I feel you are out of line to keep bothering me.*
I feel he/she/they	*I feel he should grow up.*
I feel it	*I feel it is in everyone's best interest to buy season passes.*

FEELING STATEMENTS (INSPIRED BY THE ABOVE STATEMENTS) MIGHT BE:

I feel confident. I am confident. I feel sad. I am sad. I am elated.

I feel concerned. I'm concerned. I'm impatient.

I like my space in the mornings. I am tired of hearing about this matter.

I feel disappointed. I am disappointed. I'm frustrated. I am worried.

I feel excited when I think of skiing with you guys. I enjoy skiing with you guys.

Notice that the phrase *I feel* can be usually be replaced by *I am* in a feeling statement!

SOME UNIVERSAL FEELINGS (This list is also at the back of the book.)

Feelings When Needs are Met

Affectionate	Ardent
Alert	Animated
Alive	Amazed
Appreciative	Carefree
Creative	Compassionate
Confident	Comfortable
Curious	Dazzled
Delighted	Eager
Engrossed	Energetic
Enchanted	Enthusiastic
Encouraged	Engaged
Excited	Exuberant
Friendly	Fascinated
Grateful	Giddy
Intrigued	Interested
Joyful	Jubilant
Peaceful	Passionate
Proud	Safe
Rested	Surprised
Stimulated	Tender
Thankful	Touched
Vibrant	Warm

Feelings When Needs are Unmet

Apprehensive	Afraid
Aggravated	Agitated
Alarmed	Annoyed
Anxious	Ashamed
Bitter	Burnt out
Blue	Baffled
Brokenhearted	Bored
Confused	Cranky
Crabby	Cross
Disturbed	Distressed
Depressed	Detached
Disappointed	Devastated
Disgusted	Despair
Embarrassed	Enraged
Exhausted	Fragile
Furious	Hurt
Heartbroken	Lazy
Lonely	Miserable
Nervous	Overwhelmed
Reluctant	Regretful
Sorry	Stressed out
Worried	Yearning

Your additional words:

EVALUATIVE WORDS FREQUENTLY CONFUSED WITH FEELINGS

These words imply that someone is doing something to us, and generally connote criticism. They are a combination of underlying feelings (such as irritated, confused, frightened, frustrated, hurt, alarmed, defiant, bewildered, sad, embarrassed, or hostile) plus a judgment of the other person's actions, a blaming of them for causing these feelings in us.

(Depending on your interpretation, some words from the feelings list on the last page may belong on this one or some words on this page may better fit on the last page.)

Abandoned	Abused	(Not) accepted	Attacked
Belittled	Betrayed	Blamed	Bullied
Boxed in	Cheated	Coerced	Cornered
Criticized	Discounted	Distrusted	Dumped on
Harassed	Hassled	Ignored	Insulted
Intimidated	Invalidated	Invisible	Isolated
Left out	Let down	Manipulated	Mistrusted
Misunderstood	Neglected	Overpowered	Patronized
Pressured	Provoked	Put down	Rejected
Ripped off	Smothered	Suffocated	Taken for granted
Threatened	Trampled	Unappreciated	Unfaired-against
Unheard	Unloved	Unseen	Unsupported
Unwanted	Used	Violated	Wronged

Implied Judgment	Feeling	Clearer Expressions of Feelings (plus some observations and requests)
(abandoned) *You abandoned me.*	sad lonely	*When I did not receive a phone call, I was sad and lonely.*
(bullied) *You bullied me.*	weak stressed	*When I could not find a way to get you to agree that I could stay home from the concert, I was stressed.*
(unloved) *You do not love me.*	frightened	*When you did not bring me a birthday gift, I felt frightened. (I told myself you do not love me. I would really like to hear from you what that meant to you.)*
(misunderstood) *You do not understand me.*	frustrated	*I am frustrated. (It appears to me that your response does not answer my concern. I do not know where the confusion lies. Can we start this conversation again?)*

Positive evaluations are another set of words that we might call feelings, but they are also a mix of what I perceive you doing and my feeling reaction. These seem to cause much less trouble in creating connections. These include words like affirmed, appreciated, cherished, encouraged, supported, and valued.

NOTICING FEELINGS: Follow "I feel" immediately with a feeling word. Do this three or four times a day, until the boxes are filled. (See feeling list on page 26 for inspiration.)	
I feel	I feel
I feel	I feel
I feel	I feel
I feel	I feel
I feel	I feel
I feel	I feel
I feel	I feel
I feel	I feel
I feel	I feel
I feel	I feel
I feel	I feel

SEPARATING THOUGHTS AND FEELINGS: Consider any recent conversation and try to capture separately some thoughts and feelings you had.	
I think	I feel
I think	I feel
I think	I feel
I think	I feel
I think	I feel

Do you have choices about what you are feeling?

> **Laurie:** *My mother has always told me that we generate our own feelings. However, it is always easier to blame someone for our feelings. I am in conflict with my mother right now. I want to blame her for the way I am feeling. It was her words and actions that prompted the feelings that I am having. I have trouble accepting responsibility. What about her responsibility?*

This is a hard question, which people often ask! Here are some clues, although not a final answer. NVC defines feelings as an indicator of needs met or unmet. If we investigate which needs are not met, we can certainly focus on better meeting our needs and thus creating more satisfying feelings, even at the most basic level of getting enough sleep, social interaction, and achieving our goals.

Cognitive psychologists say that feelings are responses to thoughts and past experiences, our interpretations about what is happening, and guesses about what will happen. They reflect that any stimulus goes through a thinking filter (the distortions we looked at in the first chapter.) We can make some choices about what we feel by noticing our filters—the stories in our heads that lead us to react compulsively instead of acting with choice. With an understanding of our own stories, we can decide which stories are useful to us and which ones we want to challenge. When we become aware of our filters, we can reclaim our own power more easily than if we believe others control all of our feelings. (I find it is useful to change my inner dialogue from "They made me feel" to "They invited me to feel . . . and I have not yet figured out how to decline their invitation.")

We struggled as a class to find our own way to explain it. I brought a box of matches to class and gave two students matches with heads on and two students matches with the heads cut off. Then I took the matchbox and dragged it across the matches, one by one. Of course, those with heads lit up and those without heads did not—like dynamite responding to a spark. The class decided a more helpful description of the role others play in our feelings, is to say, "The other person offers the stimulus, but unless we have a match-head, a stash of volatile material inside, there is no fire."

Everyone has accumulated over a lifetime a stash of inner dynamite. Some people have bigger stashes than others. Ways to detonate our specific triggers and to strengthen our peaceful states of mind are in coming chapters. Here is Eric's reflection on a judgment that popped out of his mouth. A few weeks later he found a possible source of inspiration for that unplanned insult.

> **Eric:** *I still feel kinda bad because I was in a less than good mood and when you asked in class last week what kind of professions use labels and judgments. I saw it as an opportunity to demean the future cops in the room, by stating their profession is nothing but labels and judgments. While I still believe my own statement, I probably should have kept that to myself.*

> **Eric** (later): *The homework activity was an interesting way for us to look at something that pissed us off and to see where the other person was possibly coming from. I chose something that an officer said to me a few months back that really made me mad. When I was all done with it and looking back over it, surprisingly I was not as mad over it. When we are able to do this it allows for a greater understanding. It made me see that I was being irrational with my thoughts towards the cop because really he was only doing his job and more or less speaking the truth.*

↓ ↓ ↓ DELVING DEEPER: NOTICING FEELINGS ↓ ↓ ↓

Recall that the first chapter invited you to notice your thoughts. This is an expanded invitation to notice and accept your thoughts, judgments, evaluations, stories, plus all of your feelings.

1. Set some time aside to deliberately notice your feelings.
Ask yourself three or four times a day, "How goes it? What's up? What's down?" Claim two minutes of complete silence here and there throughout the day to hear yourself.

2. Stretch toward accepting all of your feelings.
Try to be aware of feelings without judging or even trying to change your feelings. Feelings will change by themselves every few seconds if you do not re-activate them with thoughts or an external stimulus. Telling yourself not to feel something tends to strengthen a feeling and disconnect your communication with yourself, by sending the feeling underground. Judging yourself for having any of these feelings will interrupt your exploration of your feelings to find your underlying needs. Congratulate yourself on becoming aware of any and all feelings.

3. Find words for your feelings.
Take the time to find the exact words that describe your inner sensation. Just finding words for your feelings will often give you a sense of release. Words shift feelings slightly toward thoughts. It is easier to make choices about your actions when you know both your feelings and thoughts.

4. When you find evaluations disguised as feelings, separate evaluations from feelings.
Notice judgments in your thoughts and "feeling words." Be welcoming, even excited, to see them. Then reword them. Holding judgments of any sort as FACTS disconnects you from understanding yourself and lessens the probability that you will notice your own needs.

5. Translate feelings into information and choices.
If you increase awareness of your feelings, you may find them a valuable source of information. Please remember to also cultivate your ability to make deliberate choices on how you want to act.

Is there any value in noticing difficult feelings?

> **Katelyn:** *If you are not in the mood to talk, then say so before it gets out of control. I never thought of just telling someone that I don't want to talk at that moment. This semester, I practiced with my close friends. Just last night I was watching a movie. My boyfriend called right at the end and I told him I was going to have to call back. He was like "fine." After the movie was over, I explained and it was no problem!*

In class we generated a list of feelings that the students would not want to feel. Some suggested anger, fear, or jealousy. Others listed "irritation with a friend" because of a desire not to hurt anyone's feelings. Katelyn shares her experience with this. If she had not noticed, not made a request, there could well have been an undertone of tension between them all evening, with neither one understanding why it was there. The frequent denial of one's own feelings and needs when they conflict with one's self-image such as being nice, kind, or strong, is a common dilemma. It often goes under such phrases as "it is no big deal" or "others have bigger problems."

It was a new concept for some to see that there might be an important message from ourselves to ourselves under any feeling; like the gas gauge on a car—sometimes comforting, sometimes alarming, but generally useful. A fireman going into a burning building might want to ignore fear for a short time, but if he or she ignored it indefinitely, they could get ulcers or a heart attack. The fear might be reminding them that the safety of the fire equipment needs to be upgraded. Or perhaps they have a child and want to take fewer risks so that they live to parent the child.

Someone asked, "Isn't it character-building to do things you fear?" Several students replied that it was useful to feel the fear, apply reason, and then decide whether to use the fear as a warning and reminder of good sense or to notice the fear, consider the risk involved, and decide to push oneself to do the activity anyway. TJ offered another perspective on the value of noticing feeling.

> **TJ:** *You attract more bees with honey than vinegar. What I mean by this is that if you walk into a conflict in a bad mood, then the conflict will have a bad tone and be much less likely to be resolved. I experienced this first hand the other day when I had car troubles. I have a really old car that has never been appealing to anyone but myself. Earlier this month the engine started smoking. I took it to a station who said they knew exactly what was wrong. When I came back to pick up my car, I was excited. I paid them about $500 and was on my way. A month later the car is still smoking.*
>
> *I went back to the station in a defensive mood and got into a fight with them. Looking back on the situation, I didn't even give them a chance to help me. If I had noticed my frustration and resentment and thought about it and calmed down, maybe they would have fixed my car for free, which is what I wanted.*

FINDING VALUE UNDER DIFFICULT FEELINGS: Identify two feelings to work with. Write the feelings down in the first row. Fill the columns below each feeling.		
I prefer not to feel	a.	b.
A good time to <u>not</u> be in touch with this feeling	a.	b.
Disadvantage of never noticing this feeling	a.	b.
Potentially useful information	a.	b.

Success Script—Feelings

Title: Negotiating Housework
Name: Brian
Date: 11/17/06

Background: My girlfriend and I live in a small apartment in St. Albans. She works 3rd shift and I have a job as a school bus driver and I am a full time student. Needless to say we are usually very busy and finding time in which we can clean up the apartment is usually cause for an argument. I personally don't really care if my surroundings are overly dirty, I can live with dirty dishes, and laundry is at the bottom of my to-do list. My girlfriend however, likes everything to be neat and tidy—a place for everything and everything in its place. This means we are on complete polar opposite ends of the spectrum on this situation.

For quite a while now my girlfriend has grown increasingly frustrated when I slack off on my share of the chores. I do quite a bit including dishes, laundry and vacuuming, but there is always something more that needs to be done. Eventually she got fed up with the whole situation.

One day when I came home from school I found a sticky note on the fridge that contained directions, if you will, of what chores I need to do today. I felt like blowing up. I was so mad at her for doing something like this and had she been there, I probably would have started a huge fight. She wasn't however, and I had time to sit and think before she got home.

New Behavior: I used my anger as an alarm clock, just as Rosenberg suggested. I used it to realize what was alive in me and what needs I and my girlfriend wanted to have met. I realized that maybe I haven't been helping as much as she wanted me to and that I could probably feel good about myself if I did more around the house. When she got home I politely said that I would gladly help out more around the house but I find having a chore list for me demeaning. She agreed on certain chores that needed doing and when we would do them. The problem was solved and it was all because I was able to manage my anger.

In this example I was able to calmly see through my anger and try and see what needs we needed met. When I was able to get over the anger and use it as my alarm to wake up to what is going on I was able to meet both the needs of my girlfriend and myself.

Why I Consider This a Success: I consider this a success because I was able to see through my anger and meet our needs. Previously I might have started a huge fight over it and the issue would not be resolved and we would both get very mad at each other. Now I try and use this time as an example whenever I get mad. I am not perfect but I am making a conscious effort.

Intention for the Future: My future intentions would be to try and use this as an exemplary time when I managed my anger. I am going to make a conscious effort to use my anger as an alarm clock just as Rosenberg suggests.

Success Script—Feelings

(See directions on page 19)

Title:
Date:

Optional: create a Mind Map, a doodle, or other visual aides

CHAPTER THREE

φ

Needs

Identify which basic human needs are most alive for you today.
Actively consider which basic needs are priorities for others around you.

Brad: *Three weeks ago, after living in Italy with my Italian girlfriend for four months, I returned to Burlington for a two-week visit with my mother. I found out that I could not take all of my classes online that I need to graduate this spring as I had planned, so I decided to stay home for a semester to finish college. Marie and I have been taking the stress of this unexpected change out on each other by fighting.*

Last week, I was angered by a nasty e-mail and was planning a vicious response, when I began my homework for this class. Afterwards, instead of writing back to scold her for the things she had done and not done, I wrote asking her what she needed from me at the moment and what she needed from our relationship. Then I expressed my needs. This was incredibly freeing for me because I got to the heart of the problems without any mean words or putdowns. We had been fighting for a week straight and for the first time in awhile, her response was nice and caring.

Jenny: *It happened again—10 minutes before the class was over, everyone started to put on their jackets and close their notebooks. Professor Fraser must have thought we were rude! The good thing was that she expressed her feelings and needs—her sadness at losing the last 10 minutes of class to teach something she thought was very important. She then asked about our experience.*

Our feelings and needs were clear! It was an evening class and not one of us 19 students had eaten before the class. So now we all felt very hungry and tired of sitting. We decided to take turns bringing some snacks for the class, which made Professor Fraser and all her students satisfied. Now no one is in a hurry to leave the classroom before the ending time.

According to humanistic psychologists, such as Carl Rogers, Abraham Maslow, Rollo May, and Marshall Rosenberg, needs are the energy of life, the fundamental motivation for all behaviors. Other words for needs may be "values," "longings," "drives," "hungers," or "dreams." Feelings are the emotions of the moment, while needs are the river, the underlying flow of our lives.

Around the world, all people have the same basic needs and these needs are natural, healthy, and honorable. We will differ on the needs that are "most alive" to us at the moment. We may differ on the strategies we devise to meet our needs. Certainly some of our strategies to meet our needs are effective and other strategies are partially or totally counterproductive. Behind every action, by every person, every time, there is a hunger to meet one or more of these healthy needs.

The Business majors in our class knew a lot about needs, as their job is based on meeting needs. Several students observed that advertising tries to convince people that they will meet basic human needs by buying material goods. "Buy X and people will like you." "Buy Y to celebrate." "Buy Z to express your independence or your leadership or your uniqueness or …." Our universal human needs are translated into products to buy!

Abraham Maslow noticed that Freud formulated his theory of human personality by studying people in mental institutions. Maslow decided it would be more accurate to gather data from people doing particularly well in life and, therefore, he studied that group. In 1943, he listed five needs. Later he added Cognition, Aesthetic, and Self-Transcendent Needs. Rosenberg refers to similar categories of needs. As you can see, there is overlap on the lists. Some prefer the slightly more international list formulated by Manfred Max-Neef. A website for his list is on the next page.

Please notice that needs are not in clearly defined boxes. One activity can meet several needs.

ABRAHAM MASLOW: HIERARCHY OF HUMAN NEEDS

Physical Needs—air, food, water

Safety Needs—shelter, safety from environment and other humans

Belonging Needs—affiliation, connection with others (particular ones and community)

Esteem Needs—achievement, competence, self-esteem, recognition by others

Cognitive Needs—understanding of a subject, exploration of an unknown

Aesthetic Needs—symmetry, order, beauty

Self-Actualization Needs—realization of one's potential, comfortable acceptance of oneself and the world, identification of that which one most deeply hungers to do and action to be doing it

Self-Transcendent Needs—connection to something beyond oneself, helping others find self-fulfillment or realization of their potential

MARSHALL ROSENBERG: SOME UNIVERSAL NEEDS

Physical Well-being Needs—air, food, water, shelter, rest, movement, touch, sexual expression

Autonomy Needs—choice of dreams / goals / values, choice in plans for fulfilling them

Integrity Needs—authenticity, meaning, purpose, self worth, way to contribute to life

Celebration Needs—honoring small successes and big successes, mourning losses of loved ones and dreams

Interdependence / Connection Needs—acceptance, appreciation, consideration, community, emotional safety, honesty, love, respect, reassurance, support, trust, understanding

Recreation / Play Needs—creativity, fun, laughter, relaxing activities

Spiritual Needs—beauty, harmony, inspiration, order, peace

OTHER STUDIES OF HUMAN NEEDS

Manfred Max-Neef, a Chilean economist who studied the problems in the Third World, devised a way to measure real poverty and wealth, in terms of how well a culture meets its citizens' fundamental needs. He proposes a slightly different list of needs and discusses the qualities, things, actions, and settings that would accompany each. Max-Neef reflects that needs are basic across cultures, but strategies for meeting them vary. homepages.mtn.org/iasa/tgmaxneef.html

Here are three more models of how well a country is meeting the needs of its citizens. The Genuine Progress Indicator (GPI) has been around for 20 years. The Gross National Happiness (GNH) scale and the Happy Planet Index (HPI) are more recent efforts. Google these for more info.

Another group, **The Search Institute**, has focused on how well a community meets the needs of its youth. They list experiences (Forty Developmental Assets) that are helpful for children and have produced many studies to show that children who get more of these needs met have many fewer social and health problems. www.search-institute.org/

The Herrmann Brain Dominance Instrument, with parallel to Myers-Briggs Interest Inventory, suggests there are four major clusters of needs and that our brains are hardwired to be focused on one or more clusters. Testing and training is offered for the business world. www.hbdi.com/

MEETING NEEDS: What is one way you meet each of these needs? Example by **Daphne**	
Physical well-being / safety	*Not smoking cigarettes*
Autonomy	*Getting a part time job that relates to future career*
Celebration	*Going to dinner for friend's birthday*
Integrity	*I am a hospice volunteer*
Interdependence / Connection with others	*Calling my family whenever I get a chance*
Recreation / play	*Hanging out with friends*
Spiritual (beauty)	*Getting my nails done*

MEETING NEEDS: What is one way you meet each of these needs?	
Physical well-being / safety	
Autonomy	
Celebration	
Integrity	
Interdependence / Connection with others	
Recreation / play	
Spiritual	

THREE STAGES IN BECOMING ASSERTIVE WITH YOUR NEEDS

Western culture sometimes discourages the identification of and sharing of our needs. A frequently portrayed image of a hero is one who has no feelings, no needs, and who is tough and independent. Calling someone "needy" is an insult. I think we are slowly moving toward more human heroes.

It seems to me that our choice is to adopt a social image and then try to make our behavior line up with it or to try to find our unique, individual self by knowing our needs and expressing that self with our behavior. Decide for yourself. Look again at the list of needs. Would it be a world you wanted to live in if everyone was trying to meet these needs and supporting others in meeting these needs? In learning to value our needs, we as individuals often go through three stages.

STAGES IN MOVING TOWARD ASSERTIVENESS

First Stage	=	**PASSIVE**
Second Stage	=	**AGGRESSIVE**
Third Stage	=	**ASSERTIVE**

First Stage = PASSIVE: "I have no needs and if I had some, they are not important."

Believing we are responsible for other people's feelings, we focus on pleasing others, fitting in, and accommodating. Even when we first start to notice our needs, we feel very awkward, finding it almost impossible to share them, perhaps hinting at them or mentioning them once and then dropping the topic entirely. Rosenberg talks about the price to our health and our relationships of always being nice. Fortunately this stance is less common than it used to be.

> **Brandy:** *Something I learned this semester is that I need to take care of myself first before I can care for others. I think that society has taught us that we should not express our true feelings to others. I know that from a young age I was taught that I should be a strong person, that I should be able to lean on only myself. Expressing my feelings and fears I thought was a sign of being either weak or self-serving.*
>
> *Even when I lost my father, I handled every aspect of his death while barely shedding a tear. Later on when I had gone to see a grief counselor, I ended up bursting into tears. I remember feeling really bad and I kept trying to wipe my face while apologizing. The counselor finally asked me why I felt the need to apologize and why I didn't feel okay with needing empathy. I never went back to see her after that.*
>
> *I think that this is why I had such a hard time in class when we paired up and I was supposed to talk to someone so they could listen with empathy. Throughout the exercise I felt like I was hogging the attention and boring my partner.*
>
> **Lucy:** *I have a serious problem saying no. I can't do it! When my drunk friends called me at midnight last Sunday for a ride, I did not tell them I wasn't feeling good and had gone to bed early. They could have taken a cab or called someone else. I do not like to disappoint people, so I often end up over-exhausted for lack of a sufficient amount of sleep.*

Guy: *I can remember getting presents I did not want anything to do with, but I always said "thank you" with a huge smile. Now that I think about it, if I had shared my thoughts and feelings when I was younger, I probably wouldn't have gotten sweaters I never wore every year from my grandmother.*

James: *I sacrifice a lot of my needs for friends, family and sometimes people I don't really know. It's so common that when I don't submit, they think I am irritated or mad at them. I get tired of it and sometimes run out of energy; I just want time for myself to relax.*

Second Stage = AGGRESSIVE: "It is very important that I meet my needs, regardless of how that affects you."

We become committed to meeting our needs and are often heavy-handed, perhaps even obnoxious, and definitely not listening to other people's needs. Many adolescents are in this stage: "You're not giving me proper respect." "This is my life. Get your own life and leave me alone." "Bug off." (By this definition, some Assertiveness Classes offer only a restrained form of aggression.)

Eric: *It occurred to me that quite possibly I am somewhere in the obnoxious stage on my journey to emotional liberation. I usually do not feel that much compassion for other people's feelings. I may pretend to while in their presence but really I don't care much when it comes down to it.*

Possibly because I have too much going on in my life right now to take the time and deal with that kind of stuff. I am busy seven days a week and can barely keep up with my own needs, much less someone else's. But I would bet that it might change as I finish with my schooling and can lead a less chaotic life than I do right now.

Third Stage = ASSERTIVE: "We both have needs and all of our needs are important."

With practice, we can notice our needs and the needs of the other person / group and make choices about how we want to meet our needs. At this stage, we value deeply our own needs and also the needs of others. This leads to mutuality in a relationship. It is no longer acceptable to meet our own needs at the expense of others. Sadly, some people do not reach this stage of awareness.

Stevie: *I too have trouble asking for what I want. Maybe I am too shy or nervous to ask for what I really am needing. One of my friends went to a Patriots game with me in the beginning of the season and to this day has not paid me for the ticket. This frustrates me because I do not want to lose the relationship but it has been close to 3 months and no pay. Both the money and the friendship are important. And as everyone knows the longer a debt goes without being paid, the less likely the person is to see the money.*

So actually just today I talked to him. I explained, "I feel frustrated that I haven't been reimbursed for the Patriots ticket from before I went to school." He said that he was meaning to pay me but he has been busy and we have not seen each other in a long time. I forgave him and he is going to give my brother the money on Saturday. My friend and I made plans to hang out next weekend too, maybe bowling?

Sharaz: *I wanted to go home, but my girlfriend wanted me to wait for her on campus until her class was out. I really wanted to have some space to relax and then do my homework, lying down on my bed. Then I thought about her needs. She is going through a rough time these days. I decided that my need to be supportive to her was more important to me, so I went to the library, worked for an hour and forty-five minutes, and we went home together.*

HOW WELL DO YOU ASSERT YOUR NEEDS? Consider your primary relationships. How do you usually interact with this person—passively, aggressively or assertively?		
List your most active relationships:	**Stage?**	**Give an example**
My roommate	*Aggressive*	*I ordered him to get off the phone because I wanted it.*
My roommate	*Assertive*	*We planned together who wanted what for our party.*
My grandmother	*Passive*	*When she asks my opinion, I always say what she wants.*

NEEDS AND STRATEGIES

So, where are the needs to make money, to get "A"s, to be in control?

I do not see these as needs. I believe these are strategies to meet basic needs. In class we looked at what needs would be met by making money. Some students would pay off their loans and meet their need for more autonomy, while other students would travel and meet their needs for adventure and play. One student thought if he could buy a car, he could then get a girlfriend. Getting "A"s would also meet a variety of needs from the previous lists.

People who appear to "need control" have often had life experiences that convinced them the world is an unsafe place, that when they have not been in control, bad things have happened. Therefore, manipulating and bullying are strategies to assure that the needs for safety and autonomy are met. With awareness, a person could figure out better strategies to meet needs for safety and autonomy without sacrificing their needs for connection and interdependence.

All people have the same basic needs, although we each seem to have a few needs that are particularly important to us at any given time. Strategies to meet needs involve specific people and specific actions, but needs are life qualities, not dependent on any particular person meeting them.

Hungers? Dreams? Needs? Strategies? Huh? Why is this important?

It is easy to become confused. When we become aware of a need, we usually think of a particular strategy that would meet this need. Then, often without noticing it, we get attached to that one strategy. Some call this "a crisis of imagination," when we have shut down on thinking of other strategies.

Focusing on one strategy can limit our creativity in finding many ways to bring our own dreams into a reality. If that strategy depends on someone else doing something, we then fear we cannot meet our need unless that person cooperates in that manner. As we become fear-based about this matter, we tend to get pushy and controlling.

It would not be helpful to say, "I need you to fix me salads every lunch. My doctor just said I have to eat more salads." We may have a need for more health and a strategy of eating more salads. It will give us more options and increase the likelihood of meeting our goal if we remind ourselves there are many possible strategies to meet our need for healthy food, such as fixing salads ourselves, hiring someone else to come in and fix salads, or putting vegetables in the freezer.

The distinction between needs and strategies will become clearer when we get to the next chapter on making requests.

CREATING AN ABUNDANCE OF STRATEGIES: George, a college student, has run out of food money before the semester is over. He asks his parents for more, but they say, "No." He remembers it was a request, not a demand, so he takes a deep breath and sits down to figure out how else to take care of himself.

List 5 other strategies for George to meet his needs for food. Be creative.

Stretch yourself. List five more strategies for George.

EXPANDING YOUR OWN STRATEGIES: Now, apply this to your own life.

Identify one need in your life for which you are only using a few strategies to meet.

What are your current strategies?

Brainstorm five additional possible strategies that would meet your need.

Now REALLY stretch yourself. Brainstorm five more possible strategies that would meet this same need! Be creative!

Put a ✔ in front of any of the above suggestions that fit for you to try right now.

**If you want to understand your actions,
look at the needs you are trying to meet.**

**If you want to understand the actions of others,
look at the needs they are trying to meet.**

USING NEEDS AWARENESS TO MOVE FROM EVALUATIONS TO COMPASSION

> **Nicholas:** *The **first option** and most often used (by me, at least) is to blame the person who is giving you the negative messages. If someone tries to tell me I'm wrong, my first response is to think "No, they are wrong. How dare they tell me I am wrong?" This can cause a lot of problems and often does not lead to a good, both-parties-happy conclusion.*
>
> *The **second option** is to blame yourself, which ends up giving our self-esteem a huge kick in the gut. It isn't always right to assume that what someone says about us is true. We have to remember it is just their opinion.*
>
> *The **third option** is to get a sense of your own feelings and needs. If someone says, "You don't spend enough time with me. Obviously, you don't like me anymore," you can notice your need for time to do school work and your job, and your need for the other person to understand that.*
>
> *The **last option** is to guess the feelings and needs of the person giving you the negative messages. Your response this time might be "Are you feeling sad because we have been spending less time together and you think that means I don't like you? I want you to know I do like you and I enjoy spending time with you. It is only my need to get good grades and do my job that has kept me from having the free time I once had to spend with you." [needs = learning, trust, relaxation; strategies = good grades, getting to my job, hanging out]*

Imagine for a moment that someone who matters to you says or does something to you that you experience as hostile. What is your next thought? Your next feeling? Here are four common options:

1. **Blame the other person**
2. **Blame yourself**
3. **Find compassion for yourself by listening for your feelings and unmet needs**
4. **Find compassion for the other by imagining their feelings and needs**

Once you see these four options, you may be tempted to focus on the second two options and try to jump over the first two options. Please don't—all four are valuable to you.

If you have any blame of yourself or the other person, noticing this is exactly the most honest starting point in being where you are, being authentic, being fully alive, and moving toward future dialogue. As soon as you sense an urge to blame self or other, get your mouth shut tightly. Back off and create space to work through this. If you can get the time and space, stay with your blaming-other and blaming-self voices for a while. Do not push yourself to get through this phase.

After the charge of the emotions has settled, consider your feelings and unmet needs. As you unfreeze your judgments of yourself, and find compassion for yourself, you will likely feel the relief of being heard and accepted by yourself. Curiosity about the feelings and needs of the other person will naturally emerge. When you are ready to consider the other person's needs, you will likely notice yourself becoming aware of their humanness and feeling more compassionate. I believe that this is a more natural and sure way to reach a sense of connection than pasting on a smile and pretending to feel compassion. Try it for yourself for awhile and see if you like the end result. Here is an example and then a grid for you.

DE-BUGGING YOUR MIND: example from Nicholas, plus some imagined dialogue

Pick an action done or a statement said to you that was hard to hear or really bugged you.

"You don't spend enough time with me. Obviously, you don't like me anymore."

1. BLAME OTHER (list judgments of other)	4. COMPASSION FOR OTHER (guess the feelings and needs lying under their statement or action)
You are so wrong. How dare you say those things to me? You are so selfish. Look how you spend your time.	Sounds like she is sad and wanting more time. I know how that feels. And is unsure about my commitment to the relationship. Telling herself that I don't like her. Wow! That fear must be painful for her. I guess she wants a better connection with me.
2. BLAME SELF (list judgments of self)	3. COMPASSION FOR SELF (listen to my feelings and unmet needs)
Gosh, she is probably right. I am such an idiot. I can't believe I haven't done better in organizing my time. I'll never make her happy. I'm a terrible boyfriend. I am such an airhead.	I am working hard to get good grades and do my job. It is so hard to balance everything. I am bummed out because I really want the effort I have put into this relationship noticed. I am stressed hearing her say those things. I would really like understanding. I want to hear caring words.

Amy: *It is important to welcome feelings, even when our feelings are negative as they are a part of being alive. Once we learn to welcome all feelings, we can be at peace with ourselves.*

Just because I may have negative feelings from time to time, it doesn't mean I am a bad person, a bad student, or even that I am a negative person. It just means that some of my needs aren't being met. [I think feelings are better defined as uncomfortable rather than negative.]

WARNING: FOR YOUR EYES ONLY. NOT to be shared with person who invited this.

DE-BUGGING YOUR MIND:	
Pick an action done or a statement said to you that was hard to hear or really bugged you.	
1. BLAME OTHER (list judgments of other)	**4. COMPASSION FOR OTHER** (guess the feelings and needs lying under their statement or action)
2. BLAME SELF (list judgments of self)	**3. COMPASSION FOR SELF** (listen to my feelings and unmet needs)

Now that you have completed this exercise with your thinking, I am guessing you would find it helpful to do the exercise again, with the same or a different situation. Slow down. Give yourself time to really rant and rave, and then to be with the feelings and needs under them. Doing this, people usually reach a shift of energy and some sense of peacefulness. From that place it is a natural human reaction to become curious, concerned about the needs of the other person. This is an exercise that I personally use any time I am feeling distressed about some interaction.

↓ ↓ ↓ DELVING DEEPER: INCREASE AWARENESS OF NEEDS ↓ ↓ ↓

Here are five suggestions that can help you increase awareness of your needs. Most of us have little or no training in noticing our needs, so this will likely require some practice.

1. Look beneath your feelings.
Feelings are arrows pointing to your needs. This is the important reason to notice your feelings. Up feelings indicate needs are being met or you are guessing they will be met. If you are tense or down, you may be responding to needs not being met or that you imagine will not be met. Whether you are up or down, take a moment to notice what needs are being met or unmet and in what ways.

2. Look beneath your behavior.
Any behavior is an effort to meet a need, therefore you can observe your behavior and look for the need it either meets or attempts to meet.

3. Look beneath your judgments.
Another clue is to look at your right-wrong judgments. I hope you captured these earlier and did not devalue them and throw them away! Beneath your judgments are one or more unmet needs.

4. Dream of a totally satisfying life. What would that look like to you?
Take the time to dream, envision, and imagine what would be exactly right for you. Ask yourself what your long-term goals are and where you would like to see yourself in five years. In ten years?

5. Review a list of basic needs.
Study a list of basic needs common to all humans and think about how you meet them.

We will work on the first four ideas later in the book. Here is an exercise to address the fifth suggestion.

NEEDS MET AND UNMET: Consider the lists of basic human needs on page 36. Identify three needs you are meeting now and three needs you would like to pay more attention to.

Three needs you are currently meeting pretty well

Three needs you would like to do a little better in meeting

Success Script—Needs

Title: Renovations or Frustrations
Name: Vanessa
Date: 3/8/07

Background: *My friend, Lois, offered another friend, Charlie, and me, her older house to live in, rent-free when she moved into a newer house. We were thrilled, but upon actually seeing the house we noticed GREAT disrepair. Lois mentioned it needed some work, and that she had a little bit of money to put toward these repairs. "Repairs" was an understatement, but Charlie and I looked at it as a great opportunity to help both Lois and ourselves. We decided to renovate the house one room at a time. It turns out that Charlie and I were very good at renovating and were able to get most of the materials for FREE. We were very pleased and thought that Lois would be as well.*

At first we wanted to surprise Lois, but she insisted on seeing what we had done. She then made comments like, "Well, I never had time to do these things, but I was going to." Or "Do you think this is the best color choice for this room?" Or "How come you decided to put things this way instead of another way?" I told Charlie about how angry and hurt I was feeling and found out he had the same response. All this hard work and free material and all Lois could do was to complain and belittle us.

New Behavior: *I thought about my needs and realized I really wanted to hear "Great job, you guys. Thanks so much. I am so glad you did this." I had hoped the work would bring her some joy and I wanted recognition for my efforts. I decided to acknowledge myself for the good work done. Then I started to think about Lois and question why she would act this way toward us. All at once it came to me. When she lived here, it never looked this good. And she had moved into a new house that was not much better than the old one—it still needs a lot of work and she didn't have resources to get that house done either.*

Lois was undoubtedly feeling frustrated about her situation and possibly jealous that Charlie and I worked so well together and accomplished so much. When I explained this to Charlie, we decided to offer to assist Lois in doing renovations to her new home, if she liked.

Why this is a Success: *This was a great personal step for me. I take almost everything personally. This was the first time I was able to step back and view the situation in a new light. There was and is no reason for me to think the attacks were personal. They were just her way of letting off frustration about her own life. I was able to put myself in her shoes for awhile.*

Intention for the Future: *I believe I can focus on remembering that people's reactions are not personal attacks. With a little time and effort for self-care, I can keep from beating myself up over things that are other people's issues. Hopefully now that I know what to look for, I can apply this "step back, look and question" method to other situations where I might in the past have accepted things as personal attacks.*

Success Script –Needs

Title: What is Important?
Name: Shaun
Date: ??

Background: *I have seen my favorite band "In Flames" over ten times, yet every time they come around I feel the need to see them. If they are anywhere near, I have done whatever it took to see them. This band has been a part of my life and has influenced me in the way I play my own music.*

I found out there was an "In Flames" concert right here in Burlington at Higher Ground. It was on a Tuesday night and only cost $20. Most shows I have been to cost $50 or more. And Higher Ground is a smaller venue, which meant I could probably get closer to the band and usually the audio is better.

The day before the concert, I got extremely sick. I also knew that throughout the week I had several tests and a paper due. I could not afford to be out of class. The next day I still felt terrible, but was a smidgen better. Should I go to the concert and risk putting myself in bed for the week or play it safe, stay home and get extra sleep?

I recalled that a year ago I had wanted to go to a concert on my birthday, but I had a class so I did not go. It was my favorite comedian at the time, but I did not think I should miss class. I found out the next day it was the last time that comedian would do his routine live ever again.

New Behavior: *I decided I would not miss the concert. And I decided that only if I had a fever would I skip classes that week. Otherwise I would just suck it up and go to them all.*

Why I Consider This a Success: *I consider this a success because I took care of my needs for comfort and recreation. Although I took a risk of falling behind, I took it because I knew it would be better for my soul in the long run. The concert was amazing. The audio was great and I even got to meet the lead singer. The next day I actually felt better! Maybe it was the overall good vibes from the exciting show that made me overcome my sickness. Within a couple of days I felt as good as new.*

Intention for the Future: *I plan to really think about everything that might take place before I decide on an action and how it might affect me, positively or negatively, short run and long run. Then I can decide whether the action is worth it.*

Success Script—Needs

Title:
Date:

Optional: create a Mind Map, a doodle, or other visual aides

CHAPTER FOUR

φ

Requests

Value yourself enough to let others know what you would like.
Value others enough to make requests, not demands.

> **Rick:** *When I am at work I make requests to other officers or higher-ranking officers, but when I am out in the field [as a police officer] I do not make requests. I make demands that things get done. I have been trained to raise my voice slightly over the other people to establish a condition of control and from that, a position of trust and/or power.*

Making requests is a way that we connect with others.

How do demands differ from requests?

Demands are an attachment to a single solution to meeting a need. The speaker believes that they will not get important needs met if others don't agree to this one solution. Therefore, the speaker is very invested in seeing that their solution is accepted. Demands are often delivered in such a manner that the listeners believe they have no choice but to agree. Requests are anchored in the clear awareness that we, as adults, are entirely responsible to meet our own needs, that there are many ways this could be done, and therefore we are open to hearing "No."

We expect some people to assume responsibility for others in some situations—for example, parents, police, medical doctors, airline pilots, and teachers. This is based on a social contract wherein we acknowledge that the other person has more knowledge or a bigger picture of a situation. We decide our needs for security, predictability, and ease in scheduling are more alive for us than our need for autonomy and the absolute freedom to do as we please. We expect them to be clear and forceful in telling us what to do and we may temporarily agree to do what they ask.

If we perceive demands as meeting the needs for the well-being of a child, a patient, or the general population, we usually see them as valuable. When we believe demands are made from a desire for power over others, they are generally not seen as helpful and often stimulate much resistance. It is an ongoing challenge for parents and others in positions of authority to determine the amount of forcefulness that will be effective. In summary, when we have roles of responsibility for others, it is important that we learn how to make demands. Most encounters will go more smoothly if we treat the other person with respect and, whenever possible, make requests, not demands.

You might notice that most of our interactions are with peers wherein requests are greatly preferable. Peers tend to value equality and do not enjoy people they see as pushy or controlling. So, in addition to the challenge of taking on an authoritative role when needed, please also note the additional challenge of setting this role aside whenever it is not needed.

When will requests be more useful than demands?

> **Tucker:** *I was thinking back to conversations with my dad about mowing the lawn. When he said, "You need to cut the grass" or "I want you to cut the grass," I rebelled because the expression was forceful.*
>
> *When he said "I need some help today and I would like it if you would cut the grass" or "If possible I would like you to cut the grass," this made for a different outcome. I enjoyed doing things for my father when he needed help, especially when he let me know he appreciated my help.*

It depends on the quality of relationships we want. Rosenberg suggests we ask ourselves two questions. "What do I want the other person to do?" "What do I want their reason to be for doing it?" To build lasting relations based on equality and respect, our attitude when making a request will be: "This is what I would like—please only do this if you would find joy in doing it. I can find many strategies to meet my needs."

If we get attached to our strategy and push, threaten, nag, manipulate, or inspire guilt for non-cooperation, we may get what we want, but the relationship will suffer in the long run. Giving because one thinks one should do so takes away the joy of giving. You might want to wait until the gift or service comes to you with that quality of joy.

The

Adventure

> **To value your own needs enough
> to let others know what would enrich your life
> and
> to value the integrity, free will, and equality of others enough
> to make a request and not a demand**

TWO SURE-FIRE WAYS TO NOT GET WHAT YOU WANT

1. Don't bring it up.

I got a strange lesson growing up—that it was not polite to say "No" to someone and therefore it was rude to ask for what you wanted, which might mean someone else might have to say that awful word "No!" I learned an elaborate system of giving subtle hints and expecting mind reading, which only worked sometimes. I am sorry to report I am not alone in this.

> **Rob:** *I have trouble making requests. I am too nervous or shy to express my true feelings or needs. I guess I sort of "beat around the bush" hoping that the person I am speaking to will magically know what I am trying to say. I have at least begun to recognize that I have had an issue with stating my feelings in a vague way without ever letting the receiver know exactly what I want or how I feel and why.*

2. Blame someone else.

Another culturally habitual response when our needs are not getting met is to get angry with the other person and blame them for not meeting our needs, sometimes even when we ourselves have neglected to ask for what we want! Rosenberg calls this life-alienating communication, because instead of increasing the likelihood of getting our needs met, we are increasing the likelihood that we will not get them met. How sad!

Most people resent being told they are wrong and become defensive. They then put energy into defending themselves against the criticism or they comply out of fear, guilt, resentment, or duty, which lowers the quality of the relationship.

Sometimes we imagine that we are educating people about their mistakes. You may know parents, teachers, or even peers who frequently criticize the actions of others and focus on letting people know whenever they make a mistake. It is a fairly ineffective way to inspire change.

> **Sarah:** *Requests are often mistaken for demands when the listener believes they are going to be punished. We can avoid this by indicating our desire for them to comply only if they are willing. It's important to remember that the objective of Nonviolent Communication is to establish relationships based on honesty and empathy and not to change people.*

> **John:** *When my girlfriend says, "Don't drive so fast," I always think, "Who is she to decide how fast I drive my car? I am the driver and it's my car, so it is my decision." If she instead had said, "Please drive below the speed limit. The road is icy and I feel afraid," I would not jump to a defensive position.*

LIFE-ALIENATING WORDS OR THOUGHTS: Recall a time when you felt angry and blamed (vocally or in thought) someone. If you cannot recall any, think of blaming statements you've read, heard around you, or even heard on TV. Capture some blaming phrases.

| |
| |
| |
| |
| |
| |
| |
| |
| |

COMPONENTS OF EFFECTIVE REQUESTS

> **Katharine:** *When we read about requests, I saw I could use this. I tried it last week when I was discussing with my roommate about the bills we had to pay. I requested her half of the money, at a specific time, and reminded her I needed it in order for me to have enough money in my own bank account to cover the bills. (O, the life of a poor college student!)*

Observations are about what <u>is happening</u> out there now; requests are about what exactly we <u>would like to see happening</u> out there.

EFFECTIVE REQUESTS

1. **Get your attitude lined up before you speak**
2. **Share what needs would be met if the person were to do the thing you asked**
3. **Make positive requests for time-specific, concrete, and doable actions**
4. **Ask whether the other person wants to do this action**

1. Get your attitude lined up before you speak

> **Brad:** *Last night, sometime after midnight, I poured my soul out to Marie explaining all the reasons I thought everything was the way it was in our relationship. After about half an hour of me talking straight, I asked for a reflection. She did not want to give me one. I got frustrated and scolded her for not listening to me. Of course, this triggered her defensiveness. We ended the conversation annoyed and disconnected.*
>
> *Today, I read the chapter on making requests. I see I picked a really bad time to get into a deep conversation. Marie was very tired and just wanted to sleep. Second, after I made the initial request for her to respond to what I said, and she refused, I began to demand, totally forgetting I wanted it to be a request. Even though I was being nice and speaking in a gentle tone, it became clear I was demanding when she said "no."*

We are aspiring to indeed make a request and not a demand. If we are accustomed to leaning on someone to get them to agree, this new attitude may result in less cooperation for a while. It helps to recall we are building relationships wherein both people are free to be themselves and are encouraged to find ways to increase their own happiness.

We want to remember that needs are a natural hunger for a quality of life and there are many strategies to meet each need. If we lock onto one strategy, we will be tempted to assume that the other person has to behave in a particular way for us to find satisfaction, happiness, and peace.

That would make us powerless and may tempt us to demand they act in the way we want. Moreover, even if our words line up when we make a request, if we are thinking we want our own way and forgetting that we really want both sets of needs to be met, it may come out. The tone of our voice, our body language, our vibes, and our response if they say "No" will likely shout out our secret intention. If it was really a request, we will be okay if they say "No."

2. Share what needs would be met if the person were to do the thing you asked

> **Joe:** *I recently decided not to allow people to smoke cigarettes in my apartment. In the past I had allowed it because both my roommate and I are smokers. However, it became a problem when the smell in the apartment became unbearable. A friend of mine came over the other day and when he walked in he was smoking. When I saw the cigarette, I said, "Don't smoke that cigarette in here." My demand with no explanation of my personal needs led my friend to become angry with me. He thought I was picking on him because I had not explained to him why I stopped allowing smoking in the apartment.*

A request is often experienced as a demand if we neglect to share the reasons behind it. We relate to people's needs and are more likely to feel motivated to help them when we know their needs. We all have the same basic, human needs, so when a person shares their needs, it invites us to connect to their humanness and often inspires us to want to contribute to their happiness. Joe had a need for comfort or health, which made him want to cut back on the amount of smoke in his environment. He expressed this by making a demand, which, as he reports, was not well received.

3. Make positive requests for time-specific, concrete, and doable actions

Making <u>positive requests</u> means talking about what we <u>do</u> want, not what we don't want.

- *I don't want you to work so late.* → *I would enjoy you spending more evenings with me.*
- *Don't break the school windows.* → *If there is anything you are not happy about at school, I would like you to tell me about it.*
- *I don't need any more trouble now.* → *I want to wait and discuss this next week.*
- *Stop being such a nag.* → *I would like for you to tell me your concerns only once.*

<u>Time-specific actions</u> mean ones anchored in a specific time frame.

I would like you to:
- *talk with me about a new car.* → *talk with me, today or tomorrow, about a new car.*
- *help me with my paper.* → *help me with my paper this weekend.*

<u>Concrete actions</u> mean carefully defined, specific behaviors.

I would like you to:
- *clean your room.* → *make the bed, dust, and put your books in the bookcase.*
- *grow up.* → *write down appointments and be there on time.*
- *grow up.* → *tell the truth, even when it is hard to do so.*

<u>Doable actions</u> mean actions that are realistic to do, not something grandiose, like a change of character or attitude or even feelings. (To say "Don't feel that way" is seldom helpful.)

I would like you to:
- *be more outgoing.* → *say "hi" when I walk into the room.*
- *love me more.* → *be more affectionate by holding my hand when we go for a walk.*
- *miss me every moment while you are gone.* → *try to e-mail me a note each day.*

4. Ask whether the other person wants to do this action

Requests include a question to find out if it fits for the other person. This reminds both the speaker (us) and the listener that they have a choice and that there are many possible strategies that will meet our needs. This is part of the attitude we worked on before starting our request.

Would this fit for you?	*Does this interest you?*
What do you think about this?	*Are you willing to do this?*
Do you want to do this?	*OK with you?*
Would you be willing to fit this into your schedule?	*Will that work for you?*
Does that sound like something you would enjoy?	*How does that sound to you?*
Can you imagine doing that this week?	*Are you up for that?*

MAKING AN EFFECTIVE REQUEST: Expand the following requests to include the above four components. (Your attitude may not show up in the words.)

Clarify these requests →	Complete requests
Yo, dude, clean up the mess.	*Yo, dude. My girlfriend is coming over. Would you be willing to put your pizza boxes in the trash, run the vacuum and get the chairs back in place when this tv show is over?*
All you do is talk. You are so selfish.	
Call if you are going to be late, huh?	
Whatcha doing tonight?	
I insist you stop ignoring me.	

Wait a minute! Sometimes a matter is negotiable to me and sometimes a matter is not negotiable. Isn't it the right time to make a demand then?

> **Meg:** *I guess you could say I was kind of a pushover before I took this class. I used to let my boyfriend smoke in my car even though I hate the smell of smoke and I don't want my car to smell like an ashtray when I don't even smoke. I let him smoke because he wanted to and then I complained later. I finally saw that was just stupid.*
>
> *Now I don't let him smoke in my car at all. He hates it and I have to say "no" a couple of times for him to get that I really mean it, but eventually he does. I often pull over and let him get out and have his cigarette, but no longer inside my car. If he needs to smoke inside a car, that's too bad, we can just take his car.* [needs = recreation, relaxation; strategy = smoking cigarettes]

All needs are non-negotiable basically. Strategies are negotiable. A request that shares how important this matter is to you is a good first step. You can ask for what you want from others, but if they choose not to give that action, then you, as an adult, are responsible to find other ways to meet the needs that seem most alive to you and currently essential. If your first strategy does not work, try another and another until you get what it is you hunger for.

Meg's bottom line is that her needs for the health and aesthetics of fresh air in her car have become non-negotiable. Her first strategy was to try with her boyfriend to come up with a plan that met both needs. She respected her boyfriend's preference to continue smoking (his strategy to meet his needs for relaxation), but not to compromise her own needs. If he refused to change his behavior, her next step was to think what actions she had taken that had allowed or encouraged his behavior. She could then claim the power to change her own behavior. Meg chose to pull over when he wants a cigarette. She could have insisted on taking separate cars or refused to drive at all.

If a friend frequently calls to talk when you are trying to study, you can stop, look at your own behaviors in the situation, and change your actions. You might start with a one-time request, "I realize I have not given you some important information. I usually study between 8 pm and midnight on school nights. I would really appreciate it if you would call before or after that time. I do enjoy talking with you." No matter whether the friend says "Yes" or "No," if they continue to call, you can turn your phone off during that time or not answer it. Your actions will speak much louder than your words. Focus on your own actions. Change your own actions. If you continue talking on the phone to them and then repeatedly ask them not to call, you will be nagging. You are responsible for taking care of yourself and they are not responsible for putting your needs first.

As a parent, you have non-negotiable needs such as your child's safety. Sometimes, there is only one option acceptable to you. It is helpful at those times to first verbally acknowledge that the child wants to do some other action. "It appears that you do not want to hold my hand crossing the street. I want you to be safe, so you may either hold my hand or I will carry you. Which seems like a better idea to you?" When your child says, "No," to a request, it may seem like your only options are to accommodate or override the child. Other than non-negotiable items or lack of time, a third option is to find out what your child's current interests and needs are and the reason behind their "No," and then to work toward meeting both your needs and your child's needs. If you still choose to override their wishes, own that you understand they are objecting, tell them why you are choosing to do something else, and then accept that they may feel angry or disappointed.

REQUESTS FOR CONNECTION OFTEN PRECEED REQUESTS FOR ACTION

Matt: *Recently, I noticed I have been getting in more little arguments with my girlfriend. They always seem to be about stupid stuff. We have both been easily frustrated with one another. It troubled me and I wanted to know where the animosity was coming from.*

I decided to invite my girlfriend to look back with me at the different arguments we had within the previous week to figure out what was happening. After talking about two hours, we realized that every single argument happened when a need was not being met and it was causing us to be crabby with one another. Being hungry or being tired or not spending quality time with each other led to our harsh behavior.

When do I need to focus on connection?

The ultimate answer is: "Always! The more you aim for better connection with yourself and with others, the more satisfaction you will find in your life." The immediate answer is: "If there is any tension in an encounter, stop talking and focus on connecting." It is currently one of my stretching points to remember this more often. Let me share a recent failure and my process around that.

I was the greeter for an activity and a woman with whom I have had several tense conversations in the past, put a large bouquet of forsythia on a table near the door. Some of the branches were in the line of traffic, so I said, "Will you please cut the branches back—people may bump into them." To my surprise, she became angry with me. When we returned to the conversation a few minutes later, I discovered that she was distressed that I wanted them to be cut as she has pain about people not appreciating nature in its wild state. She was agreeable to rearranging them out of the way.

I thought about what I could learn from this unpleasant encounter. I noticed I often see a problem, think of a solution, and suggest the solution with no context. (This rests on several assumptions: that efficiency is everyone's first priority, that everyone sees the situation the same way that I do, and that others will be grateful for my insightful solutions! As you can guess, this sometimes alienates others.) I next shared the encounter with an NVC friend who suggested it would help if every time I told myself "I have a problem," I reframed it as "I have an opportunity to connect."

As I would like to increase connections, I sat down to brainstorm some ways to improve. I could:

- Be more regular in taking quiet time

- Remind myself when I leave my home, to look for opportunities to connect

- Notice actions I appreciate around me and share my appreciation more often

- Be especially attuned when I see someone with whom I sometimes feel tense

- Make connection my first priority when talking about an emotionally charged issue

- If I sense tension in either of us in the middle of a conversation, stop, change focus

- Remind myself to be curious instead of angry or irritated

- Remind myself that everyone is trying to meet the same honorable needs that I am

If I had recalled these, perhaps I would have said:

"Sophia, thanks for bringing in the lovely bouquet of forsythia."
(Noticing my appreciation of both the flowers and her efforts, I share this with her, which invites connection.)

"I have a concern that people may bump it as they walk by."
(My need is for ease, comfort for people arriving, perhaps a subcategory of safety, which I translate out of a formal need statement into commonly used language.)

"Do you see this as a problem?"
(This invites her opinion and is open to hearing her solution before offering mine, both of which are connecting stances.)

Isn't this just part of the first component of making an effective request—to get your attitude lined up before you speak?

Good catch! Yes, it is. I thought the details of my stretching might be helpful. Some people who are practiced with NVC say that if you get a solid connection with yourself, wherein you easily and regularly notice your feelings and needs, and then aim at connection with others, you create more space for everyone to be attuned to what is most alive in the moment. I touch this space on occasion, but I do not live there. Perhaps some of you are better at this than I am.

BUILDING BETTER CONNECTIONS:
Brainstorm four ways you could better connect with yourself.
Brainstorm four ways you could better connect with someone you especially want to connect to or with people in general.
Of these suggestions, which ones, if any, fit for you to give more attention now? Put a ✔ before any that you are ready to address.

Success Script—Requests

Title: Asking for Time
Name: Janie
Date: 10/28/08

Background: *My boyfriend is in a band and band practice takes up a lot of his time. We've been together for five years and I wish I was more included in his life. I work about 20 hours a week on top of going to school full time. My boyfriend works 40 hours a week. With this kind of busy schedule it is hard to see one another. On top of working, Steve practices with his band twice a week. The time he spends with his band takes away from the time we could be spending together. This has been really stressful for me because I would like to go to practice, and I have hinted at it, but I am never invited.*

New Behavior: *Saturday I flat out asked Steve if I could go to band practice with him. I used the technique in* Connection. *I said, "Steve, I am feeling sad. I would like to spend more time with you. Can I go to the band practice with you tonight?" He said, "Of course you can come. The other guys' girlfriends are there and I would really like you there, too."*

Why I Consider This a Success: *I think this conversation was a success because I got my feelings and needs across to Steve and he accepted them and wanted to include me. I know that this isn't a big deal in our relationship, but I think we are learning to communicate better. Steve didn't ask because he thought I did not want to go and I did not ask because I was worried I would get rejected. I think this tiny example has shown me I need to vocalize requests, instead of hoping he will catch on. I see that women are trained not to share needs and make requests. This makes relationships very difficult, because I think and feel a certain way and never vocalize these emotions. I expect Steve to read my mind, and this is unfair to him.*

Intention for the Future: *I intend to get more comfortable with making requests. I know I was not taught as a child, so now when I make requests, I feel too bossy. I think this technique will really allow me to open up to Steve. To make any serious decisions, we have to consider both people's needs and feelings. I want to learn how to express myself in a positive, assertive way. This success will encourage me to try again.*

I do have a question—what is the next step if your request is going to be turned down by the other person?

(The next step would be to switch to a listening mode and ask what need of theirs would <u>not</u> be met by doing what you ask. When you have both sets of needs on the table, then you can try again to figure out a way to meet all the needs. This is covered more extensively on pages 117- 120.)

Success Script—Requests

Title:
Date:

Optional: create a Mind Map, a doodle, or other visual aides

CHAPTER FIVE

φ

And an Attitude

**Realize the deep satisfaction of connecting with yourself and others.
Intentionally reach for that connection.**

Jay: *I see I need to develop more self-compassion and stop dissing myself, like, "Wow, way to go, Jay. You really screwed that one up." That just makes me feel down, depressed, and angry. I never even thought about getting in touch with my needs. All I know is that I don't agree with my actions. This has been a major problem for me.*

Doma: *Every human being talks with their own inner soul. People who talk with the inner soul before taking an action can know whether it is right or wrong to do something. Such people are able to have good relationships and can handle conflict easily. People who talk to their inner soul after the action will more often have regrets about what they have done.*

An attitude is the mindset, the core beliefs we carry with us into any situation. The four NVC steps we have been working with rest on the assumption that people's deepest satisfaction can be found by connecting fully to our own needs, including our need to be supportive to others in meeting their needs. NVC and many others see the most basic energy of the universe as one of cooperation, connection, and compassion—that our hunger to give and receive these is our core motivator.

Maslow's hierarchy suggests it is a process, a journey. As one set of needs, such as safety, are met, we are drawn to address another group, such as belonging needs. I personally find this journey exciting, terrifying and difficult at times, satisfying, painful, humbling, and fulfilling, and to me it is all worth it as I become more fully alive and find more compassion for myself and for others.

Perhaps you already experience the satisfaction of connecting with yourself and others. If so, you have noticed this is the underlying attitude in Connection. If this attitude is less familiar to you, then Connection is an invitation to try this viewpoint on, walk this path for a while, and see if you like it. At this point in your life, do you want to take the time and effort to get to know yourself better? Perhaps you want to put more energy into better connecting with someone particular in your life? Or perhaps you are ready to improve the way you relate to people in general? Only you know your priorities and your timing.

The following exercises will invite your attention in those directions.

 **Our hunger to connect with ourselves and others
is more vital
than any communication tool we can learn.**

RELEASING ENDORPHINS WITH AN ATTITUDE OF GRATITUDE

> **Katelyn:** *All my life I have been very hard on myself. I decided in this class to be more compassionate. At first I started to let go of smaller things I used to get angry about, like spilling a drink or hitting my head on the wall over my bed. Now I have moved to bigger situations where I can provide compassion to myself. Yesterday I took a Property Law test. I studied and studied some more, but when I got the test, I froze and ended up with only an 88. I managed to let it go and not stay up all night worrying about it. I am really proud of myself for this.*

In Water the Flowers, Not the Weeds, Fletcher Peacock reminds us to give our attention to parts of our lives we want to encourage. It can be habitual to see only the parts of our gardens, and our lives, which need fixing. We often forget to acknowledge parts of our lives that are working well.

Rosenberg recommends that every day we take twenty minutes journaling about the just-right-ness already existing, life-affirming decisions we made, and our inspired positive actions. Here is a three-part exercise on appreciating self, life, and others.

Start with yourself. Journal or look in the mirror or at least take a few quiet minutes daily to notice and appreciate, to yourself, some things you have done that pleased you. Make an observation and then identify the feeling and the need met. (No request is needed.)

I made it to the gym today. I am proud because I followed through on a commitment as well as getting healthier.

I took time to call my sick aunt. That was satisfying. She has always taken time for me and I really liked being able to give something back to her.

When Jeremy asked me to go out partying last night, I said, "no, thanks" because I wanted to get more sleep. I felt rested this morning and full of energy.

I had a great time partying with Jeremy last night. I got to see some old friends and I took a much-needed break from my studies.

I APPRECIATE ME: Craft a 3-part appreciation (Observation, Feelings, and Needs met) of something specific you did yesterday that pleased you or brought a moment of satisfaction.

☺ THE NEXT STEP IS VERY IMPORTANT. GIVE IT SOME TIME. ☺

Reflection: Take two minutes to sit with the feeling from the above exercise. How did it taste and feel? Let yourself get the benefits again of that energy going through your body. This practice will literally change your body chemistry by releasing more endorphins.

A second area to look at with appreciation is life. Catch life doing something you enjoy and take a moment to notice it. And then notice it again. Re-feel the moment. Smile.

The snowflakes were awesome this morning.

I'm lucky to have so many cool friends living on this hall in the dorm.

That dinner really hit the spot—looked good and tasted marvelous.

Hey—I found a parking space first time around the block.

I APPRECIATE LIFE: Write a practice statement here.
Reflection: Take <u>two minutes</u> to sit with the feeling from the above exercise.

And the third area for gratitude is to become aware of the kindness, the blessings that people around us bring to our lives. It is easy to take it for granted, to become blind to it. A relationship-building practice is to notice daily and comment on specific actions that please you, but for this exercise, just cultivate your observation and gratitude.

Practice gathering appreciations. Notice the specific moment of beauty. Focus on the action that brings you joy. Really see it and feel it. Breathe it in. Taste it.

I noticed how graciously Pat took it when I brought home extra guests tonight. I am grateful.

I remembered again how much I like Christopher's sense of humor—we were all laughing.

When Jean brought fresh flowers to my home, I imagined being out in the meadows and relaxed.

The young boy who was playing so earnestly with his dog today at the park, warmed my heart.

I APPRECIATE THE ACTIONS OF OTHERS: Write a practice statement here.
Reflection: Take <u>two minutes</u> to sit with the feeling from the above exercise.

CLAIMING A MORE CHOICEFUL LIFE

> **Tom:** *Rosenberg pointed out something that really opened my eyes: "Human beings were not meant to be slaves. We were not meant to succumb to the dictates of 'should' and 'have to' whether they come from outside or from inside ourselves." I am constantly saying to myself how I have to take school more seriously or I have to start eating better or I have to work out more.*
>
> *According to Rosenberg I have to figure out my needs behind all those desired activities and really figure out why I want to do them so badly and only then will the self-judging stop. Instead of saying to myself "I have to start taking school more seriously," I could say "I choose to take school more seriously because...." Perhaps I'll have more luck accomplishing things for myself if I find the true needs behind them.* [Notice that Tom hears Rosenberg's suggestion as another "have to." This is a good example of how we continue to repeat patterns of thinking, even we want to change.]

How much choice do you have in your life?

Some people think they have few choices because they believe that they need to follow the rules, be accepted by peers, and make everyone around them happy. Others think they have few choices because of their genetic makeup or their social upbringing. You can find more freedom in your life if you rethink these assumptions. NVC says you always have a choice in every situation whether you like your choice or not. What seems true to you?

Experiencing control over your own life is such a basic human hunger that expanding your choices is often invigorating. Listening in on your inner dialogue and then changing your self-talk can increase your options. First, make a list of all the things you tell yourself you "have to do" (= "I should, I have to, I need to, I must, or I ought to.") Start each sentence with the phrase that fits for you. Then re-write the list using this template: "I choose to ___ because I ___."

Peggy: *I should clean the house every day.*

> *I should spend more time with my mom.*
>
> *I should not spend money on my credit card.*
>
> *I should be more involved with the community.*
>
> *I should take the dog out more often.*

> *I choose to clean the house daily because I like it to be clean.*
>
> *I choose to spend less time with my mom because we argue.*
>
> *I choose not to use the credit card because I want to have good credit.*
>
> *I choose not to be more involved with the community because I have no time.*
> [It would be more accurate to say, "I prefer to do other things with my time."]
>
> *I choose not to take the dog out because it has been so cold lately.*

A CHOICEFUL LIFE: Example by **Suzanne**
List five things you tell yourself you "have to do" = "I should, I have to, I need to, I must, or I ought to." Start each sentence with the phrase that fits for you.
I should teach Sunday School.
I should sub at preschool.
I should feed my friend's cat.
Write your list again, substituting "I choose to" for the "have to." Then ask yourself why you would choose to do this? What need does it meet? Give your reason.
I choose to teach Sunday School because it meets my need for community and contribution.
I choose to sub for only an hour and a half at a time for the preschool because I want to see the children. (I worked with them full time over the summer and I miss them.) I choose not to sub a full day.
I choose to watch my friend's cat because I will feel guilty if I don't. [Note that guilty is a feeling mixed with an evaluative thought.]
Reflection: Which of these actions makes your life more alive and satisfying?
Teaching Sunday School
Reflection: Which actions do <u>not</u> contribute to your well-being? Explain.
Feeding my friend's cat is unnecessary—I have to go way out of my way to go there and the cat has a huge bowl of dry food and feeding him is adding resentment to our relationship.
Reflection: Which actions call for further thought?
I would like to see the children, but maybe I would like to visit them, instead of subbing.

> **Lucy:** *I decided to notice when I say the word "should" and to ask myself to find the choice underneath it that would enhance my life; to ask whether this is something I would like to actively pursue or to get off my case about. A month ago, I heard myself say, "I should go abroad." Immediately I stopped myself to consider whether this was really important to me. I decided to pursue it. I then set up a meeting with the professor in charge of studying abroad and began to look at my options. I am now planning to go to India, my first semester senior year.*

What if your list includes activities such as feeding a baby at 2:00 am? You are tired and plan to get up for an early class and for a few minutes you feel great resentment that you "have to get up." You can make it worse by blaming yourself—calling yourself an unloving mother or father. Or blaming the baby—thinking of it as a spoiled brat.

A happier alternative is to acknowledge your need for sleep. Next ask yourself what other needs you have? Let yourself find the aliveness of your own needs and then notice the needs the baby is expressing. What needs would you meet to get up and feed the baby? Perhaps it meets your need to contribute to the baby's well-being. Perhaps you have a need for integrity—to know that you follow through on commitments. It probably meets several needs. When you focus on these, you can likely move your resentment into satisfaction.

A CHOICEFUL LIFE

List five things you tell yourself you "have to do" = "I should, I have to, I need to, I must, or I ought to." Start each sentence with the phrase that fits for you.

Write your list again, substituting "I choose to" for the "have to" phrase. Then ask yourself why you would choose to do this? What need does it meet? Give your reason.

I choose to

I choose to

I choose to

I choose to

I choose to

Reflection: Which of these actions makes your life more alive and satisfying?

Reflection: Which actions do <u>not</u> contribute to your well-being? Explain.

Reflection: Which actions call for further thought?

WORKING WITH ENEMY IMAGES OF OTHERS

> **Charlie:** *Last summer there was an incident between my boss and I over a paycheck. I had done him a favor by working on a Saturday, but when I got my paycheck, it was short the extra eight hours I worked. I was furious. I was convinced he was trying to screw me out of the one hundred and thirty dollars. I started thinking how I could get back at him. The next day I found out that work done on the weekend before payday was always paid on the following paycheck. My problem was my self-applied blinders. I was fixated on the belief that he was trying to pull a fast one and did not even think about other possibilities.*

If we choose to connect, we need to confront our cultural habit of projecting enemy images on people with whom we disagree. Before we can kill people, they have to become non-individuals, non-persons, in our minds. All Vietnamese became "Charlie." A soldier reported that Iraqis are often called "Rag-heads" or "Hajjis." If we saw them as students, brothers, boyfriends, and young men with dreams fairly similar to those of young men everywhere, we could not easily kill them. Even with friends, we can decide that they are acting out of a negative motivation, that they are intentionally harassing or misunderstanding. It is often a response to not liking their strategies. When we assign enemy images, we lessen our ability to see clearly. It is a challenge to back off from these assumptions and choose to become curious about how things look to them, instead.

(This is not to say that all behaviors need to be accepted—some actions are not okay with us, for cultural, personal, or safety reasons. We may choose to put effort into stopping the behavior.) When we remember that all actions are strategies to meet basic needs, then our dialogue will focus on identifying and meeting their underlying needs with less costly strategies. This will resolve problems more effectively than blaming and evaluating the other—whether friend or stranger.

The class did an exercise to stretch themselves toward seeing the needs of the individual behind some actions or words that irritated them. On the next page is a grid for you to do the exercise.

> **Tom:** *The only statement I could think of was when a guest at my apartment was playing with my drums and said in an arrogant manner, "Your bass drum is obnoxious." I felt insulted and hurt. (I take anything said about my drums personally.) I really wanted to have my experience recognized and my authority in picking a good drum acknowledged. I guess he was feeling nervous and excited. Maybe he wanted the drum to sound like his own or maybe even that I recognize his authority of knowing something about drums.*

> **Laurie:** *The situation I used was something that my mother had recently said that made me feel sad and hurt. My needs were belonging, love and support. After doing the exercise, I was able to imagine what my mother was feeling or needing during the time of our interaction. This was important to me because I was able to see our interaction in a new light. I did not see her as a mean person any more. I just saw her as just a person like myself with feelings and needs that are not being met.*

> **Nicholas:** *For our homework, I used a small situation that dealt with me and a roommate and comments made after an intense round of Halo. At first I thought he was just being a pecker head, but after doing this exercise I realize that maybe he was just needing to be acknowledged for his good game play. After seeing this, I realized I was not mad anymore and I wasn't going to think about it any more either.*

WARNING: Another FOR YOUR EYES ONLY

WHY IN THE WORLD DID THEY SAY (OR DO) THAT?	
1. Think of one action done or a sentence said by some other person that puzzles you or frustrates you when you think of it. Describe briefly what happened.	
2. List all of your feelings that you can identify related to this incident.	**3. List all your needs that you can identify related to this incident.**
4. List the feelings you guess the other person may have been having when they said or did what they did.	**5. List the needs you guess the other person may have been experiencing in this incident.**
6. Can you identify any shift in your feelings and understanding after doing this exercise?	

If you rush through this exercise, you will likely not experience any shift of feelings or viewpoint. On the other hand, if you take the time to sit with your feelings and needs, and then go into the feelings and needs of the other person, it is probable that the situation will seem different to you.

If you want to repeat this exercise, you can find a template online at www.theexercise.org.

⬇ ⬇ ⬇ DELVING DEEPER: THE EXERCISE ⬇ ⬇ ⬇

You may want to do this exercise again with another issue. And again with another issue. And yet again. This work of repeatedly changing enemy images into an awareness of our common basic needs lessens the time we hold onto these images before reclaiming our shared humanity.

When I am frightened, I often want to see myself as RIGHT and the other person as WRONG. Claiming rightness makes me feel secure, safe from the chaos and pain in the world.

The exercise invites me to let go of this false security. I aspire to do so in order to find a neutral ground to communicate with others. It also helps me clear out a distorting filter and embrace reality instead and therefore be more open to the world, more alive, more connected.

TRICKS OF THE MIND THAT PERPETUATE CONFLICT

This section is a change of pace. I hope you will stay with me here. Several years ago, I read an article in the New York Times (July 24, 2006) that continues to inspire me. The writer, Daniel Gilbert, a professor at Harvard, entitled his essay, "He Who Cast the First Stone, Probably Didn't." The article talks about how kids and nations use two justifications when confronted about being in a fight: "He hit me first" and "He hit me harder."

Gilbert explores these. We label those who give punches #1, #3, #5, etc, as the instigators of the fight. When we think we are giving punches #2, #4, #6, etc, we can convince ourselves that we are the victim and the blameless one. <u>In this context, our actions are seen by us as reactions</u>. We tend to perceive a conflict as starting when we first feel pain. Therefore, it is natural to experience that the other person offended first and that we are only responding with even-numbered punches.

(A story for you, in italics) <u>*CHAPTER ONE:*</u> *Kenny and Benny are children who often play together: the same neighborhood, same age, and same size. They fight a lot. Who starts it? Kenny is sure that Benny is the one who starts and escalates their conflicts and that he only does what he has to do to defend himself. But when you talk with Benny, he will tell you that Kenny is the one who starts and escalates everything, while <u>he</u> just does what <u>he</u> has to do to defend himself.*

In his article, Professor Gilbert refers to a psychological study done at the University of Texas, by William Swann and colleagues. Pairs of volunteers are assigned roles as world leaders in conflict and then asked to dialogue about whether to initiate a nuclear strike.

<u>*CHAPTER TWO:*</u> *Our fictitious friend, Ken, now a college student, needs extra money, so he volunteers for the Swann conflict study. He is paired up with a stranger, Fred, for the experiment. After the initial dialogue, volunteers were shown some of <u>their own statements</u> and asked what was said <u>before</u> and <u>afterward</u>. Ken looked at a list of his own statements and tried to recall what Fred said before and after these statements. Like the other pairs of volunteers, Ken could usually recall the statements made before his, i.e. Fred's statements that he, Ken, had responded to. But Ken could seldom recall the statements Fred said after his (Ken's) statements.*

When shown <u>the other person's statements,</u> it was in reverse. Ken looked at the statements Fred had made and could recall the after statements - his replies to Fred's statements, but not the before statements of his which had preceded the statements made by Fred. Fred followed the same pattern of strongly seeing his words as reactions to what he heard, but seldom seeing or remembering how his own words may have elicited the response that he got from Ken. This documents the tendency to see ourselves as being reactors rather than causers, always throwing the even-numbered punches, so to speak.

(You can see why modern parenting instructors often report that it is a counterproductive starting point to try to determine who started it. The only way out is to announce boldly, "Something has happened. Let's see what needs each of you are trying to get met.")

We see other people's actions and hear their words more easily than we observe our own words and actions. We have access to our inner dialogue; therefore we usually know the reasoning behind our actions. Our behavior makes sense to us, and, therefore, our words and actions are less jarring, less memorable to us.

Compounding this, Gilbert refers to another study done by Sukhwinder Shergill and colleagues at University College London, addressing "He hit me harder."

CHAPTER THREE: The next semester, Ken is studying abroad in London. Ken's old friend, Ben, is visiting. They have gone to all the tourist sights and are bored. They do not have anything better to do on a Thursday afternoon, so they both volunteer for Shergill's study. Volunteers are wired to a device that measures the pressure each applies to the other's fingers. They are instructed to exchange touches of equal force. Ken and Ben concentrate to follow instructions. Even with the best of intentions, like the other volunteers, they routinely increase the pressure on each other. Across the board, volunteers applied about 40% more pressure than they received, each time! Why? The pain we receive is more tangible / real to us than the pain we give to others.

Recent studies find that our brain numbs out our awareness of sensations that are familiar and/or expected. It overrides our continued noticing of the chair we are sitting in or the mildly pinching shoes we have on. We do not hear the noisy fan and traffic, but the much softer cry of a baby gets our attention. If we initiate a physical action toward ourselves or others, our brain registers less than if someone else does the same action. When a friend massages our feet, our brain will take more note of it than if we massage our own feet, especially when they make unexpected moves.

CHAPTER FOUR: That very weekend, Ken and fiancée, Polly, get into a terrible argument. They yell at each other. They say unkind things. He storms out. She is in tears.

CHAPTER FIVE: Polly calls her friend Molly and tells her how wounded she is because of all the cruel things Ken said. Molly listens for nearly an hour to a list of Ken's devastating comments. Ken and Ben go out to a local pub where Ken relates to his friend all the hurtful, mean things that Polly said to him. They agree she was a bitch and maybe he should not get married after all.

CHAPTER SIX: So, shall we make this story have a happy ending? Shall Ken receive in the mail a few days later, the report on what the recent Shergill psych study was all about and, by some odd coincidence, on the same day shall he read in the paper an article on the Swann psych study he participated in the last semester? And with even greater coincidence, shall Ben go with a friend to a workshop on Nonviolent Communication? Shall Ken then call Ben, who is at home by this time, and shall they confer about how they could apply all of this information to understanding the fight Ken had with Polly? Shall they then consider what steps Ken might take to invite Polly to join him in digging themselves out of the hole they together dug themselves into?

I leave the ending to you.

Here is a summary of the ways our brain misinforms us.

- We usually perceive a fight as starting when we first experience pain, therefore everyone involved can easily conclude that the other person started it.

- We know the details of our own lives and our own thinking, therefore, our words and actions seem to us to be reasonable, logical, and ethical.

- We seldom know the details of the life and the inner dialogue of the other person, so their words and actions can often seem unreasonable, jarring, and startling.

- We notice stimuli that are surprising to us more than those familiar to us.

- The physical and mental pain we receive is more real to us than the pain we give to others.

Throughout <u>Connection</u>, we will look at many ways to get beyond the illusions of our minds.

CATCHING AN ALIVE ILLUSION OR TWO
1. Think of any interaction you have observed in person or on TV that might illustrate any of the above ideas. Describe briefly what happened.
2. Think of one interaction between you and a friend wherein they said or did something you did not appreciate. Can you find or imagine any words or actions of your own that they might be reacting to? Describe briefly what happened.

DEEPLY HONORING TWO SETS OF NEEDS = WIN-WIN SOLUTIONS

> **Jeff:** *A win-win orientation is achieved by viewing conflict as a set of problems to be solved rather than games in which one person wins and the other loses. A neutral observation describes the problem without focusing blame on the people or making any judgmental statements. Then they look for the needs of each person. Then the discussion would focus on whether we want to get another pizza, rather than who ate the last piece.*

> **Brad:** *Before I left to study and live abroad for a year and a half, I sold my car. Now that I am home for the semester, I don't have a car. I can walk to and from school, but on the weekends, I like the use of my mom's car. Usually she is okay with that, but recently we both wanted it at the same time. After some discussion, we saw that we could not come up with a plan for both of us to use the car this weekend. So, we compromised. Her immediate need was clearly greater than mine so she took it this weekend and I get it next weekend. We also thought I should get another cheap car for now.*

> **Jessica:** *My ex-boyfriend has not sent any e-mail for a while. I usually say something like "I don't know why I am writing this e-mail because you never write e-mails back," which is an evaluation. But in this case, I thought about just trying to express my needs and to notice his. I did not get angry, nor did I get down on myself. I said, "I know that you are busy with work, and you need time to think about things, so you should take your time. I would really appreciate a reply, it would mean a lot to me." And I got a reply back saying "I will read over your e-mail, and write a response when I have time." I was pleased.*

We live in a society that often thinks in terms of win-lose, that sees only the options of fight or flight. Many TV shows are based on people fighting, whether with weapons or with wits, each struggling to get their own way. When individuals or groups are in a competition mode, they are defensive and somewhat fearful. This is not a productive energy to be in when we hope to create new solutions. The problems stand firmly between us.

If you play an instrument or read your poetry or even make a speech to a class, think about how much easier it is when you are sure the audience is accepting and appreciative of your effort rather than looking for ways you might fail. Students often have no idea that their own attitudes affect the tone of a class. If we want to find win-win solutions, we will pay attention to doing everything possible to create a safe and affirming climate.

It may take some discernment on our part to look beyond competition and see the vital third stance that is possible—wherein one does not fight, fly away, nor freeze; but stands boldly asserting one's own needs and also listening to and honoring the needs of the other party. As we explore this way of approaching life, it becomes increasingly solid, real, and effective in meeting needs, in solving problems, and in building community. This stance requires vision and a willingness to be open to the other person. If this is a new concept, it may seem elusive to you, especially at first.

When we stand together to face the problems, the shift in position creates an alive, zestful, compassionate space wherein new satisfying strategies are likely to emerge. With cooperation, two people or even a group can often craft a better solution than any individual can come up with. Holding this intention shifts our focus from who is wrong, who is at fault, to what needs are being met or unmet. Refocusing changes the way we perceive a situation and unleashes new creativity.

If we are stuck in the competitive model of I-will-win-and-you-will-lose, we will always create more tension. Some people believe that competition is good for bringing out the best in people. It is possible that this is true in sports and business, but it does not contribute to the close personal relationships that most people want to live in. Nor does it create a peaceful world.

Ironically, even if we aspire to give in all the time, we still set the stage for more tension. Some part within us will tend to get angry with the other person for not noticing our unspoken needs, and the other person may get bored that we are not bringing our whole selves to the relationship. It seems to me that if we want to build strong relationships, we have to aim for win-win.

The problem is between us   Together we will face the problem

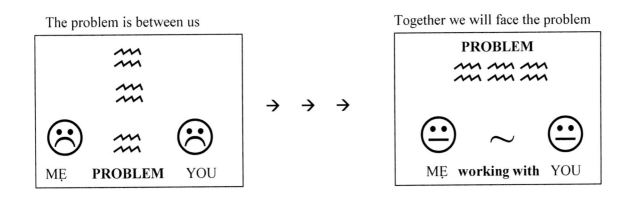

Can you always meet everyone's needs?

Almost always. Still there may be times when both sets of needs cannot be met at the same time or with the strategies presented. Honoring everyone's needs means knowing and valuing each need, and refusing to lightly set aside any need, but working for strategies wherein everyone wins. If a need cannot be met at this time, it is connecting to notice that together.

Many are surprised to discover that when they get clear about their needs even when they are not currently met, this self-connection alone brings them a sense of peace. Try it for yourself.

Is there any place for compromise solutions?

> **Jay:** *My mom told me that on Christmas Eve we were going to her friends' home and to a Christmas Eve service. I threw a fit. I had bad experiences at a religious school and would rather stand outside in the cold than go to church. Later we talked about the menu for Thanksgiving dinner. I love turkey and wanted her to fix it. She is a vegan and does not like to have meat in her home. We compromised that I would go to the Christmas Eve service and she would get turkey for my brother and me.*

For compromise, you win part of what you want and lose part of what you want. The other person also wins some and loses some. It is useful to resolve <u>minor</u> conflicts. It takes less time and effort. For win-win solutions, we need more time to get beyond the initial apparent conflict to explore the needs under each person's preferences, positions, and strategies. Then we will look together on how to meet all the deep needs. This process will be explored in detail in Chapter Twelve.

Success Script—Attitude

Title: Remembering my Intention
Name: Andy
Date: 9/24/06

Background: *At my job, working with youth, we have a room known as "the planning room" where students go to check in with staff about challenges or to be isolated during a tense or unsafe situation. One of the planning room's most frequent customers is a 15-year old named Mike. He has been neglected, physically and sexually abused, and has a late onset of puberty, and regularly has issues with peers and staff.*

The last time Mike was sent to the planning room, his regular staff person was headed to a meeting, so I was asked to be Mike's support staff. Mike was distressed and his mission seemed to be to get someone else distressed too. He shouted that the staff were all "fucking idiots and liars," that we were all "big failures, wasting our lives here." I tried to argue with him point by point that we indeed were not liars and failures. Eventually I became frustrated and had to remove myself from the situation.

New Behavior: *Several days ago I was in the planning room again with Mike. He again yelled at me, "You are a big, fat loser, Andy; get a life." He continued for quite awhile like this, trying to bring me down. This time I saw beyond the "punk kid" who was insulting me, and focused on the young man who had faced unbelievable adversity and was trying his best to work through it. I thought of the good interactions we had shared in the past, the rides home from work, and positive gains Mike had made in the program. The big picture got me through. I remembered that Mike did not really hate me—he was just having a tough day.*

Why I Consider This a Success: *A co-worker told me that self-care was one of the biggest challenges in the field of social services and that it was impressive that I could listen to Mike rip me apart and stay solid in remembering the bigger picture of myself and of Mike.*

Intention for the Future: *I am going into the field of social work and I plan to continue my good work around self-care.*

Success Script—Attitude

Title:
Date:

Optional: create a Mind Map, a doodle, or other visual aides

Part Two: Grounding Through Self-Care

Amy: *I am finally getting it—that it is important to look kindly at ourselves rather than seeing our actions as punishable failures or expressions of our limitations. Judgments of self-hatred, shame and guilt are not very effective motivators. Instead, it is enough to let change be stimulated by a clear desire to enrich lives for ourselves and for those who contribute to our lives.*

Brent: *How can you be happy with yourself if you don't know what you are feeling and needing? I know for myself, whenever I'm feeling down, I go to my room where I can have some peace and be alone. I then slow myself down, think of what's going on and look at the bigger picture and what my needs are, then go from there.*

Some think that the youth of today are too selfish and self-centered and that we should return to old-fashioned virtues. Here's why I think this "me-first attitude" is valuable for both society and the individual. Identifying inner values and finding the courage to live by them is based on self-understanding, self-respect, and self-care.

There is a shift in the underlying paradigm in the U.S. and in the world—from kings to democracy; from the common distrust of people's basic nature to a wider acceptance that the core motivation of humans is to meet needs we all share, as proposed by Maslow; from an emphasis on obedience to one of cooperation.

Perhaps a contributing factor was the explorations of consciousness and the movements for social justice in the 1960s. (Full disclosure: I was in college in the early 60s, so I am partial to attributing long-term consequences to the youthful efforts of my generation! ☺)

I believe that when individuals are seriously committed to becoming familiar with and meeting their own needs, they become responsible people. Knowing one's own needs leads directly to a deeper understanding of the needs of others. When one becomes more aware of the value of creating situations wherein everyone's needs are being met, one is on the road to conflict resolution.

This is known as enlightened self-interest. It is also the basis of a democracy.

Today's youth—at least those I meet at Champlain College—report learning at home the value of thinking for themselves, and the willingness to question any authority. They are developing an internal value system to weigh their actions. I hope readers will be patient with them and/or yourselves through the awkward moments in this transition. Moving from a system of power over and power under into a system of power sharing, is difficult—both personally and for our society.

We are all cultivating the skills we will need tomorrow, and we are still in training today.

**If it is not fun,
why do it?
--Ben & Jerry's slogan**

How would self-care help us professionally?

CAREER CHOICE

> **Sam:** *Students need to be exposed at a young age to the questions of what are your feelings and needs. The idea of focusing on one's own needs and aspirations is most important in order to make it clear that no one should dictate what you should or shouldn't do with your life, for example, making a student attend a 4-year college right out of high school even if it's not truly what they need at the time.*

Today's culture often encourages people to believe that their deepest needs can be met by owning many things. This message permeates most media channels. Unless they are reminded to pay attention to their own interests, many college students make the earning of a lot of money their highest priority. Unfortunately this choice will likely postpone making their own vital connection with their life energy, their vision, their calling, and their needs. They may miss the deep satisfaction of spending forty hours a week in a job they love.

ENERGY ON THE JOB

> **Kiki:** *In our group of social work students, we were able to come up with many ways in which self-care is essential to a successful career. As a social worker, we will be in regular need of self-evaluation and check-ins with ourselves. Our clients will be dealing with heavy issues that could easily find their ways into our daily lives. Working with people who need help and being the type of person who wants happiness for everyone, it may become difficult to see clients I care about stumble and fall. I need to make sure I re-center regularly.*

If a person focuses on caring for others and neglects to take care of their own needs, they are less effective in their caring—professionally as well as personally. They are candidates for burnout. This is especially true in careers where one works with people having difficulties in their lives.

CLEAR COMMUNICATION ON THE JOB

> **Laurel:** *I had requested of my supervisor to add an agenda item about a mail procedure to our meeting coming up. My supervisor replied, "We can talk about it, but my answer is not going to change." After thinking more about this interaction, I decided to practice using OFNR steps. When I approached her again, I said, "I would feel more encouraged attending this meeting, if you waited until after the meeting to make your final decision. Would you be willing to postpone your decision?"*

> **Abby:** *By showing us how to focus on what we truly want rather than on what is wrong with either others or ourselves, Nonviolent Communication gives us the tools to create better understanding with others on the job as well as at home.*

Most jobs include working with co-workers, even if you are not working with the public. Job satisfaction and effectiveness are often based on how well co-workers communicate. When employers talk to colleges about training their graduates for on-the-job skills, their number one request is for better communication skills!

I thought relationships are about giving to someone else. Self-care in a close personal relationship sounds really selfish to me.

Jay: *I decided to break up with my girlfriend. She thought she loved me and maybe she did, but she would barely give me any time for myself. She told me it was hard for her to leave me alone because she liked me so much and she felt safe and happy with me. This was one of the nicest things I have ever heard. Every time she was afraid, she called and I talked her through it. I tried hard to be there for her, but I was getting more and more emotionally drained.*

I found myself biting my tongue often when I was feeling irritated at her. She said she would try harder to give me more room, but she said the same things two months ago and she hasn't changed her actions. I could not figure out how to get my space. This frustrated me so badly I realized the only way to fix the problem was to break up with her, even though I did not want to hurt her feelings.

Sarah: *I would really like some time for myself, to not be running around all the time trying to complete tasks for everyone else. I think this is harder for women. Women naturally want to help everyone they care about and to be there for them. They often forget to take care of themselves. Last night I wanted to stay home and work on this paper, but my boyfriend wanted my attention and I couldn't say "No." I am now up this morning typing my heart out with my coffee at my side.*

It is very hard to maintain personal relationships if you prioritize taking care of the other person. Many people find that when they start with noticing their own needs and then the other person's needs, they are more likely to find outcomes that work for everyone. Both Jay and Sarah reflect how poorly their own needs were met when they put their entire focus on their partner.

Perhaps when Sarah looked inside, she would have found two honorable needs in apparent conflict—her need for connection and her need for achievement. "I could spend the evening hanging out with my boyfriend or I could write my paper." At this point she might choose to put both of these needs on the table and tell her boyfriend what is happening inside for her and find out what her boyfriend is feeling and wanting. "I am feeling torn. I would love to spend the evening talking—that is important to me. And I am also concerned about getting my paper written for class tomorrow afternoon." If he does not even know about her conflicting choices, he misses the opportunity of supporting her in her scholastic endeavors. She misses knowing about his support.

And they miss the chance of weighing together whether the urgency he feels to share this evening is more important than doing the paper. Looking together at all the needs, people have a better chance of working out ways to respect all of the needs. If one party makes the decision without consulting the other person, they lose a valuable chance to connect, to strengthen their relationship.

This section of the book will help you clarify what is or is not bringing you satisfaction, health, energy, and connection. Students are not the only ones who often rush through their days without taking the time to do any examination of the quality of their life. The upcoming chapters are full of invitations to become more self-aware and more self-nurturing. With a clearer picture of what you want and need, it will become easier to figure out what actions would start moving you toward your goal. Making deliberate choices will enhance your life, both personally and professionally.

Don't ask yourself
what the world needs.

Ask yourself what makes you come alive
and go do that

because what the world needs
is people who have come alive.

--Howard Thurman

CHAPTER SIX

φ

Self-Care, Nurturing Body and Brain

Renee: *When I was in High School, I had extremely bad anxiety. My mom didn't want to put me on drugs to fix it, so instead of drugs, she started teaching me about meditation and breathing techniques. Now I regularly remove myself from a situation and breathe to clear my head. The fog begins to clear when I start my meditation. My heart rate comes down and my adrenaline goes out with each and every breath. Then I can see the real issues. I used to think you had to deal with situations right away. Now I know that eventually you do have to deal with them, but not right away.*

OBSERVATIONS—UNDERSTANDING YOUR BRAIN STRUCTURE

Neurologists who study the brain have made many discoveries lately. A human brain has different sections that serve different functions. The most basic is the brain stem, sometimes called the Reptilian Brain, which activates the fight, flight, or startle response. The next layer up is the limbic region, sometimes called the Emotional Brain, which contributes our ability to feel emotions, create emotional memories, and read the emotions of others. The third major part of the brain is the prefrontal cortex, sometimes called the Thinking Brain or Executive Brain, which provides our capacity for reasoning, planning, imagining, creating, and fine tuning of our emotional response. Left-brain or verbal functions and right-brain or non-verbal, creative functions are both part of the Thinking Brain. Stimuli perceived as life-threatening will activate the Reptilian Brain with its fight, flight, or freeze response. When a situation is perceived as distressing, it activates our Emotional Brain, where the events of our lives have created stories, emotional memories, and filters that interpret events. These occur a fraction of a second before our Thinking Brain kicks in.

So what does this have to do with me?

Several pieces of this information could be helpful to you. If you are between 16 and 24-25, you are in a stage of physical development wherein your brain structure is actually working against you on making thoughtful choices! Scientists have shown that the limbic region that feels and enjoys strong sensations has a surge in growth several years before the similar surge in growth of the prefrontal cortex that reminds you to think it through and consider the consequences!

If you are in your late teens or early twenties, knowing that you are more susceptible to emotional overloads, could be important information. You might deliberately choose to put calming factors into your life—enough sleep, regular exercise, healthy food, a balance between work and play, more hanging out with friends, and following any spiritual practice that has meaning to you. Obviously, if a situation could be difficult, you do not add to your ability to handle it well by drinking or drugging. Think carefully about your choices.

FEELINGS—CALMING YOUR OVERLOADED FEELINGS BY BREATHING

> **Caitlyn:** *My boyfriend lives with four other guys. I am over there a lot and we are all pretty close. The other night we all got back from the bar, I threw on some short shorts and a big shirt to go watch TV with everyone. My boyfriend got really mad at me and told me to go change because I should not be wearing those in front of the guys when they were drunk. I did not think it was a big deal, but he kept yelling at me and getting madder.*
>
> *I could have easily flipped out right back at him, but I took the time to stop and breathe. I got up and went to the other room to regroup my thoughts. I hate it when I get yelled at, so I really needed some kind of self-support. No one was giving me any support. I waited awhile and thought about it. After I calmed down, I was able to talk with him later. I was pleased that I remembered to breathe rather than create a scene.*
>
> **Hannah:** *The tips on how you can support yourself in a conflict that were most helpful to me were: don't take it personally, attempt to change your current perspective, and remind yourself to breathe! I tried it out with my dad on the phone. He was upset with me about money, the usual argument.*
>
> *Instead of "throwing up my guard" when he confronted me, I took a couple seconds to breathe and think about what I was going to say. It didn't solve the conflict, but I believe it really helped me to understand his position more and I think he may have actually listened to what I was saying for a change!*

When we experience a flood of emotions such as anger or fear, our thinking doesn't work as well. William Donahue and Robert Kolt, authors of a college text on conflict management, say that being in crisis makes the brain "get stupid." We tend to distort what we hear and to misperceive the other person's motives because we degenerate into black-white thinking. Biases we long ago set aside may re-emerge. We frequently imagine we are in danger and need to defend ourselves in any way possible. We often neglect to think about our options. This especially happens when we imagine or experience an attack on our freedom, dignity, or self-esteem. Threatened people quickly move into a stance of protecting themselves rather than being able to think productively about the problem at hand. And it is only a short step further to counterattack.

If the only thing you remember from this book is to stop, shut your mouth, and breathe when in a difficult situation, your relationship with yourself and with others will likely improve noticeably. This reminder is pertinent to a person of any age.

The second thing I hope you remember is that you will invite this self-defensive response in others when you are perceived as demeaning them about character qualities they hold dear even when it appears to you that "they started it." It will help you both move to resolution of any problems if you regularly help those around you to "save face." In other words, never hit below the emotional beltline. You can choose to be a safe person and to invite people to activate their Thinking Brain.

Knowing how easily a person can lose perspective, we can plan ahead some simple, useful responses, and then practice them until we use them even in the storm. Obviously, if we can get calm before making decisions or taking actions, we will make wiser choices. (The following calming sequence was developed by Bonnie P. Peplow, based on work by Becky Bailey.)

EMERGENCY CALMING SEQUENCE

1. Notice your stress, anger, fear, or giddiness.
2. Stop what you are doing. Withdraw if you can.
3. Take a slow, deep belly breath. Hold it.
4. Relax your jaw, your shoulders, your arms, your entire body.
5. Breathe out slowly.
6. Repeat the breathing and relaxing sequence several times.
7. Tell yourself:
   "I am safe at this time, in this place," which calms your reptile brain.
   "Because I am breathing and relaxing, I am calm," which soothes limbic brain.
   "Because I am safe and calm, I can deal with this situation in a productive way," which activates the thinking brain.

CALMING EXERCISE: Set aside five minutes and slowly do each of these steps.

Imagine for a few minutes a situation that has invited some tension in you.
Take a slow, deep belly breath. Hold it.
Relax your jaw, your shoulders, your arms, your entire body.
Breathe out slowly.
Take a slow, deep belly breath. Hold it.
Relax your jaw, your shoulders, your arms, your entire body.
Breathe out slowly.
Take a slow, deep belly breath. Hold it.
Relax your jaw, your shoulders, your arms, your entire body.
Breathe out slowly.
Tell yourself "I am safe at this moment in this situation."
Tell yourself "Because I am breathing and relaxing, I am calm."
Tell yourself "Because I am safe and calm, I can choose my best actions."

NEEDS—TAKING CARE OF YOUR VEHICLE

David: *When I went to college, I wanted to see if I could do the homework and not be a star athlete. Therefore my exercise went from doing 3 sports regularly to nothing but video games and homework. Looking back, I find that I was not functioning well. I got angry quickly. People tiptoed around me hoping that I wouldn't have a mood swing. When I made the connection that I use exercise as a tool to deal with stress and anger and to better function, I began lifting weights with a friend for an hour or two a day. After a few weeks, people started to notice and said that I was acting differently in a good way.*

Justin: *I recently broke a habit I have had since my 8ᵗʰ grade year. I used to always prioritize my homework above all else. I recently had two choices—to get an A on my homework or to meet my needs for recreation. I accepted the invitation to go over to a friend's house. We spoke for hours, listened to music, played guitar, rode a long board, and she taught me how to solve a Rubrics cube. When I arrived home much later, I made the choice to get some sleep so I could function the next day.*

I do respect the fact that this new behavior may not be in my best scholarly interests, but the happiness it brings me is worth it. I will not forget that I also have needs for learning and achievement, but they are not the only needs that are important to me.

Self-care starts by asking what is happening in your life and whether your life is going in ways that satisfy you. Everyone has choices to make daily. How are you making those choices?

Let's look at the most fundamental level of human needs. We are physical beings. If we get enough sleep, eat well, and exercise, we will be more stable and better able to handle stress. College students' bodies usually need more sleep than college students get. Doctors consistently recommend eight hours or more a night for good health, fewer colds, and clear thinking. We also have deep needs for connecting with others in recreation, laughter, fun, and conversation. Sometimes one gets busy and forgets.

REALITY CHECK LIST: For one week give yourself a + , an OK or a – daily.							
	Sun	**Mon**	**Tue**	**Wed**	**Thur**	**Fri**	**Sat**
How much sleep are you getting?							
Are you eating healthily?							
Are you drinking enough water?							
Are you exercising regularly?							
Are you relaxing regularly?							
Are you socializing regularly?							

Imagine for a minute that you are responsible for a young child. Would you recommend they get the same care you give yourself? How are you doing with basic care for your vehicle? As you consider your Reality Check List, what is working for you, i.e., what needs are being met and what needs are not being met? Are there any actions that you could add or subtract which would improve your basic care for your vehicle? Would it fit for you at this time to request of yourself to modify one or more of these actions?

HOW WELL ARE YOU PARENTING YOURSELF?
Needs being met
Needs not being met
Actions you could add or subtract that would improve your basic self-care
Actions that you are ready to request of yourself to modify   **(Remember to request, not demand.)**

Jenny: *Needs are important, because they are a cause of why we act or say something. A person's needs are also a main cause behind anger. It's very seldom that John and I are yelling at each other. Every time we are angry at each other we haven't eaten anything for a long time, and are very hungry. Because we know that when we are very hungry we are not in a good mood, we have identified what need has not been met, and then we could do something about it. Instead of trying to solve why we are angry at each other, we make something to eat. Then we realize that we were quarreling about some rubbish.*

Not only are we more effective in learning, but our ability to handle conflict increases when we are at a solid place in our daily lives.

REQUEST OF YOURSELF—CREATE A FIRST AID KIT

> **Brady:** *It is important to have a first aid kit for stressful moments. I want to remember to get enough sleep, eat healthy, and take a walk or go to the gym to discharge emotions from my body. These strategies will be important to me in every aspect of my life, especially in the criminal justice world. Police must remain calm even when we see criminals do a lot of sick things. You can't take your anger out on them or you will ruin your career.*

You, your parents, and your coach probably have a first aid kit with items ready for emergencies. You can deliberately make plans ahead of time that will support you in getting through tense situations with some dignity, maybe even some grace, and getting your feet back under you ASAP.

FIRST AID ITEMS

1. **Breathe**
2. **Make an emergency exit**
3. **Use your plan to regroup fairly quickly**

1. Breathe

> **Nick:** *A good example of how I have gotten better with conflict happened the other day. I was at work. I was pretty sure a co-worker had misplaced his lunch tickets in with mine. I brought the issue up and politely asked him to check over my tickets and see if any of them were his. My co-worker got defensive and started to get verbally aggressive with me.*
>
> *Instead of my usual Nick response, I took several deep breaths and said, "Maybe you're right. Maybe none of these are yours, but it would mean a lot to me if you would just look. I can't afford to pay for meals I didn't take. That's all." After that, he sat down, went over the tickets and did indeed find two that were his. He apologized for getting so heated.*

As we discussed a minute ago, remembering to take a slow deep breath and then another is probably the strongest on-the-spot response. You could learn to give more attention to your breathing by noticing your breathing during calm times of the day. Can you take a moment now to take a slow and deep breath that expands your belly? Some people recommend that you teach yourself to breathe like this all the time, as the additional oxygen is good for your health.

2. Make an emergency exit

> **Kelly:** *Recently Mom and I were discussing where I am going to live next year. I could see that my voice was raising and that I was angry. When Mom and I argue, we both think we are right. To help this discussion go a little better, I withdrew and called my friend. She makes it so when I call upset about something, I am in a better state of mind when I am done talking to her. I realized that life is too short to always be arguing. I took good care of myself to leave the situation until both Mom and I cooled down.*

Katie: *I was eating dinner and playing with my friend's cell phone and he had asked for it back twice. I did not see it as a big deal and thought we were just playing around when he threw a bottle of relish at my head. (My friend is developmentally disabled and when he apologized to me he told me that it made sense in his head because he had already asked me twice and he is used to just throwing stuff at his roommates.)*

At the time of the incident, I was not interested in explanations or apologies. I was fuming. I knew my anger was only a result of embarrassment because our table had become the center of attention in the cafeteria, so instead of blaming or crying, which I desperately wanted to do, I took a deep breath, stood up and walked out of the cafeteria. Instead of possibly further worsening the situation or engaging with my friend, I chose to remove myself, a more mature decision than I've made in a while.

An explosive or even a tense situation often does not give you the time to arrive at a thoughtful handling of the situation. With planning, you can usually create valuable space between the stimulus and your response. It is helpful to plan out and memorize a few emergency exit strategies. If you ask often, "Am I enjoying myself?" you will be aware within seconds when you start experiencing distress. Consider strong feelings like the red light on the dashboard of your car. This is a reminder that whatever reactive words you are about to say are likely to decrease the possibility of you getting what you would like out of this situation which is having the other person hear your concerns and interests and you hearing the other person accurately.

If you can, take a deep breath and say, "I need to think some more about what you said—I'll give you a call soon." Another great exit line, especially to your parents, is to say, "Thank you for your concern. I will think about it and get back to you." I have read that Japanese businessmen say, "We need time to consider your very important idea. We will talk again tomorrow." Some people respond to any request, "I need to sleep on it." (I am trying to make that my habitual reply.)

In a close relationship, you might choose to share openly, "At this moment, I am feeling so scared and so disconnected from you and from myself that I fear that anything I say right now will not bring us closer together. Would you be willing for us to take a two hour (or a ten minute) break before we continue this discussion?" This stance may take some extra practice!

3. Use your plan to regroup fairly quickly

Audrey: *When I was in the dining room asking one of the servers to prepare my sandwich, I was rather angry because she was not really nice (according to me) and she did not understand what I wanted. My first reaction was to think she misunderstood on purpose because I was a foreign student with a bad accent! (This reaction was based on my experience while spending one year in [another country]. I wasn't well treated there.)*

But I took a walk and thought about it and realized that maybe it was me who didn't make an effort to articulate and to speak louder. Then I also realized that this woman was certainly tired of seeing so many students in one day and likely bored of always doing the same task. Finally I was satisfied because this event did not disturb me anymore, when I found some potential reasons for her behavior.

IF YOU PLAN AHEAD, YOU ARE MORE LIKELY TO DO THESE CALMING ACTIVITIES

- Go to your room and journal for an hour. Or write on loose paper and destroy it or on your computer and delete it. As you get accurate words around your feelings, you move toward thoughts and you will likely feel calmer just by that alone.

- Go out to the lake, or find a place alone and yell out your judgments. Then yell out your feelings. When the steam subsides, notice your unmet needs.

- Call a friend and explode. Who might you call on as a reliable source of understanding? (You want friends who won't reinforce blame with comments like: "yeah, he's a real jerk" or "oh, you really deserved that." Go to one who will listen.) After taking the time to do some uncensored ranting and raving, share your feelings and your needs.

- Is there some place you can go that is peaceful to you? If not an actual place, can you call up a place in your mind that calms you?

- Identify music you find mellow. Do you have that music on hand? A "chill list" on your Ipod? Throughout history people have used music to influence their feelings.

- You could also discharge the emotions from your body by physical action—a walk, working out at the gym, playing Frisbee, or gardening. And then return to thinking about the matter with a clearer head.

CONSTRUCTING YOUR OWN FIRST AID KIT: Choose an item for each category	
A place to go to or visualize	
Music that calms me	
A calming activity I could do	
Two friends or family members I could talk with during a stressful situation	
Improve on physical care—getting enough sleep	
Improve on physical care—consuming healthy food and enough water	
Improve on physical care—getting both exercise and relaxation	
Improve on physical care—regular socializing	
(Your suggestion)	
Are you willing to pick two of the above strategies or two strategies of your own and decide to start putting them into your life? If so, put a ✔ in front of them.	

AND AN ATTITUDE—BEAM ME UP, SCOTTIE

> **Rick:** *Some of the stuff in our homework did not seem to match my situation. Then I came to the slogans. "This is not about me." and "Shut your mouth and breathe." were drilled into me in basic [police] training and honestly they do work. This situation is not about me. I am responding to a call because I am needed there. So don't get hot-headed. Just go do your job.*

When Star Trekkers found themselves in a difficult situation, they had the fall-back option of signaling to the mother ship and requesting a quick rescue, "Beam me up, Scottie." You can create in your mind, a rescue beam for yourself, for the times you are on total overload, thinking brain degenerating by the moment, <u>if</u> you take the time to build it carefully.

12-Step programs such as Alcoholics Anonymous, repeat a number of simple slogans, again and again. They are on posters on the walls, they are given by sponsors to their sponsees, and they show up in the talks regularly, because they are an important part of the safety net for a recovering alcoholic, such as: Easy does it. First things first. One day at a time. This too shall pass. Nothing is so bad that a drink won't make it worse. Live and let live. Let go and let God.

If you would like a beam-me-up rescue sometimes, you can do this too. Gather a few short slogans, affirmations, or words of wisdom from your family or any other source. Lines from a song are especially powerful. A personal mantra you have chanted for hours is a solid transport beam back to sanity. Pick a slogan that reflects one of your truths, that really speaks to you. To be effective, the slogan needs to be short and positive. When your brain is flooded with emotions, a short statement is more likely to be there than a long one.

After you have one or two, commit them to memory, say them in the mirror to yourself, write them on post-it notes and put them on your computer. Extra progress points for singing them to yourself or saying them while walking because of the non-verbal associations. If you say them at least several hundred times, you may recall one of these slogans even when emotions cripple your clear thinking and your brain starts to "get stupid." This parallels the breathing exercise we looked at a few pages ago.

Lately I have valued Leonard Cohen's lines in Anthem: "Ring, ring the bells that still can ring. Forget your perfect offering. There is a crack, a crack in everything. That's how the light gets in." It gets me unstuck from my tendency to be a perfectionist. (Yes, I also have some shorter slogans!)

Here are some common statements that some students have found useful. Try any of these or gather a few of your own. What slogan do you lean on?

- It is not about me
- I always have choices
- HALT—if I am hungry, angry, lonely, or tired, I will call a friend
- Shut your mouth and breathe
- There is nothing that God and I can't handle
- Everyone is just meeting honorable needs

Success Script—Nurturing Body and Brain

Title: Getting More Active
Name: Matt
Date: 10/26/06

Background: *I have always been a very active guy. In the summer you won't find me inside any time. I love hiking, fishing, swimming, skiing, you name it. Outdoor time lets me relax and not worry about other things in my life. I also am often with friends. It meets many needs—recreation, spiritual, physical and connection.*

This fall I found myself indoors a lot. The weather has been lousy, so I have been picking up my video game controller and sitting in front of the TV. I have been getting stressed about school work and testier with my emotions. I also felt tired and lazy—generally not in a mood to do anything.

New Behavior: *Our workbook assignment on Self-Care included a "reality check" to see how we were meeting our physical needs daily. As I went through each item, I started noticing a pattern. Not only was I not getting enough outdoor exercise, other needs were not being met due to the lack of this important time for myself.*

I decided to call some friends and go for a hike no matter the condition. It ended up raining again, but we didn't care. We got all our necessary gear, food, and water and made the trek up Mt. Mansfield. It was muddy and sloppy every step, but we were having a great time—splashing in rivers and talking about good old times. We hiked all day, ate lunch at the top, and then took a different trail to the bottom. It took us about six hours for the entire trip.

I think it is important to me to get outside at least once a week. Since that Saturday, I have been consciously trying to get more active. I have been shooting hoops in between classes, walking to and from school, and getting out a little while at least one of the weekend days.

Why I Consider this a Success: *I have generally been feeling a lot better and I have been friendlier with everyone. This is kind of weird, but I have actually been sleeping better too, which makes me more energized throughout the day. It was also a success because I looked back on a week and figured out why I was feeling down in the dumps, and then found a cure that was as simple as going for a hike with some friends. I think it is amazing how one little activity can change how you are feeling.*

Intention for the Future: *It is obvious that outdoor time is very important in taking care of myself. If I am ever feeling down, I need to look within myself and my actions to figure out why and how to fix it. I am going to try to not let this fall period get me down again. I need to realize that I must spend time with friends outside, or my whole life starts to spiral in the wrong direction.*

Success Script—Nurturing Body and Brain

Title:
Date:

Optional: create a Mind Map, a doodle, or other visual aides

CHAPTER SEVEN

φ

Self-Care, Doing Inner Work

Jody: *Two nights ago I received an email from a teammate stating he didn't think I cared about his ideas for our project and that I would report what I wanted regardless of his input. Receiving this email, I perceived it as an insult accusing me of not caring. I felt hurt and upset and I wanted to shoot off an email in defense of myself.*

Instead I reminded myself to stop and pay attention to my inner dialogue. I decided to listen to myself as if I were my own best friend. I saw I wanted better understanding from my teammates. Then I thought about what needs he could be having. I found compassion for him when I saw that he needed more acknowledgement and appreciation from me. I e-mailed to tell him I heard his concerns and did appreciate his input. He thanked me.

OBSERVATIONS—TRACKING YOURSELF

There are different words for the practice of stopping all action, slowing down, and observing our thoughts and feelings. Regardless of the name for it, many traditions identify a calm center within every person, a quiet witness, which is capable of observing our inner process with detachment, like watching a show. This is applying our skills in making neutral observations to the way we watch our internal workings.

Journaling, formal meditation, yoga, some martial arts, or talking to a friend who listens well can all help you develop this quiet inner center. Even knowing that this calm center exists and reaching for it can increase your balance and ability to make more beneficial decisions.

Rick: *In law enforcement, it does not pay to get angry. Officers need to have their mind clear of all distractions, in order to fully comprehend their surroundings for their own safety and the safety of others. The presence of anger should be the first alarm the individual needs to wake up and observe the situation.*

Why are they getting angry and how can they deal with this issue? Anger must be dealt with or we will react to a situation without thinking, in a sense of vengefulness. This could easily make a difficult situation worse. It is necessary to remember that anger comes from inside ourselves and not from others. Anger also needs to be expressed for an individual to be healthy.

Here is a model for a structured look at some situation in your life that you are stressing about. This is a combination of outer observation and inner observation. The model is followed by some student examples, and after that a grid where you can do it yourself.

A STRUCTURED LOOK OUTSIDE AND INSIDE: Here is the underlying OFNR (Observations, Feelings, Needs, and Requests) frame for this exercise.	
Observations:	1. Notice your situation (with observations, not evaluations) • Your current inner dialogue • Your current actions
Feelings	2. Notice your feelings
Needs:	3. Notice your needs
Requests:	4. Ask yourself • Do I want to continue my current inner dialogue and actions? • Do I want to change my inner dialogue and actions? • If so, in what direction?

Rob: *What happened yesterday was that my teacher said I was a slacker. I felt resentment, embarrassment, and frustration. I thought the teacher was a jerk. I knew that if I were a robot I could have gotten the assignment finished. I also know I am a full-time student and I have an internship. I chose to take time to sit on the couch and relax the other afternoon. I needed some down time, so I took the time to mentally get away from school. The teacher could grade me down for not getting the paper in on time. That would be fair. The teacher does have the same guidelines for everyone in the class. But I did not deserve to be called a slacker. Maybe I will go talk to the teacher so he will have an honest understanding of what is going on for me.*

Kelly: *When I started taking a computer class, I thought the professor was way too hard. He gave huge assignments and never explained them clearly. At first I complained to a lot of people about his teaching tactics and just got madder. I finally gathered my courage and went to his office. I explained the problems I was having in his class. I also told him that I felt there was too much homework and that I needed more time to complete the assignments. He did hear me and he now gives the assignments earlier, which allows me more time to complete them. I am also more assertive in asking him to explain stuff I don't understand. If I had not talked to him, I would have failed the class. I guess getting aware of my fear of failing is what gave me the courage to go see him.* [felt there was too much homework = softened thought]

A STRUCTURED LOOK OUTSIDE AND INSIDE: Example by **Allyson**	
Your situation	*I hate public speaking; I am thinking about skipping a presentation and taking a zero.*
Current inner dialogue	*Presentations are an unfair way to judge a student.*
Current actions	*Complaining to friends*
Feelings	*Fear, shame, stressed out, frustrated*
Needs	*Esteem needs and contribution needs*
Continue my current inner dialogue and actions?	*No*
Change my dialogue and actions?	*Yes*
If so, in what direction?	*Suck it up and give the presentation. Focus on how good I will feel when it is over.*

A STRUCTURED LOOK OUTSIDE AND INSIDE: Try your own irritating situation.	
Your situation	
Current inner dialogue	
Current actions	
Feelings	
Needs	
Continue my current inner dialogue and actions?	
Change my inner dialogue and actions?	
If so, in what direction?	

Byron Katie (www.byronkatie.com/) does some interesting work in having people ask themselves whether their current dialogue and resulting actions are helpful to them. She challenges them to imagine that the opposite of what they believe may be true. I have read some of her earlier books and am intrigued by the title of her latest book, Who Would You Be Without Your Story?

FEELINGS—TRANSFORMING PAINFUL MEMORIES TO NEEDS AWARENESS

Tom: *Often we can be too hard on ourselves when we do something that we don't like. We waste time judging ourselves. Instead we should figure out what needs were or were not met by the action in question and approach the situation from that angle. I deal with it on a daily basis. Whenever I don't do assigned work for school, even if I consciously choose not to do it, I am often very hard on myself internally.*

Laurel: *Recently my supervisor's boss asked me a procedural question. I was thrown off by the question, so I said I did not know. In fact, I really did know that answer. My unmet needs were expressed through my moralistic judgments of myself, "What an idiot you are—you are such a loser." The needs underneath that judgment were the need to communicate and the need to contribute on the job. Once you start to hear your underlying needs, the self-forgiveness process starts.*

Most of us tie up much of our energy by feeling regret or even judgments about our past behavior. It is part of the inner stash of dynamite which is easily set off by events that remind us of this sore area and lead to explosions or compulsive behavior. The next several pages will lead you through an exercise for the healing of painful memories of things you have done and feel sad about. Here are some student responses to this exercise, an example of a recent experience I had laid out in this format, and then a grid for your work.

Kelly: *Observation: I got really impatient with my boss when I had to close the restaurant because she wasn't empathetic about my need to go home and study for my Child Psychology test, so I swore at her.*

My self-judgment: I was a horrible person for yelling at my boss.

Needs not met: my need for acting maturely. [needs = integrity and mutual respect]

Needs met: the need to study for the exam and to express my frustration with my boss. [need = achievement; strategy = studying]

My current feelings: disappointment in myself.

Awareness: I want to tell my boss before any upcoming exams that I have an exam and I want to leave early in order to have enough time to study! And I would prefer next time not to use profanity at all.

Marcus: *One time I was driving up the mountains for a ski trip and I did a really dangerous and unnecessary passing of a slower car. I think "I shouldn't have passed like that—it was really stupid of me." My unmet need was security and caring for my friends. I would never forgive myself if my friends had been in an accident I had caused.*

When I looked at which needs I was trying to meet when I did this passing, I see I was trying to get to the cabin as fast as possible to be able to have fun with my friends. It was the need for joy. When I think about this, the few minutes I saved passing that car were not worth the mental pain and the risk. I could plan an extra day with my friends or avoid traffic by going in the middle of the week.

Jessica: *Observation: I did not return my mother's call. Self-judgment: I am selfish, spoiled and sorry. Current feelings and needs: Disappointed in myself; would like to have had more compassion for my mother. Honorable motive for my action: I need to have my own space. Strategy for the future: to try to call my mom before I take a weekend for myself so she does not call in the middle of my time for myself.*

TRANSFORMING PAINFUL MEMORIES TO NEEDS AWARENESS: Example by **Bonnie** (teacher and author of this book)
What is one thing you did in the past that you regret having done? Tell a brief story, using clean observations.
This week, a student wanted to drop a seminar I teach and came to my office five minutes before the class started to get my signature. I was already tensing myself a bit as my supervisor was coming to observe. I tried to find out why she was quitting, listen reflectively, argue with her, tell her to come back later, and finish getting ready for class—all at the same time! I gave up and was real snippy with her. I said, "Okay, I will sign it." By that point both the student and I had tears of frustration welling up in our eyes and I was late to class. [It was my guess, my evaluation, and <u>not</u> an observation, that her tears were also because of frustration.]
What self-judgments did you have?
I felt horrified to see myself communicating in ways that did not follow what I was teaching and what I believe is connecting. My self-evaluation was that I lacked integrity.
What needs of yours were NOT met by your actions—i.e., why did you pick this incident?
I did not express any of the caring I have for this particular student. My actions did not reflect my values of respect and connection. I completely abandoned <u>my</u> need for gaining a clear understanding of the student's reasons for dropping the seminar.
What needs were you trying to meet by taking this action?
I wanted to resolve the conflict immediately to meet a need for ease. I ended the conversation and got to class, meeting my need to be respectful of my students and my supervisor. I did meet the student's need for support in getting the form signed.
What action could you have taken or could you take now that would meet both sets of needs? Take time to notice and acknowledge any needs that were not met.
I would have liked myself to have calmly said: "I understand that all you need is my signature and you cannot understand why this is complicated. I have a strong hunger to understand your experience. I want to talk with you before signing the form and I do not have time now. Can we set up an appointment later today or tomorrow?" What I did was to send her an e-mail and apologized for my attitude and asked her if she would be willing to help me understand her choice. I got a short answer, but the chance to explore her concerns was gone.

Here is a grid for you to do this exercise. It is a chance to observe your own past behaviors, to replace the evaluation with an understanding of needs and to re-file the incident. Please try this exercise with a <u>small incident</u> before you tackle more difficult sticking points in your memories. Write up another grid for repeating this exercise.

TRANSFORMING PAINFUL MEMORIES TO NEEDS AWARENESS:
What is one thing you did in the past that you regret having done? Tell a brief story, using clean observations.
What self-judgments did you have?
What needs of yours were NOT met by your actions—i.e., why did you pick this incident?
What needs were you trying to meet by taking this action?
What action could you have taken or could you take now that would meet both sets of needs? Take time to notice and acknowledge any needs that were not met.

NEEDS—FINDING YOUR NEEDS UNDER YOUR JUDGMENTS

Ryan: *Early in this class I shared about yelling at my mom to get off the phone so I could use it. Not only did she not get off the phone, but she also did not want to be more considerate of my needs for the phone in the future because I was not considerate of her needs for respect.*

When we learned about needs under all judgments, I looked for my judgment which was that she was inconsiderate. My underlying need was for connection with my friends on the phone, so I felt sad and frustrated when it wasn't happening. I thought about her needs and realized she has a new boyfriend and wanted connection, too. Finally, I talked with her in an honest and polite way, which allowed us to come up with a solution—that we would let each other know when we were planning to use the phone and for how long.

Kate: *The other day while I was parallel parking, I accidentally ran into a snow bank (this would be the stimulus.) Running into the snow bank caused me to think critically to myself, "I am so dumb for not being able to park correctly." However, I then thought about the feelings and needs behind my critical thought in order to gain a better understanding of why I had the critical thought. I determined that I felt angry and upset, and that my need was to keep my car and me safe. By recognizing the needs and feelings behind my critical thought, I was able to feel less guilt and shame for my action and in the future, I will be better able to understand myself in similar situations.*

It is time to bring out that collection of judgments and evaluations you have been saving up. I hope by now you are noticing your critical thoughts of others and finding more skill in holding them to yourself. And I hope you are viewing your self-criticism with more equanimity also. Judgments are a direct route to an essential piece of information—what is going on inside? What needs are not being met in your life? What deep hunger do you have for things to be different?

I do not respect myself for judging others. I pity myself for all the places I fail royally. And you want us to look at all this? Yukko!

I know it might seem painful to become more aware of other-blaming and self-blaming statements, but I assure you they are useful to explore. Self-hating and self-pitying freezes the situation and makes it temporarily unworkable. It is a crisis of the imagination, an assumption that there are no options to meet your needs. When you isolate the feelings and then notice the unmet needs they point to, you may find feelings like "discouraged" and "despairing" because you are hungry for "movement," "change," maybe "support." To be in touch with that hunger, that need, unfreezes your thinking and invites you to start considering strategies to meet those needs.

Increasing your awareness of what needs are alive for you today is a vital, life-giving skill. In the next chapter, we will work on more strategies for meeting your needs. It starts with awareness.

Look for any judgments, "should thinking" that has been in your mind recently. The amount and ways of criticism we have for others is usually closely related to the amount of criticism and ways we have for ourselves. As I did not stop harshly judging myself until in my mid 30s and am only recently finding more beauty inside, I am guessing most people will be able to find some examples.

FINDING PEARLS IN OYSTERS: Can you find any judgments in your thinking?" (If not, make some up.) Then turn them into observations, feelings, and needs. Examples are drawn from above quotations by **Ryan** and **Kate**.

Judgment: My mother is inconsiderate.	**Judgment:** I am so dumb.
Observations: My mother refused to get off the phone.	**Observations:** I ran my car into the snow bank.
Feelings: sad, frustrated	**Feelings:** angry, upset
Needs: connection with my friends	**Needs:** Safety

Judgment:	**Judgment:**
Observations:	**Observations:**
Feelings:	**Feelings:**
Needs:	**Needs:**

Judgment:	**Judgment:**
Observations:	**Observations:**
Feelings:	**Feelings:**
Needs:	**Needs:**

Judgment:	**Judgment:**
Observations:	**Observations:**
Feelings:	**Feelings:**
Needs:	**Needs:**

REQUEST OF YOURSELF—ENVISION WHAT WOULD ENRICH YOUR LIFE

> **Jaycee:** *I never knew how important it was to listen to our self and to be able to recognize what was going on. At first I didn't like to do the ups and downs we did every class period, but the more we did them, the more I saw how important they were. I find that I am usually so busy doing schoolwork and working that I don't keep track of how I am feeling at that moment. This goes along with if you are enjoying life.*

In addition to asking yourself how you are doing day to day, most people find it useful to take time once in awhile to revisit long-term goals, dreams, hopes. If you imagined your life going exactly the way you would find most satisfying, what would that look like? What would make your life more fulfilling? What would make your life more wonderful?

Industrial engineers, who go into factories or businesses to analyze how they can become more efficient, have found that if you can get everyone to come up with a clear vision of what ideal would be like, and then work back toward realistic restraints, you get a significant gain over what you can accomplish if you just look at what is and think about how to improve it. I think this holds true for personal dreams as well. By getting a clear vision, you have activated your motivation to move in that direction and you have the material to set concrete and doable goals for yourself that exactly fit for you.

Moving toward a goal because of your clear awareness of the need it will meet is naturally easier than taking on someone else's goals and then telling yourself you "should" meet them.

Many people report experiencing that if one gets very clear about their vision and goals, the universe cooperates and brings people and opportunities to help one reach these goals.

WHAT WOULD ENRICH YOUR LIFE? Example by **Amy**
What would make your life more wonderful?
A fairly new car   *A job that uses my skills and pays well*   *A vacation trip to celebrate graduating from college*
Pick one of these dreams and list the needs you would like to meet.
A fairly new car —Autonomy, freedom as soon as possible after I graduate
What is your preferred strategy to meet these needs at this time?
Getting out of debt
What could you request of yourself to move yourself in that direction?
I ask of myself that I stop using high interest credit cards.   *That I study hard so I can get a degree and pay back the loans to come to school.*
Decisions: Which of these requests, if any, fit for you to make at this time?
I will stop using the credit card.

WHAT WOULD ENRICH YOUR LIFE? Refer to the Needs List at the back of the book if you would like help clarifying needs under strategies.
What would make your life more wonderful?
Pick one of these dreams and list the needs you would like to meet.
What is your preferred strategy to meet these needs at this time?
What could you request of yourself to move yourself in that direction?
Decisions: Which of these requests, if any, fit for you to make at this time?

What if my request is of someone else? When I look at my requests, I see I often do not ask others for what would make my life better.

> **Daphne:** *My answer would be to not be sick anymore, seeing how I have been sick for quite some time now with mono. My request was that I wouldn't have to attend class until I was feeling better. The action I decided to take was to ask my teacher if I could have time off without risking failing as long as I made up the work. I did not use negative language.*
>
> *I made a compromise with the teacher and my request was met.*

I agree with you that the decision to make requests starts with inside work to get clear about your needs and your request. Speaking your request is outside work, covered in the upcoming chapters.

AND AN ATTITUDE—NOTICING SATISFYING ACTIONS

> **Rebecca:** *This past weekend, I realized I had just made a demand rather than a request. We did an exercise in class to remind us that learning to communicate in a new way is an ongoing process that takes time. I was expecting too much of myself. There have been several times when I have thought after the fact, about how I could have used nonviolent communication and gotten frustrated thinking about what I should have done.*
>
> *After the exercise, I realized that even thinking about it after the fact, is a step in the right direction and that instead of concentrating on what I should have done, I could acknowledge that this is new to me. Then I focused on how I could go back and clear up the miscommunication. I ended up speaking with that person again, restating my request in a clearer way and getting a much more positive response.*

Taking time to focus on the stuff that <u>is</u> working in your life helps you maintain balance, sanity, and relaxation. We live in a world where bad news sells and many people still think they can "criticize someone into better behavior." You have many opportunities to think poorly of the world, others, and yourself. A steady dose of this kind of thinking is very hard on both your physical and mental health. Again, we are working on increasing the endorphins in your body, which add to your health.

CATCH YOURSELF DOING SOMETHING WONDERFUL: (All right, at least something that pleased you a bit)	
	What are two things you did today that pleased you?
Sunday	
Monday	
Tuesday	
Wednesday	
Thursday	
Friday	
Saturday	

Success Script—Self-Care, Doing Inner Work

Title: Noticing my Stress was Helpful on the Job
Name: Robert
Date: 11/28/07

Background: I work at a gas station and am known by most of my customers as a friendly attendant who works hard to make them happy. I try to avoid conflict with customers, my co-workers and my boss. I have worked there for four years and have problems off and on with how my boss acts toward me.

In the summers, I have no problems with my boss, but as soon as school starts, we begin to have disagreements. My boss, Dave, wants me to work more and I want to work less. By the time we are through setting up the schedule, we are both unhappy.

He has accused me of being lazy and not dedicated enough which makes me feel really depressed and worthless, but I never confronted him about it.

New Behavior: I asked myself what would improve my life and that made me think about my stress at work. I noticed the fact that it happens this time of year regularly. Then, I tried to see it from his point of view and noticed that he works over 50 hours a week and wanted more help from me. I had a talk with him and told him that we had different priorities. I told him that work was not my top priority, although I do value and appreciate the job. And then I suggested that we hire another part time employee to pick up the slack and maybe even take over a few of his hours so he can spend more time with his family because I know how hard he works. He agreed with me.

Why I Consider This a Success: We now have a new employee in training who will pick up one of my days and one of Dave's days. Now I have more time for school and he plans to take some time with his family. Hiring a new employee is a huge relief to both of us. It creates a win-win situation. This will also reduce the tension between us.

Intention for the Future: I will certainly try to change my attitude by noticing my stress and thinking about what the other person might be needing when I start to feel pressure from a boss. I can see that it certainly worked out very well for me in this specific scenario and I bet it will continue to work well.

When there is no pressure and both people understand one another, an environment can change from tense to relaxed overnight.

Success Script—Self-Care, Doing Inner Work

Title:
Date:

CHAPTER EIGHT

φ

Self-Care, Taking Action

TJ: *All choices that you make are catering to some need you have, but the trick is to find out which needs you want to fulfill and the needs you can put off for awhile. If you're home alone and your friend comes over in his dad's new Porsche and says "hop in—my dad is out of town until tonight," you must weigh your needs. From every angle of every situation you are meeting some need.*

To get into your friend's dad's car you may be meeting your need for excitement and recreation. This is usually the first need your mind jumps to. However you also have a need to not get into trouble or disrespect your friend's dad and you need to not get arrested. The true-life value of realizing all of my needs is another way of weighing all the consequences. It is like the motto: don't do the crime if you can't do the time. [needs = safety, freedom of movement; strategies = stay out of trouble and not get arrested]

Megan: *I've always been a person to just do what has to be done and not even question why, or anything. If I had a paper to write, even if I was tired, I would do it anyway— whether the paper was a big part of my grade or a very small part. Since taking this class, I have been asking myself why some things needs to be done and what needs it will be meeting for me in the long run and the short run.*

Last weekend, I had to get up really early to help Chris build our house. I was really tired and grumpy because I had not gotten much sleep. I thought about the benefits of getting up vs. sleeping in. I did not want Chris to hurt himself by trying to lift heavy things alone. I was getting closer to moving into my own home and when it is time to move in, it will feel more like home because I helped build the whole thing. And, although the house is taking up a lot of our lives right now, we are making sure to do relaxing things like go out to dinner and spend time with friends. When I remembered the benefits for me, it was easier to get up and have a good attitude.

The goal is to discern what will bring you more aliveness and satisfaction, and then to choose options that support this goal. Some choices are obvious—if you want better self-esteem, you will act in ways that you would respect if you saw someone else doing this. Other decisions call for a more careful weighing of your options and looking at both the long-term and short-term results.

This is where the rubber hits the road. Like many others, I have more ideas of actions that would be enriching to my life, such as exercising four or five times a week, than I carry through on. It helps when I let go of a few of the expectations that come from society.

Please recall that most of our needs are met in relationships with others. Enlightened self-interest is the clear awareness that being supportive of others, actually creates a better world for ourselves.

OBSERVATIONS—HOW IS YOUR LIFE GOING?

Kathlyn: *I took this activity very seriously because I had many things going on in my life that were not working out, causing me to become edgy and overwhelmed. I do realize the issues will not go away simply by ignoring them. I need to do a better job understanding and supporting myself before I can support others when they need my assistance.*

Sometimes we get caught up in the day-to-day matters and forget to look at a bigger picture, to notice the patterns, the changes from last month, last year. Start by sitting back a bit and taking an overall look at your life these days.

LIFE TODAY: 1. Imagine you saw a movie of your life this week. What five or six things would stand out? Try to make neutral observations in this section. 2. Comment on these.

1. The camcorder records:

2. When you look at your typical week, what parts of it do you like? What parts do you not like? What feelings and needs are you aware of having?

FEELINGS AND NEEDS—USING NEEDS-BASED DECISION-MAKING

> **Tiphaine:** *I like when others are pleased thanks to me. Last week I made crepes for the entire dorm. I was really pleased because they seemed satisfied. However, I was also frustrated because I tasted just one crepe! At first I felt angry because I blamed the others, but in the end, I blamed myself. I was too nice. I shouldn't have given away all the crepes.*

Tiphaine noticed her need for contribution, but not her need for self-care. Sometimes meeting all of your needs seems impossible at any one point in your life. Other times you will see that strategies appear to be in conflict. Rosenberg says that you can meet all of your needs, although sometimes not with the timing you had in mind, nor with your initial strategy.

How can I use awareness of my needs to make my life better?

First, identify your needs in a challenging situation. Remember that needs are universal, and strategies are possible ways to meet these needs that involve specific actions by specific people. As you look at the needs you bring to a situation, you can understand why it may be difficult.

Second, recall that there are many strategies to meet every need. So, take time to brainstorm strategies / actions you could take that would meet more or all of your needs. While you are brainstorming remember to freely generate a list of ideas without any evaluation. To judge each idea as you go will interfere with your creativity. (More brainstorming tips are on pages 197-198.)

Third, decide which options to put into action. After letting your creativity generate possibilities, return to your list and weigh which ideas best suit you to follow through on, at this time. A decision to try this out or a very short term commitment is enough for now. This relates to making requests of yourself rather than demands of yourself. Fourth, act on your decision and evaluate the results. If you have more thoughts, return to the last three steps and do them again.

NEEDS-BASED DECISION-MAKING 1. Identify challenge. 2. Brainstorm. 3. Decide. 4. Act and evaluate results. (example)
1. Challenge: *I see tension between my need for connecting with peers—especially finding a girlfriend, and my need for achievement—good grades and a good job when I graduate.*
2. Brainstorm: *Study during the week and party on the weekends* *Party every other week and study alternate weeks* *Study this semester and party next semester* *Party this semester and study next semester* *Go to the parties and take my book along* *Go to the library between classes and finish homework so I can go out after supper* *Put an ad in the paper for a female with a good sense of humor who also likes study dates* *Ask my roommate's girlfriend to set me up with a friend of hers who is serious about her grades.*
3. Decision: *I think I will go to the library between classes and finish with homework so I can go out after supper, and ask my roommate's girlfriend to set me up with a friend of hers who is serious about her grades, too.*
4. Act and evaluate results.

NEEDS-BASED DECISION-MAKING 1. Identify challenge. 2. Brainstorm. 3. Decide. 4. Act and evaluate results. (example)
1. Challenge:
2. Brainstorm:
3. Decision:
4. Act and evaluate results:

Can you identify another challenging situation and use these steps to change or expand your actions?

So, sometimes the hockey game is tonight and the paper is due tomorrow and there is no strategy that is going to meet both responsibilities. What then?

First, translate them from responsibilities to two honorable, basic human needs. Sometimes we double book ourselves and cannot meet all the agreements as we had hoped to. Getting clear about our basic human needs and being honest with ourselves about what is going on, is the first step.

Check yourself—is there any way to meet both needs? One strategy might be to finish the paper and go for the second half of the game. Another strategy would be to check the syllabus and see if the teacher will accept late papers with only a grade lowered. Can you think of other strategies?

Let's assume for a moment that these activities are mutually exclusive. Then carefully consider each option—go to hockey <u>or</u> stay home and finish the paper. Ask yourself these questions:

- *What needs would be met by each choice?*

- *What needs would not be met?*

- *How will I feel tomorrow when I hear about the game, if I have gone to it?*

- *How will I feel tomorrow when I hear about the game, if I did not go to it?*

- *How will it be tomorrow when I go into class, if I have written the paper?*

- *How will it be tomorrow when I go into class, if I did not write the paper?*

- *Which will give me more satisfaction to remember five years from now?*

Thinking is only the gathering-of-information part of this process. If you only think about it, you may be tempted to focus on the outside rule system rather than what actually fits for you, at this moment in your life.

As you pay attention to your basic human needs, sit quietly and breathe a bit more. Which ones are more alive for you? It is likely that one need will rise in importance for you for the moment. Honor any sadness you have around not meeting the other need at this time. And then go forward with sureness to enjoy fully the option you chose and to accept comfortably the consequences of not taking the options you decided against for now.

TRY THIS ON A CONFLICT OF YOUR OWN: What did you decide?

REQUEST OF YOURSELF—MAKE DELIBERATE CHOICES OF SELF-CARE

Jana: *I have realized over the past few weeks, that I have a very strong way of taking out my frustrations on people who have absolutely no responsibility for the reason I am frustrated or angry. I have gone back and apologized several times now. One day I was frustrated about work and was* <u>this close</u> *to taking it out on a co-worker. I stopped myself and was able to take a deep breath and continue doing my job.*

I consider being able to apologize to people and be able to acknowledge when I am wrong a huge success. I feel a great sense of responsibility when I do this. Actually remembering to take a deep breath and shut my mouth instead of flipping out on someone was another success. I like when I think about the possible outcomes of what I am about to say or do before I actually commit the acts.

Matt: *The other day in class I was trying to take notes. It was difficult because I was writing, listening, and trying to compute all at the same time. The guy next to me asked a question. Then out of the blue, the teacher asked me a fairly specific question about the reading. I was caught completely off guard and had nothing to say. The teacher told me to keep my mind on the class. It made me feel bad.*

After class, I went to the teacher and told him why I had responded the way I did. He reminded me all of the notes were online, so I could download them and then just follow along. That was very good advice for me. I am now paying more attention in class and my grades have gone up. My intention is always to reduce the number of distractions. I also remember to eat before class so that I am not thinking about food, and to do the reading and take notes before class. I try to keep my school and social life separate while in class.

Emily: *So here's the situation—I am often not very nice to myself. One would think, with all my fantastic academic and personal achievements, that I would be a proud, confident and self-accepting young woman. I'm not.*

But I am slowly learning to sort out my conflicting needs and to make choices that respond more positively to them. Last night instead of pushing myself to complete my assignments on time, I recognized my feelings of exhaustion and need for rest. I took a shower and rubbed lotion on my feet, fixed lunches for myself and the kids and got to bed a little early. I celebrate my little successes.

When a baby is born, parents take on the decisions for the safety and well-being of the infant. Thoughtful parents set up situations wherein gradually the child takes on more choices, more responsibility for the consequences of their choices. By the time the child becomes an adult, hopefully they take complete responsibility for everything they do, i.e. when they turn in a paper late, they accept the lower grade without protest or guilt. (Yes, some adults have not arrived here.)

YES, WE CAN: Claim responsibility for better meeting one need in your life today.	
Name one unmet need you would like to meet more fully today.	

⬇ ⬇ ⬇ DELVING DEEPER: NEEDS-BASED ACTIONS ⬇ ⬇ ⬇

Thanks for the examples of people who have taken responsibility for meeting their needs in one situation. I am not there. I am sporadic in even thinking about my needs, hours later. Now what?

> **Audrey:** *It is true that sometimes we do things we don't really want to but we do them anyway. For example, today I had a meeting with a friend, which was planned earlier. I didn't want to go because it was far and it was snowing heavily, but I still went to meet my need for integrity. I didn't want her to think that I don't show up for meetings.*
>
> *If I had changed "I have to go to this meeting" into "I will go to this meeting because I want to be a person with integrity," it could have made me have a good feeling about myself. If I wanted to meet both needs—not going outside and still not canceling the meeting, I could have invited this person over, and offered her coffee and cake. This would have met even more needs, like recognition, relaxing and hosting.*

Not there? Not to worry. Just start where you are and become more aware. That is all we can do.

Notice the last time your actions did not take care of yourself in a way you would have liked to. You probably "shoulded" on yourself. Study the incident. Take it apart. Think of alternative responses. Brainstorm a few strategies. If you rework recent incidents in your mind, not to scold yourself, but to think about what you might like to do differently in a similar situation in the future, you will gradually create a different frame of mind. Eventually these thoughts will come to you in time to put them into effect. Be patient with yourself and give yourself kudos for being willing to rethink a difficult situation. Here is a grid for you to get started with this.

BE THE DIRECTOR: Replay the scene until you get it the way that suits you.
What recent situation comes to mind wherein your actions did not bring you much satisfaction?
Which needs of yours did you meet or were you trying to meet with your actions?
What needs of yours did you <u>not</u> meet?
What needs do you guess were most alive for the other person?
What other strategies might you have suggested that might have met both needs?

CHOOSE MORE ACTS OF SELF-CARE

Another way of being more choiceful is to consciously add life-enhancing activities to one's schedule. Many people nurture those around them on a regular basis and forget to give the same deliberate attention to themselves. What do you do for self-care? Some of my students' answers:

Laugh whenever possible

Have dinner with my family weekly

Go to my bedroom and take my kitty with me

Make sure I have time to snowboard

Satisfy my craving for chocolate

Play with my dog and cats

Take time on Sundays to plan my week

I keep up with my friends

Drink orange juice

Buy fresh flowers for my room

Pump iron

Have sex

Light some candles, listen to music

Kickbox / dance / go to the gym

Listen to music a lot—I have a chill list on my iPod

I am faithful to my boyfriend, so our relationship will last

Running and swimming keeps me healthy and centered and relieves my stress

I always make sure I'm comfortable in the things I wear

Listen to country music because it makes me feel good and sometimes gets me up and dancing

Making sure to get enough sleep—I get really cranky and unmotivated without enough sleep

Writing in my journal always makes me feel better if I am low—it puts things into perspective and helps me to be open and unafraid

Rent a "girl movie" and watch it alone, so my boyfriend doesn't sigh and make comments at the most romantic part

COMMITTING ACTS OF SELF-CARE: What do you do for self-care?

AND AN ATTITUDE—SAYING AND HEARING "NO" IN A CONNECTING WAY

Brady: *The word "no" is often one of the hardest words for people to say and hear. People need to realize that every "no" has a "yes" to it. For example, if my friends ask me to go to a party on a school night, I say "no." I am saying "yes" to doing my homework and getting a good night's sleep. This idea is useful to me because I like to work out and have some time to myself, but it has always been hard for me to tell my girlfriend when I need alone time. I think if I explain it to her as a "no" really equals a "yes," she may not get offended if I want a night off from her every once in a while.*

Jody: *I've always imagined that by saying "no" I was being selfish or worse. Because of my discomfort with saying "no," I automatically took offense when someone told me "no." I have learned in this class that saying and hearing the word "no" is just another way of saying and hearing "yes"! It reminds me of my macroeconomics class where we learned that everything you say "yes" to is a "no" to something else. From the economic standpoint, this is considered "an opportunity cost," the cost of passing up other choices.*

Renee: *The more you say "no," the easier it is to hear "no." If someone asks something of you, stop and ask yourself, what are your own needs. Then you guys should discuss what you both need. All of my life I have had trouble saying "no," but I am learning. Last week my roommate wanted me to help her study and I had a huge paper due. I told her my situation and we decided to study after I finished my paper. We were both satisfied.*

One way we neglect to choose actions that enhance our lives is by freezing when someone asks us to do something we don't want to do. Look with me at the big picture first. Every choice we make is saying "Yes" to one option, and "No" to many other options. If you sleep in, you don't watch the sunrise, you don't make it to breakfast, and you don't make it to your first class. Or you go to your first class and you do not get the extra sleep or the elaborate breakfast. If you focus on practicing your skateboarding, you may be doing it at the expense of listening to music that hour.

Suppose a friend requests you to do something, anything. You check with yourself and you notice, "Oh, bleh! No! I do <u>not</u> want to." Stay with that feeling. You may bump into the thought, "I would be a selfish person if I don't say 'Yes'." Stay with that too. Listen to yourself until you find your needs underneath it all. I confess that my self-judgment was so strong that at first I could not even find an unspoken "No" inside. I had to start by noticing any discomfort when I said "Yes!"

Ask yourself, "What need of mine would not be met by doing what they ask?" or "What would I be saying 'Yes' to instead, if I were to turn them down?" Perhaps when you look inside, you will see that you have no room for saying "Yes" to their request, even if it is very urgent to them. You <u>might</u> say briefly, "Thanks for the invite—it does not fit for me today." Or you <u>might</u> let them know what you are saying "Yes" to instead, i.e. why you cannot meet their request. Or you <u>might</u> want to work with them to try to come up with a strategy to meet both your needs and their needs.

**Every choice we make
says "Yes" to one option
and "No" to many other options.**

WAYS OF SAYING "NO": Based on the initial dialogue, expand ways for the SECOND speaker to say "No." 1. To give a friendly refusal. 2. To share what they are saying "Yes" to. 3. To suggest a way to meet both needs. Use your imagination to capture missing details.

Initial dialogue.

Robin (1st speaker): *Let's go to the movie tonight.*   **Gail** (2nd speaker): *Nah. I don't want to.*

1. Rewrite the second speaker's line to give a friendly refusal.
Gail: *No thanks, it does not fit for me.*

2. Rewrite the second speaker's line, sharing what they are saying "Yes" to.
Gail: *No, thanks, I am in an exciting place in my novel and really want to read it tonight.*

3. Rewrite the second speaker's line, suggesting a strategy that could meet both needs.
Gail: *I'll be finished with my book by tomorrow evening. Want to go to a movie then?*

Terry: *Come to Kenya with Linda and me.*	**Doris:** *No way, Jose.*
1. Doris (friendly):	
2. Doris (sharing "Yes"):	
3. Doris (strategizing):	

Scott: *Those look good. I am hungry.*	**Taren:** *Do not touch my Fritos.*
1. Taren (friendly):	
2. Taren (sharing "Yes"):	
3. Taren (strategizing):	

Cyd: *I need to borrow your motorcycle today.*	**Ellen:** *Not going to happen.*
1. Ellen (friendly):	
2. Ellen (sharing "Yes"):	
3. Ellen (strategizing):	

Greg: *Turn the tv off and come play a game of ball.*	**Tim:** *Go away.*
1. Tim (friendly):	
2. Tim (sharing "Yes"):	
3. Tim (strategizing):	

Lori: *I need you to invest $1000 in my coffee shop.*	**Jamie:** *You think I'm made of money?*
1. Jamie (friendly):	
2. Jamie (sharing "Yes"):	
3. Jamie (strategizing):	

Tami: *We are going to hike the Grand Canyon. You should come.*	**Jane:** *Sounds awful.*
1. Jane (friendly):	
2. Jane (sharing "Yes"):	
3. Jane (strategizing):	

OK. I see how maybe I could say "No." What about when the other person says "No"? That one is even harder.

Many people find it difficult to hear "No." First of all, turn to page 54 and review the components of an effective request. Your mindset going into this has to be focused on honoring their needs as much as your own. You are not trying to force, guilt-trip, threaten, bribe, override, or use any other such demanding method. You are really aiming for a win-win solution that works for everyone. So check on your attitude as your starting point.

Rosenberg suggests that a yardstick for making a true request, not a demand, could be, "Do not do what I ask unless it would bring you the joy of a young child feeding a hungry duck!" So, maybe that is a bit much for you. Please lean in that direction as far as you can go. After you get your win-win attitude lined up, you are next aspiring to invite the other person to join you in this frame of reference. This can become your habitual way to approach differences.

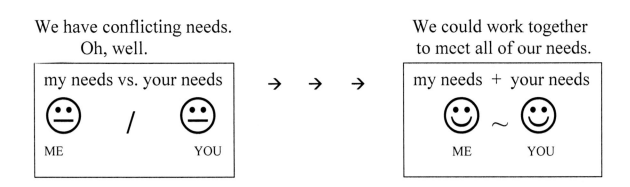

After getting your attitude in order, start with a complete request that both states your interest and clearly refers to their choice. If they say "No," you next want to respectfully ask for more information, so you can start thinking of ways to meet your needs and theirs. You may find a way to combine your needs. As you share the importance to you of what you asked for, they may change their "No," and as you hear their feelings about their needs, you may want to change your request. Or, perhaps, either or both of you will find a way to get your needs met by a strategy that does not involve the other person.

So, Robin asks Gail to go to a movie and she says "No." When he finds out she is interested in finishing her novel, he could make suggestions. Gail might also offer suggestions.

Robin: *This is the last night for the movie that Andy and Jessie recommended so highly. Knowing that, might you be willing to set your novel aside for one more day?*

Gail: *I have been looking forward to this novel all afternoon. Why don't you call your daughter, Cami, and see if she wants to see the movie with you?*

Robin: *I would really prefer doing something with you tonight. What about we take turns reading your book aloud? We haven't done that for awhile. Does that sound enjoyable?*

REACHING FOR A "YES" WHEN YOU HEAR A "NO": From the perspective of the FIRST speaker: 1. Make a more complete request. 2. Find out what they are saying "Yes" to. (3. Create a line for the SECOND speaker that offers what they are saying "Yes" to.) 4. Suggest a way to meet both needs. Use your imagination to capture missing details.

First speaker's initial effort at a request. **Robin** (1st speaker): *Let's go to the movie tonight.*   **Gail** (2nd speaker): *Nah. I don't want to.*
1. Rewrite the first speaker's line to make a more complete request. **Robin:** *I want to go to the movie tonight and would love your company. Interested?*
Gail (2nd speaker): *Nah. I don't want to.* **2. Rewrite the first speaker's line, to find out what the other person is saying "Yes" to.** **Robin:** *Hmmm. I am curious. Do you have other plans for the evening?*
3. (Create a line for the second speaker that shares what they are saying "Yes" to.) **Gail:** *Yes. I am in an exciting place in my novel and really want to finish it tonight.*
4. Rewrite the first speaker's line, suggesting a strategy that could meet both needs. **Robin:** *If you are finished by tomorrow evening, would you like to go to a movie then?*

Amie: *The baby needs changing.*   **Matthew:** *No way—it's your turn.* 1. Amie (request):
Matthew: *No way—it's your turn.* 2. Amie (ask for info):
3. Create a "Yes" for second speaker. Matthew:
4. Amie (strategizing):

Claudia: *You and Cierra have to come to our barbeque.*   **Michael:** *Mom, don't be a nag.* 1. Claudia (request):
Michael: *Don't be a nag.* 2. Claudia (ask for info):
3. Create a "Yes" for second speaker. Michael:
4. Claudia (strategizing):

Rob: *Here's fresh snow peas—you must fix them for supper.*   **Patti:** *No—put them in the frig.* 1. Rob (request):
Patti: *No—put them in the frig.* 2. Rob (ask for info):
3. Create a "Yes" for second speaker. Patti:
4. Rob (strategizing):

Success Script—Self-Care, Taking Action

Title: The World Has Not Fallen Apart Even Though I Said "NO"!
Name: Laura
Date: 10/20/06

Background: *I am the Secretary of the Tenants Association in my building. I find I am doing more errands and tasks than I want to and not having enough time for myself.*

I tend to do what is asked of me unless I have a very pressing need that conflicts with the request. I am a people-pleaser (emotional slave!) and like to feel needed. I was talked into the Secretary position because the Chairperson just had everyone else on the Board resign and was seeking people she thought would be acceptable to fill the empty slots. I was needed. The secretary position started before my college classes started. And I am the only Board Member with a car. The job has become a nuisance because I get all of the go-for jobs. I have been run ragged by the Chairperson.

New Behavior: *After reading class material on needs and self-care, I have finally realized that I can take care of my own needs and do not have to say "yes" all the time. I need to have time to study, do my housework, be with my husband, rest, and just have space to be with myself with no "have-to"s.*

Recently, I have begun to actually say "No, I cannot go to Costco this week." "I can do this, but not that." I even said "I cannot help you at all."

Why this is a Success: *I am getting more sleep. I'm happier and I am NOT feeling guilty. I have not even gotten negative feedback from the Board or the Chairperson. No one has yelled at me or changed their behavior towards me. (There will still be challenges. It is much easier to say "no" to the Board than to my mother or my husband!)*

Intention for the Future: *This is an ongoing lesson to be learned, practiced and someday to become embedded in my soul. I want to say "no" when it conflicts with my needs, "yes" when I want to do for people I am involved with and care about. I am trying to accept myself as I am and to not try to prove my loyalty or love by giving in to all requests. My intention is to take better care of myself and to listen to what is inside more often. I have years of programming to overcome. I want to get to the place where I can take care of me without feeling guilty. I am on my way there.*

Success Script—Self-Care, Taking Action

Title: It Was the Alarm Clock's Fault
Name: Dorrie
Date: September 28, 2006

Background: *Every single morning I was late. I could never just be on time. I tried and tried to hurry but there were many mornings when my boyfriend arrived to give me a ride to school and I was not ready. My boyfriend knows I am slow in the morning. I know he knows how slow I am, but I always blamed his wait on something else without taking responsibility for my own tardiness.*

Every morning I had another reason. "My alarm did not go off." "Last night my mother called and I ended up having to talk with her FOR-EV-ER." "I couldn't find my brown pants and then did not realize it was so cold out today, so I had to change my outfit after I spent twenty minutes getting it ready." Last week, he was sitting anxiously on the arm of the chair as I was brushing my hair and making coffee simultaneously. He asked, "Why can't you just be ready?"

New Behavior: *I was about to turn the situation around and accuse him, when I saw that he was slouched over, clearly as tired as I was, and annoyed that he could have been sleeping a few extra minutes instead of waiting for me. I saw that I really was totally responsible for my choices—it was not my mom's fault or the alarm's fault and certainly no fault of his.*

I apologized instead and have made more effort to be ready when he arrives. I am still incredibly tired in the morning, but I now pack my school bag, set up my coffee and breakfast the night before, and listen to the weather in the evening so I can at least ball park my outfit.

Why I Consider This a Success: *It has improved our relationship and I sleep better at night knowing I will not be as rushed in the morning. I have played a blame game a lot through my life, not taking any responsibility. I am trying hard to just own up to my own mistakes instead of quickly accusing someone.*

Intention for the Future: *Ideally I would like to be zapped or something when I blame someone else for what I have caused and created. I notice I am a bit more careful with my words, slower to blame someone else. The five minutes it takes me to prepare my things the night before makes a world of difference in my lifestyle. I hope I continue that too.*

Success Script—Self-Care, Taking Action

Title:
Date:

Optional: create a Mind Map, a doodle, or other visual aides

Part Three: Communicating for Connection

Brent: *This listening with empathy is a new business for me. I don't often find myself being empathetic. It is something I am willing to try, but honestly it doesn't fit my personality too well. I'm one of those people who give solutions and be done with the problem. I usually don't find any need to talk about thoughts and feelings and such—too mushy for me, really. I am not against the idea, but it comes very hard to someone like me.*

We are social beings and we meet or try to meet most of our needs through our interactions with others—from the chitchat we exchange with a stranger at the grocery store, the gossip we share with our neighbor, the conferences at work to plan a new project, to the many levels of potential intimacy between partners, and the carefully planned negotiations between countries in conflict.

What kinds of relationships do you have with others? At home, with friends, at work? What kinds do you want? Only you can decide. Here are some questions to aid your reflection.

- As you look at your interactions with people, are you pleased with what you see?
- How would it benefit you professionally to have stronger people skills?
- With specific individuals, are you as close as you want to be?
- How much energy do you want to put into your relationships?
- Is avoiding conflict lessening your aliveness in a relationship?
- Is losing your temper lessening the quality of your relationships?

Doesn't everyone have their own style of communicating?

Yes. Every culture develops its own language system—words, grammar, and a complex set of subtle customs about what topics will and won't be talked about and in what ways. Within a society, families have further subsets of customs. Any group of people develops its own vernacular, including couples. If they come from similar backgrounds, they may have similar expectations of how people relate and seldom find conflict arising. When there were traditional roles for men and women, many marriages ran fairly smoothly by following them. For some friends, shared activities or a high tolerance of differences, mean an equally low need to process.

And you may seldom think about this until you move into a culture with a noticeably different language system—such as a foreign country, a college dorm, a marriage, or a communication class. Or you study this book.

To these language systems, you need to add individual personalities. Many personality tests reflect that some people find listening easier than talking, and others find talking the easier part of a conversation. Some prefer a large amount of personal sharing, others thrive on much less. Some are slow to anger, some quick. Some people are nourished by many relationships, while others are quite satisfied with only a few contacts.

Therefore, it is likely that you will find some tools in the upcoming chapters more useful to you than others. Various readers will resonate with different ideas. I do not want to imply that we all "should"—or even can—excel in every skill. I encourage you to start where you are and move cautiously—try out a few of these ideas and see which ones enhance your current relationships. If one tool does not seem very useful, set it aside for now and try another that looks promising to you.

This strategy will let you walk into new ways of talking and thinking, if and when it fits for you, rather than throwing yourself at some ideal, which can be bruising. Really! I hope you will honor your own journey in this matter and trust your sense of what works for you.

OK—so go slow. Don't expect perfection of myself. And take what fits. Got that. Now, what's the big picture of the communication skills for moving into dialogue and dealing with anger?

We are recycling through the basic tools—sharing our observations, feelings, needs, and requests, while listening for the observations, feelings, needs, and requests of the other. Plus holding the entire conversation with an attitude, an intention, of deeply valuing ourselves and the other person.

Here are my ideals, my goals:

- Replace my evaluations with observations
- Notice and accept all of my thoughts and feelings exactly as they are in this moment
- Be quickly aware of my anger, and shut my mouth so that my words might be choiceful
- Translate my feelings, criticisms, and judgments into needs
- Take the time to notice and value my needs
- Connect with others by speaking openly of my feelings, needs, and requests, as appropriate to the situation
- Listen carefully—wonder about the needs and feelings of the other person
- Hold the possibility that what they are observing may be different from what I am seeing
- Make reflections of what I hear and check them out to assure that I understand the speaker
- Translate all the criticisms and judgments I hear into needs and requests
- Cultivate an attitude of appreciation and respect for myself and others
- Value getting everyone's needs on the table, and met, if at all possible

This list sounds impossible. Do you actually do all these things?

No. Like everyone else, I find some skills easier than others. Some I have done for years. Others are less familiar to me. Studying, practicing, teaching, and writing about NVC remind me to focus on the importance of needs. I slowly, steadily improve and I like the results.

When people earn my respect, then I will treat them with respect.

Hmmm! I notice that the word RESPECT has two quite different meanings. One is a feeling of admiration or appreciation of a particular person wherein I might wish to hang out with them or model my behavior on theirs or write them a good reference letter. To me, this is the only portion of RESPECT that people either earn or do not earn.

The second meaning of RESPECT is a decision to be polite and considerate. RESPECT is a set of behaviors that I aspire to act on consistently because of my own values, because of who I want to be in the world. As the old saying puts it: "There is a low below which I will not go." On the job, it is important to treat bosses, co-workers, and customers with courtesy that is not dependent on their actions. It is part of being professional. It is your choice how you want to behave around people whose actions you do not like.

So how many of these skills are useful in managing conflict on the job?

Most jobs probably have some potential for conflict between people or groups and some jobs are situated in the midst of conflict. So, I would say that the above list of skills would be useful for anyone who interacts with others in any capacity on the job. Because Connection is an introduction to concepts, it focuses on improving connection and managing conflict between you and the people currently in your life. Most people practice and learn new communication skills in daily interactions. As these skills become part of your repertoire, you will find more places to apply them.

There are NVC materials available that focus on communication in the work place using these same tools. (If you wish to explore this, I recommend the books and training workshops of Martha Lasley, leadershipthatworks.com for a well-rounded, zestful, and effective program.)

A decision to act with respect for everyone is one of the most basic tools for lessening conflict. It is easier to work with someone who consistently treats everyone as if they had value. Another across-the-board useful skill is to be able to translate concerns into requests rather than taking the same concerns and expressing them as complaints and criticism.

Tension in the midst of a friendly conversation really throws me off—whether to talk or listen, especially.

I have noticed that when I get tense, I sometimes simplify the situation by quite disregarding either myself or the other person! Either I focus on the other person and scurry about in my mind looking for ways to make them happy, to make things peaceful again; or I lose any sense of them as a person and talk louder and faster about what I am thinking. Sometimes I do remember to reach for the third position of staying in connection with both of us.

In most relationships, both people will contribute to the conversation in a somewhat turn-taking manner—talking—listening—talking—listening. Robert Bolton, in People Skills, his classic book on communication, suggests that this simple exchange of ideas and feelings would benefit from the regular use of reflective listening or paraphrasing.

As you attend to words of the speaker, you wonder in your mind about their observations, feelings, needs, and requests; and you periodically let the speaker know what you understand them to be saying and you check it out with the speaker. This gives the speaker the chance to let you know if the message you received is the same as the one they intended to send. This may seem time-consuming, but in the long run, it will save time and misunderstandings.

Reflections are important because we bring different interpretations of the meaning of words, and because what we <u>expect</u> to hear from an individual or from the world is often <u>all</u> that we hear. (He offers to bring her coffee in bed. She may think, "He loves me and wants to tell me in little ways." Or she may think, "He wants me to get up earlier and get the house cleaned more thoroughly.") As you talk together, you can identify miscommunication, listen to each other carefully, and get it cleared up before tension between you moves into conflict between you.

When any tension arises, slow way down, breathe, connect with yourself first, and double your effort to listen carefully without any communication barriers. If you are really distressed, create some space to withdraw a bit. Go for a ten-minute walk.

After you have gotten at least somewhat calm, think about whether you want to connect by listening or talking. Are you able to listen? Do you guess that the other person is calm enough to listen to you? When one's mouth is full of words, one's ears cannot hear well. If it appears no one is able to listen at the moment, you have two forwarding options: to take a few more deep breaths and see if you can find the space to listen first; or to withdraw, refresh yourself, and then return to listening. Many more skills for improving connection and resolving conflict are ahead.

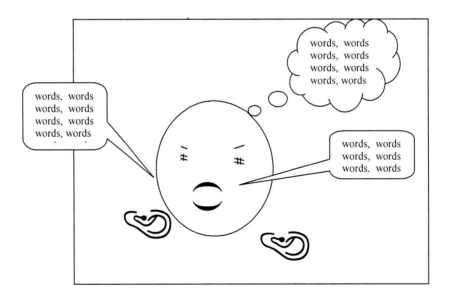

When your mouth is full of words, your ears do not work well.

When their mouth is full of words, their ears do not work well.

CHAPTER NINE

φ

Listening for Connection

Nick: *About two weeks ago I met a girl, who I will call Rachel. We hit it off right away and are now in a relationship. It's kind of a long distance relationship and last weekend, she happened to come to Burlington. I decided to try out some listening skills. I made myself constantly aware to talk less and listen more. The end result was pretty impressive.*

She even made a comment before she left that she really liked how good of a listener I was. Needless to say, that is not a compliment I receive often. There is some hope for this method of deliberate communication, but I also know that now that Rachel has gone back, this style is going away. It was draining. I can see however, this method used in small doses, could be very effective in many situations.

Aren't some people natural listeners? Can I even become a better listener?

Maybe and yes. According to personality tests such as Myers-Briggs, some people listen more easily, while others speak more easily. That does not condemn half the world to being poor listeners. If you want to become a better listener, there are many behaviors you can practice. Everyone can expand their listening skills if they have the intention to do so.

And the starting point for becoming a better listener is . . . ?

The first step is, of course, to focus on your intention, your hunger to connect and really understand another person. This will carry you further than any other skill in this chapter.

The second starting point is to become aware of your choice. To listen or to not listen is a decision. Do you want to listen to this person at this time or not? You probably do <u>not</u> have the time or the energy to listen carefully to everyone who crosses your path. We have many needs, and connection is only one of them. Mindful listening literally burns calories, similar to studying.

So when a person approaches you and starts talking, check with yourself to determine what needs are currently alive for you, and then determine how much energy you want to put into listening. It often works for both of you that you listen casually for the few minutes between classes or other events. Other times, a short conversation or a casual one may not be enough. Someone launching into a long monologue is a request for your attention, even if they forgot to verbalize that request. Your decision to listen carefully is a gift you may decide to give to a stranger or a casual friend, but you may also decide not to give it. If listening does not suit you at this time, you might want to review the discussion in the previous chapter on respectful ways of saying "No."

OBSERVATIONS—AVOIDING COMMUNICATION BARRIERS

Mary Ann: *I could relate to the list of common barriers to listening. When I was talking to my friend Karen about her loser boyfriend, I would advise her by saying "I think you should..." or "Why don't you..." before she had even finished her story.*

Even when we want to listen, we usually have many habitual responses that invite the other person to stop talking about things that matter. Here are the most common barriers to mindful listening. Stress and conflict situations will increase the negative impact of using these roadblocks.

- **Judging**—telling people they are wrong (or right) "How could you be so stupid?" "That was wise of you."

- **Giving Advice**—"You just need to . . ."

- **Cheering People Up**—"It's not that bad."

- **Changing the Subject**—"That reminds me of the time . . ."

- **Interrogating**—"Why did she stop you? Where were you? How long . . ."

- **One Upping**—"You think you had a bad date. Let me tell about mine."

- **Lecturing / Educating**—"That is exactly the point I was making last week."

- **Correcting their Version of the Story**—"It couldn't have been Tuesday."

- **Pretending to Listen**

COMMUNICATION BARRIERS: Check the barriers that are most irritating to you when you encounter them in conversation with a friend or family member. Give an example.		
	✔	Example
Judging		
Giving advice		
Cheering people up		
Changing the subject		
Interrogating		
One upping		
Lecturing / educating		
Correcting their version of the story		
Pretending to listen		

Wait! Maybe there are good reasons for not listening.

**Not knowing the question
It was easy for him
To give the answer**

(This is from Dag Hammarskjöld, Swedish diplomat and the first Secretary-General of the UN.)

There could be a variety of understandable reasons. As Hammarskjöld's haiku reflects, our world is less complex when we do not listen. Real listening may call upon us to challenge our deepest beliefs about ourselves, others, and life. It is possible to avoid that challenge by only talking and seldom listening. Please note that it is also possible to hide in listening and seldom sharing.

Sometimes we forget to take the time to listen. Perhaps we are busy meeting other needs and the need to connect is not the need that is most alive for us at this time in our lives. Perhaps listening is not something we do easily.

Bolton proposes another reason we don't listen—that we imagine we know the thoughts and feelings of the other person. He recommends that we always assume a need to learn more. He says we tend to underestimate our lack of knowledge of the other person. We usually do not even know how much we do not know!

You will learn more about both yourself and the other person, if you stretch yourself to listen.

I read somewhere that judging people was the worst barrier.

> **Mary Ann:** *I was in a conversation with my mother and she was saying not very nice things about my father's side of the family. Instead of interrupting her with my judgments: "I don't want to hear you speaking poorly of these people," I decided to put myself on a neutral ground and to listen until she finished talking. I looked at her needs and could understand why she did not want to attend a family gathering.*

Yes, many communication experts will tell you that the single biggest roadblock to careful listening is judgment. All the work you have already done on noticing evaluations and translating them to observations, feelings, needs, and requests will pay off as you move into listening.

Our habits of Faulty Language Usage keep us from seeing people as they are. Projecting enemy images or hero / saint images on another person, and then locking them into that category, distorts everything we see and hear and understand about the other person. If we can shift our thinking from black-white categories to the awareness that all people have the same hunger to meet the same basic needs, this leaves us more room to see individuals in their many facets. Everyone does things we appreciate and things we don't appreciate. When seeing reality, we make better choices.

When we assign rightness-wrongness, goodness-badness, hero-enemy terms, we also encourage people to protect themselves by sharing defensively and selectively. The more we maintain a neutral ground and refrain from judging, the fewer barriers we place between ourselves and the person we wish to listen to.

Giving advice is bad?? Cheering people up? That's what I go to my friends for.

> **Stevie:** *The other day I forgot my speech until the day before it was due. I made the decision to stay up all night and get it ready. I thought it was an awesome speech and Power Point presentation, but when I got to class, I tripped all over my note cards. I received a 75. I spent the rest of the day complaining to my friends how I stayed up all night and didn't even get the grade I wanted.*
>
> *My friend one-upped me by saying he stayed up all night for a test that was cancelled. Another friend shut me down by trying to cheer me up. In the end I decided to focus on having compassion for myself.*
>
> **Laurie:** *I have a brother who is a heroin addict. We all went through hell for about four years. We wanted desperately to save him. I remember talking with him and, on many occasions, I would advise him or console him. I finally realized I needed to just listen to him, and focus all my attention on what he was expressing to me. I listened for hours. I also told him about my fear for him. This year, he has thankfully gotten clean.*

The recommendation to avoid dispensing advice and cheer is one of the hardest for most people to make any sense of. For some, it is habitual to give friends advice and good cheer. When you know friends well, you can often see after a few minutes what you would do to solve their dilemmas and how they could proceed. It is tempting to tell them what they should do.

I recognize that your intention is to be helpful. But are you being as helpful as you could be?

Sometimes, they do want your advice. And other times what a person needs even more than your opinion, is your company through the difficult moments of their life, your willingness to just listen with attention and care, or even to just hang out if they are not ready to talk yet.

Staying present to them in their discomfort requires you to have more trust in your friend and more patience with their process. When you jump in, your advice or cheer may say loudly that you are unwilling or unable to be with them in their down times. It reflects that you cannot bear their pain. Your actions may also signal that you don't trust they can figure it out or that you think their situation is so dangerous that you must pull them out of it quickly.

Is this what you wish to convey?

Kudos are often given in our culture for saying positive, uplifting things under any circumstances. Our culture has many popular slogans about the virtue of always looking on the sunny side of life and not letting yourself feel any sadness. Sometimes cheering up is exactly what a person wants, but please be aware of the possibility that they might prefer a friendship wherein they could count on your company while looking at the parts of their life that seem to be dark at the moment.

If a person is asking for information that you have and they do not have, help them, of course. This is often what is requested on the job. Be careful not to expand that category by thinking they need your wisdom and advice instead of their own. If they are asking for your experience on a matter and you decide to share it, remember to talk about it in terms of what happened for you, not as the solution for anyone in a similar situation.

I am sometimes amazed to observe how easily I dispense advice to people who absolutely do not need it, did not ask for it, and are often irritated by it! I get an idea how a person could be more efficient, for example, in fixing a cilantro salad. I get excited by my idea, so I tell them without thinking about how many times they have already fixed this salad or whether they have any interest in efficiency as interpreted by me. It would be progress if I at least asked if they wanted my great wisdom! Half of my friends have the communication skills to say, "No thanks." Or, "Sure. I won't promise to follow your suggestion, but I am up for hearing it." Worse yet is how much it irritates me when someone else gives me unasked for advice. I imagine I am being disrespected, and am sad that the other person does not see how much I already know! Whew!!

When a person is thinking a matter through to sort out their feelings, thoughts, needs, and potential actions, I can tell you that by giving the speaker your answer, you risk throwing off their process of deliberating. But, do not trust my word over your own experiences. Try it out for yourself.

Skip giving advice or cheer, and just listen. Avoid all the listening barriers, and just listen. Or, at least listen twice as long as you usually do before offering any answers. Listen to understand, not to reply. I assign this in every communication class, because we all need our ears stretched. You may have heard the saying, "We have two ears and one mouth for a reason." Here are reports of the listening efforts of three students, followed by a grid for you to record your experiences.

> **David:** *When people tell me their problems, I view them as whining and to stop the whining, I usually offer a solution to the problem or change the subject. When my mother is cooking, she often says, "I hate cooking and I am not good at it." My usual response has been, "Take a cooking class" or "You're fine." It never seemed to make her feel better.*
>
> *Luckily, I had just been working on my homework on listening when she started in again. This time, I just said, "So, you don't like cooking and you think you are not good at it?" This allowed the door to remain open in the conversation without me shutting it with a solution. She replied, "I never seem to be able to find the time to cook and when I do, the chicken is burnt and the mash potatoes are too runny." As I kept listening, I discovered she thought I did not appreciate her cooking, while, in fact, I like chicken very crispy and mashed potatoes on the runny side. The overall conversation was the best I have ever had with my mother about her cooking.*
>
> **Megan:** *When I was in high school, my friends and I always ran to each other for advice. I remember giving advice all the time. I did not think about whether they really wanted it. I also did not think about the fact that we are two different people and every person handles things differently, so why would what I would do in a certain situation fit for someone else? It wouldn't.*
>
> *Just the other day, a friend was telling me about her boyfriend going on a website to meet other girls. They have been together for 4 years so this was really shocking to her. And the website was sexually explicit, not like match.com. She told me and then straight out asked me what I would do. I told her I really did not know what I would do because I had never been in that situation and that it is her life, not mine, so I could not make decisions for her. She kept on talking and eventually figured out for herself how she wanted to respond. I think we just need to talk out loud sometimes and things become clearer for us. It feels good to learn something and then put it to good use.*

Peggy: *My best friend, Mary, came to visit this weekend and Saturday, she was upset about her boyfriend. She is constantly calling me up crying about the awful things he does to her. And I get frustrated because, even though I tell her over and over again that she should dump him, she never does. Instead she ends up mad at me.*

This time I decided to try hard to just listen. For two hours, I barely spoke a word. She talked herself out. Finally, at the end of the evening, she started rattling off the things she was going to do to change her life, including breaking up with her boyfriend! Even if she does not follow through, I realize the choice is hers, not mine. Even more important, it was the first time in months she was completely honest with me, and our conversation ended without us being angry at each other.

STRETCHING YOUR EARS: Report on three of your experiences of trying to listen for twice as long as you usually do, without giving advice or cheering up a person.	
Conversation with____ about ____	**Results**

Pretending to listen is a barrier? Sometimes it is rude <u>not</u> to pretend.

Pretending to listen is a survival skill for many people—young and old. You always have the option of letting the teacher or the guy down the hall know that what they are saying does not interest you, telling them what you would prefer, and seeing what happens. But most of the time, people do not choose to do that and I cannot honestly recommend that you do.

Sometimes, pretending to listen is the best option you can find to do in a situation.

Maybe ease is more important than intimacy to you with casual friends. Ask yourself, "Do I want my friends to pretend to listen to me?" Ask your friends. Maybe you <u>do</u> want people to pretend to be interested and they prefer this pretense. If so, you both know what the other person would prefer, at this time, and you now know more accurately what their listening means to them.

WHAT FITS FOR YOU AND YOUR FRIENDS? Ask two friends and report on your findings. (Do you believe them?)	
Friend:	**Says they prefer:**

What about pretending to listen to my good friends or my partner? I am not going to say "No, I don't want to listen to you."

> **Laura:** *My best friend, Erika, called me Monday night to talk about herself and her boyfriend. I was in the middle of studying and then I had to go to work, but she immediately started talking. I allowed Erika to continue talking for a few minutes, then I realized I did not really know what she was saying. I tried to interrupt her, but she continued to talk.*
>
> *I finally got up the courage to say, "Erika, I am not listening to you." She stopped talking long enough for me to explain what I was doing and to plan a time to talk later that night. I was a much more focused listener later when we returned to the conversation.*

True, there are other options that would attend to both your needs and theirs. Many friends choose to be more deliberate about a decision to talk together. I have one friend who always begins a phone call with the question, "Is this a good time to talk?" Even when you can see the other person, you may not guess accurately whether they want to listen. Regularly asking, "Is this a good time to talk?" is a courteous and time-saving skill to use in a workplace.

You could also make it a habit to let the speaker know about your availability even when they do not ask. Taking responsibility for whether your ears and your heart are present requires openness and allows for better listening. If the timing is not good for you, you may decide to request a postponement of listening. And you probably want to tell them what you are saying "Yes" to instead of listening to them.

- *I am in the middle of studying right now. Can I find you in three hours so I can give you my undivided attention?*

- *I'm good for about twenty minutes. Does that work for you?*

- *I am expecting a brief call from Rob. It will only take a minute or two, but I want to take it. So, if you are good for a short interruption, I can listen now.*

- *I am fixing supper and I am half listening, but this sounds important. Shall I stop fixing or do you want to plan a time to talk later or are you ok with me giving you divided attention?*

- *I am exhausted and not really able to bring much energy to listening right now. Can we possibly postpone this discussion until next week?*

- *I am on the other line—may I call you back in about ten minutes?*

- *I am really into this game on the TV. Could we wait and talk at the next commercial? Or is it urgent enough to you that I should turn the TV off and give you my full attention?*

- *You know, I could listen much better if you give me two minutes to go to the bathroom and get a glass of water. OK?*

- *I am running behind on my project and will have to work late tonight. It would be really helpful to me if you could make an effort to be brief and to the point. Ok for you?*

- *I am in a silly, playful mood and probably don't have much wisdom right now. Want to take your chances?*

LISTENING FOR FEELINGS & NEEDS—WHAT'S ALIVE IN THE OTHER PERSON?

Tucker: *Looking back I see that if I had listened better, I could have avoided a fight with my father. Last holiday, I talked about getting a job, but deep down I thought I deserved a break for completing a successful semester at school. I was content with hanging around the house or with friends, going to the gym, taking a midday nap. My father started making snippy remarks, "I see you did nothing today," but I just assumed he was in a funk.*

I finally sat down and thought about his perspective. He gets up at 4:00 a.m. to work out before going to work to lead his company and deal with employees and problems. When he returns home worn out, he finds me asleep and the house a wreck. When I guessed his viewpoint, I was glad to do dishes, clean the living room and generally help out after my workout at the gym. I do care about my father and want to make him feel better.

We will take apart the natural sequence of listening and talking, in order to focus on listening.

Mindful listening starts in your head. Let's consider what is going on in your head first—the first three tips. Then we will come back and consider what your mouth is doing—the next three tips. The last three tips relate to particularly challenging situations.

TIPS FOR MINDFUL LISTENING

1. **Make a decision to get present to the conversation**
2. **Try to understand the context of their story—their observations**
3. **Listen for their feelings and needs—expressed or unexpressed**
4. **Make frequent reflections of what you are hearing**
5. **Use respectful interruption, as needed**
6. **Make room for silence**
7. **Be patient with the person who does not want to talk**
8. **Be flexible about using reflections**
9. **When you notice tension, deliberately slow down, breathe, and listen**

Now, what is happening in my head while I am listening?

1. Make a decision to get present to the conversation

Doma: *Good listening does not mean shaking your head and saying "yah" every moment. It is hearing with the ears, the eyes and the mind. When I am thinking about family and stuff going on in me, at that moment my spirit of listening is not with me.*

Amber: *Just the other day I was talking with a friend of mine when I hear my phone ringing in my bag. Usually I would get it, but this time I simply let it ring. I remembered that even looking at who was calling would have been distracting to my friend. I wanted the person to know that listening to them was important to me.*

Start with a decision. Can you bring your attention and energy to the conversation? When you focus your full attention on the present conversation, your attitude will shift and your quality of listening will be different, so do what you need to do in order to get totally present.

This could require only a shift in your focus or you might benefit from some actions of self-care. If you are distracted, notice what is on your mind. Make a mental or actual note of the source of your distress that says: "Come back to this." It may be enough to clear your head. If your physical needs are distracting you, or might be in the near future, it is helpful to take a minute and deal with them—such as getting water to drink, going to the bathroom, eating some protein. Sit down, if possible, to state non-verbally that you have time to listen. Take a breath, let go of the outside world, let go of whatever occupies your thoughts, and get present.

2. Try to understand the context of their story—their observations

> **Stevie:** *When I go home, my father often walks in when I am watching a movie or television show and starts asking dumb questions, "What movie is it?" "Who is that character?" "What are you doing this evening?" I thought he was rude. Instantly I have gotten angry, ignored him, or delayed my answer. When I thought about why he did that, I see that he misses me because I have been gone for a year and just wants to be part of my life. I like that he cares. I won't be angry next time.*

That which inspires their comments may seem obvious to you, but your perception may be different from theirs. We bring different meanings to words. We bring different interpretations to events. People really see matters differently, especially if either one or both of you are tense. TV sitcoms are often based on two people thinking they are talking about the same thing when they are not. Look for it. It is useful to hold the awareness that you may be on different pages of reality.

3. Listen for their feelings and needs—expressed or unexpressed

> **Joe:** *I was talking with my mom about nonviolent communication and how we try to figure out the feelings and needs we have and others have. A little while later we were talking about me and my dad. We don't get along very good—especially about me finishing school. She said maybe I could use my new skills. When I tried to figure out his feelings and needs, I was able to see where he was coming from. He never went to college and wants me to get a good job. It made me realize I had been judging him wrong.*

> **Jeff:** *If my mom tells me she cannot live with my messy dog anymore and I'd have to get rid of it or live somewhere else, I could get angry and tell her how selfish she is or I could ask her if she wants more order and cleanliness in the house, because it has become a real burden on her. If I hear her needs and share my needs we can probably figure out how to make both of us happy.*

As you have gained some skills by now in listening specifically for your own feelings and needs, you are turning this same sensitivity to the other person. (Actually, you are also still open to information from within about your own feelings and needs while you are listening.) Are you connecting with the specific emotions and needs this person is feeling and experiencing?

So I have my thoughts in order. Now what is my mouth supposed to do?

4. Make frequent reflections of what you are hearing

> **Marcus:** *This week I have tried to reflect back to others what I thought they were saying. This felt a bit awkward, because I felt so sure about what the person meant, I felt stupid to ask. However, my interpretation of what the person was saying was not always correct.*

> **Hannah:** *I have been really focusing on my main problem—my dad and our usual financial arguments. Last time we talked, we started to argue and I remembered to simply listen while he said everything he wanted to. I even reflected back to him his core concerns. It worked. He did not need to repeat himself so I did not feel like I was getting a lecture and it did not turn into a huge fight. We were both a little surprised.*

Rosenberg, like Bolton, recommends regular paraphrasing—reflecting back to the speaker in brief summaries what you heard them to say. This will give the speaker an opportunity to correct your interpretation if you are not hearing their message in the way they meant it. If you are reaching for connection, it will come across on your face, and in your tone of voice and your body posture.

The key to mindful listening is in the music, the heart-space, not in the words. Reflections are usually best when they are short, 20 words or less. Reflections or paraphrases are a guess you are checking out. The tentative way you speak them will convey they are actually between a question and a statement. This is <u>not</u> an exam to test whether you can recall all the details; it is a time to reflect the gist of the conversation, what it feels like to the speaker. Take your time. This allows you to be more confident that you are understanding their observations, feelings, needs, and requests, in the way they are intending them.

Observations: It is often useful to start by finding out explicitly what is being seen, heard, sensed, recalled, or imagined that is stimulating this conversation. Do not pretend to understand.

- *I am puzzled here. Which party are you talking about?*
- *You said that the people were rude. Would you be willing to give me some more details?*

Feelings and Needs: Listening mindfully means noticing the feelings and needs in, under, and through the actual words. Saying, "I know how you feel." is inaccurate and often disconnecting. When you reflect the underlying feelings, it invites the speaker to recognize and feel their own feelings. It also validates that their feelings are acceptable material to talk about with you.

(To my readers who are just learning NVC: while it is vital to <u>notice</u> feelings and needs, excessive sharing of your guesses about their feelings and needs and then asking them about the accuracy of your guesses often interrupts their free flow of speaking. Go easy on this one.)

- *Sounds like you are frustrated because you want more ease in this situation?*
- *Really bummed because you value . . .?*

Requests: Are they requesting anything of you? Recognizing their request does not mean you have to say "Yes."

- *Are you wishing I would . . . ?*
- *I am guessing you had hoped I would . . . ?*

Paraphrasing or reflecting is particularly important before you act, or argue, or criticize.

💣 **Warning: Increase slowly the number of reflections in your conversation**. If you jump from one an hour to one every five minutes, you will drive your friends and yourself crazy. Move from one an hour to three or four an hour. See how that goes. If you like it, add a few more.

5. Use respectful interruption, as needed

> **Brian:** *I find myself frequently cutting off my girlfriend when she is speaking so I can get my point across before she expresses her thoughts. This is not a great listening skill.*

Yes, interrupt! Well, not exactly in the way Brian reports he did. NVC recommends you interrupt in order to reconnect with the speaker, not to change the topic.

Push in and say, "Wait, I am not with you here. Would you go back to that last statement?" Or, "Let me see if I am following you. You are frustrated about . . . ." Or, "I don't understand and I would really like to. Do you mean x or y?" "I'm lost—what do you mean by the phrase . . . ?" Or, "I notice I am running out of listening energy. I would like us to bring this conversation to an end soon. OK with you to bring this to a close in a couple of minutes?"

When you regularly check in with yourself, you will notice if the conversation stops holding your attention. If you are finding yourself confused, bored, disconnected, or otherwise not present, don't tough it out or pretend you are listening. Trust you have a good reason for not being present. Notice how your ears and heart are doing and make a request that you can imagine will reconnect you to the aliveness of the conversation. If they are into their head and talking about facts and ideas, you may want to inquire about their feelings and wishes in this matter.

Sharing your restlessness may be a profound gift to the speaker—it is easier to for them to hear about the disconnect than to sense it and not understand where they lost the listener. Also, talkers sometimes get their "talk button" stuck on and are relieved when a listener helps them reconsider what they really want to be sharing.

6. Make room for silence

> **Guy:** *When I was growing up, silence was a sure sign that something bad was about to happen. Now I have come to see that silence could be a time to gather one's thoughts in order to state them clearly. Before seeing this I tried to just get through a problem quickly and fix things. Hopefully now I will remember that silence is an important part of conversation and I will respect it.*

Regularly leaving times of silence in a conversation can be a very rich practice. It can say that the other person will have air time without having to push for it, that you value their time enough to choose your words carefully, even that you enjoy their company beyond words.

What about listening tips for really challenging situations?

7. Be patient with the person who does not want to talk

Sometimes you want to listen, but the other person doesn't want to talk. Remember that your ultimate goal is to connect with them as they are. If they do not want to share with you, it is important to respect that. If you are demanding they talk, you are already not listening to their silence. When you honor their timing, you increase the safety of the space between you, which builds trust in future encounters.

In Chapter Twelve, page 191, we will look at possible responses when you are in conflict with someone who does not want to talk.

It is also helpful to check yourself: "How safe and non-demanding a space am I offering? If the other person does not wish to talk with me, is it a reminder in any way for me to improve my listening skills? And am I listening to myself about my feelings and needs in this situation?"

8. Be flexible about using reflections

There are times when almost any reflection is counterproductive. In some cultures, some families, and some groups, personal reflections are uncomfortable or even taboo. If you are accused of being rude, insensitive, impolite, or "using that NVC stuff" or "doing psychology on the speaker," please stop it. The goal is connection, not education.

If you focus on <u>hearing</u> their feelings and needs, your attitude will shift from one of criticism to one of acceptance. Your attitude will be heard without any spoken reflections from you. As you continue in this stance, the relationship may become more peaceful and there may eventually come a time when it is appropriate for you to share your thoughts on the value of feelings and needs. (Think in terms of two months or two years, here, not two minutes.)

9. Deliberately slow down, breathe, and listen, when you notice tension

> **Kelly:** *Every year around this time my mother and I have a conflict about where to go for Thanksgiving that usually leads to anger. I would like to go to my grandmother's home and my mother thinks we should go to my great-grandmother's home because she is so old and won't be around many more years. When we started talking about it, I noticed that I was getting very angry, telling myself I was right. I was not seeing my mother's side of the story. I realized I needed to walk away from the discussion, so I did so. I stopped to breathe. I also remembered that I wanted to find a solution that met both my needs and my mother's needs, so I had to let go of being stubborn.*
>
> *When I returned to the conversation, I did a better job of keeping track of needs for both myself and my mom. We decided to stop in at my great-grandmother's home for a short visit on Thanksgiving Day, and then we are going to go to my grandmother's house for a meal. I was pleased with our decision and that I helped us focus on our needs.*

When you notice tension arising between you, or an argument starting, let it remind you to focus. It is most helpful at this moment to very deliberately slow way down, breathe, and get present to yourself. Use any re-centering techniques that help you return to yourself, to get grounded.

Then reach for strengthening your connection with the other person. Counterbalance any urge to talk faster and louder by getting slower and softer. Take time for careful listening, and extra reflections of what you are hearing. How does it look to them? What are they saying "Yes" to?

If need be, review your options of emergency exits and use one. Take responsibility to initiate a return to the conversation soon.

Donahue and Kolt remind you that you do not need a relationship without conflict. Instead, you want one wherein you together create a sure path through the conflict. As you repeatedly get through differences in a respectful manner, you are strengthening your relationship.

What next? Conflict often takes several, even many, conversations to untangle. Only on TV does everything get resolved neatly in an hour or two. Here are some goals I think are realistic for a single conversation in the midst of a conflict:

- Remaining respectful with the other person
- Staying connected and willing to keep working on the issue at hand
- A bit more insight gained by either of you

Bonus tip: After any conversation, give thought to how you listened. Notice if you would like to do it differently next time. Imagine that revised conversation. As you imagine listening in a different way, you are creating new neural connections in your brain in the same manner as if you practiced in a real situation. If you are patient, this will yield a slow and steady improvement.

INVERTORY OF LISTENING SKILLS: Review a recent conversation with family or friends. Check the skills you used. Check the skills you would like to improve upon.		
Skills	Did these	Could have done more of these
Made a decision to get present to the conversation		
Tried to understand the context of their story		
Listened for their feelings and needs		
Made frequent reflections		
Used respectful interruptions, as needed		
Made room for silence		
Was patient with a non-talker		
Was flexible about using reflections		
Slowed down, breathed, and listened when I noticed tension		
What was your experience of this conversation?		
Go back to the above chart and place a * in front of the one or two skills you are willing to particularly focus on in the upcoming week.		

REQUEST OF YOURSELF—TRANSLATE: HEAR ALL COMPLAINTS AS REQUESTS

> **Katie:** *The DREAM program was on a day trip to Montreal and we were eating pizza outside. Joey, age nine, had run away from the group and seemed upset. Joey tends to avoid me, so I went over to his mentor, Josh, to find out what was going on. He had also noticed that Joey was having difficulties, but he did not know what to do. I suggested he ask Joey what could happen for Joey to not feel so upset, to help make his trip better for the rest of the day. Josh reported back later that evening—by following my suggestion, he found out that Joey wanted pepperoni pizza, not cheese. That was easy to remedy. What seemed overwhelming and scary was easily solved by helping Joey formulate his request.*
>
> *In a similar instance, the DREAM program was at a barbecue at UVM and a bunch of us were sitting up on a hill eating our hot dogs and cheeseburgers. All of a sudden, Joey comes barreling out of nowhere and pushes another child over, very hard. I got quite upset at this, especially when Joey ran away laughing. I yelled at him and asked him to come back but soon realized I was getting nowhere. I took a deep breath and walked over to Joey. I asked him why he had pushed the child over. He said it was because she was being stupid, which did not give me much information. I tried again, asking if he was having fun at UVM, he told me "no, it is a stupid and ugly place." That set me off so I had to stop and breathe again. Then I asked him what could make it better for him. He was speechless. I don't think he was expecting someone to care about his wants or needs.*
>
> *I started listing off activities we could do and he turned all of them down. He ran off again and this time I didn't run after him. Less than two minutes later, Joey had gotten a hold of a Wiffle ball set and was asking me to play with him. Other mentors were confused as to why he had just hated me and now suddenly wanted my companionship like mad. Since that day Joey and I have been best of buds and there is a new level of respect between us.*

Effective listening calls us to constantly translate everything we hear from the language of stories, complaints, and criticism to hearing only in the language of feelings, needs, and requests.

⬇ ⬇ ⬇ **DELVING DEEPER: TRANSLATING** ⬇ ⬇ ⬇

Glenda Mattinson, an NVC leader, challenged us to translate all demands that we hear into requests. Even if the speaker believes they are making a demand, we, the listeners, have the choice to label it a request and choose how we will respond. We may not like our choices, but we always have a choice (NVC Leader-full Training, Albany, NY, 2006).

Identify some of your own demands and translate them into requests. Then find some of your complaints and translate them into requests.

TRANSLATE
all complaints you think or hear into requests
and
all demands you think or hear into requests.

AND AN ATTITUDE—CULTIVATING YOUR DEEP LISTENING SKILLS

> **Renee:** *Last week my neighbor got in trouble with the school for experimenting with drugs and alcohol. She talked with me about it. It was hard not to share my stories because my ex-boyfriend was heavily into drugs and I have some past experiences too. I remembered to just listen. I let her talk and talk. When she finished, she said "Thanks—you are the only one who did not lecture me or try to influence me." Since then, she has slowed down and has become more responsible. Listening helped more than I thought it would.*

> **Caitlyn:** *My roommate's father died unexpectedly and when she returned from her home town in Massachusetts, she was really upset. I knew I wanted to remember to be a good listener to her, to keep my mouth shut and really let her talk and talk until she let everything out. There were many things I wanted to say, but I remembered to be quiet. The most awkward times for me were when she was silent. I thought I needed to say something. It was kind of weird at first to not say anything. But it was effective. She told me things she had kept on her chest for a long time. She thanked me for listening.*

Deep listening? What is it? How do you do it?

Deep listening starts with an attitude of truly valuing the other person exactly as they are. It is the practice of bringing your focused attention to a person and then listening and listening and listening. Your goal is to be present, in the moment, with the person. You add your energy to theirs to help them explore this part of their world as they work on untangling the issue that is perplexing them. You are following them into their world, not trying to lead them into your world. You are not giving frequent reflections and not interrupting; just offering your focused attention and your comfort with their unfolding.

This kind of listening creates a cozy-by-the-fireplace space and then holds that space for the speaker to express their own thoughts and feelings. Deep listening is particularly helpful to a person who is experiencing strong feelings (such as discouragement or even great enthusiasm), or when they just want to sort their feelings out. If someone has lost a loved one or has been through some other traumatic event, often the best comfort you can give is just hanging out with them and being open to listening if they want to talk, or to doing whatever they want to do if they are not ready to talk. Your presence is your gift. It is only a variation on deep listening.

As he matured, Carl Rogers, a psychologist famous for his ability to give unconditional positive regard to his clients, reflected, "I become less and less inclined to hurry in to fix things, to set goals, to mold people, to manipulate and push them in the way I would like them to go. I am much more content simply to be myself and to let another person be [themselves]."

I asked my friend, Patti Peplow, who is an excellent listener, how she gathers the attitude she brings to her deep listening, how she would describe exactly what she does. I found her words helpful. After setting aside any potential distracters, she takes a few moments to deliberately clear herself of her own agenda in order to hear the speaker without her stuff intruding. She brings herself to the present, to the here and now, and becomes the curious witness. She listens as if watching them draw a picture and refrains from adding any suggestions, "Wouldn't it be balancing to draw in a bird just left of that tree?" She trusts it will be enough to offer the gift of presence.

Ok—start with a connecting attitude and then . . . ?

> **Kate:** *The exercise in class taught me that even when there is silence, you can stay focused on the speaker and wait. I tend to get frustrated when there is silence during a conversation. I have now come to the realization that it is important for silence to occur sometimes. It can help both the speaker and the listener to clarify their feelings and needs.*

> **Jeff:** *Last night, my girlfriend called me long-distance, crying because a kid had just gotten shot near her home, the sixth shooting this month, and her sister was right in the area picking up three girls she baby sits for. She said if her sister had arrived a little earlier, it could have been her sister who was shot. She had baked some brownies for the girls and had them playing games to keep their minds off of what had just happened, but she still felt frantic herself. I could see she needed to vent and she did not need any advice from me, so I just listened and listened until she calmed down.*

Your willingness to sit in attentive silence and wait peacefully while the person you are listening to gathers their thoughts is helpful. If you are thinking about your next words, you are missing being present to this precise moment.

Robert Gonzales, a well-known NVC leader, recommends only speaking when you are losing connection or when you sense the other person is wanting to hear something from you (NYIRT, NYC, 2005). The speaker may make a self-conscious comment, such as "Well, I have been talking your ear off." or "This must be boring." A brief response could be "I am appreciating hearing about your life. Do go on." Or "Are you wondering how I am doing with listening? I need to go in about 15 minutes and meantime, I am right here. Please continue."

If the speaker asks your opinion, communication coaches recommend that you deflect answering such questions until the speaker has finished their own thoughts, has gotten as far as they can go, and indeed may be ready for your input. Instead of answering their question, a more helpful response might be, "You seem puzzled and not sure what to do next." Surprisingly, this will usually launch the speaker into a renewed consideration of the problem and the options.

In times of intense feeling by the speaker, a single word or two capturing the feeling and reflecting it is enough. You might find yourself using some of the following door-openers to let the person know you are with them:

- "Ummm" "Aaah" "Mm hmm"—a variety of listening grunts
- "Bummer" "Puzzling" "Whoa" "That sucks" "Interesting" "Tell me more"

In summary, you may wish to cultivate your ability to listen at this deep level, to a friend or a stranger. If your friend's topic and decisions do <u>not</u> impact you, it is easier. When your own interests and concerns are involved, it is almost impossible to listen with complete acceptance of their unfolding. Notice your own needs. On the other hand, the longer you can bring yourself to really listen, the more easily you will get through any conflict. And as you develop stronger listening skills and more comfort with seeing and accepting all parts of yourself, your ability to temporarily set aside your agenda and attend to theirs, even when it does impact you, will improve.

Success Script—Listening for Connection

Title: A Different Kind of Concert
Name: Justin
Date: 10/25/07

Background: My brother and I don't seem to talk much unless he is drunk. We usually have pretty surface conversations, meaning we don't get too deep. I normally find myself just waiting for my turn to talk with him because he does the same thing with me.

New Behavior: My brother and I were driving in my car on our way to a concert at Wasted City in Fort Ethan Allen. We were excited to go see it and were talking about having a good time. His phone rang and he answered it. It was his girlfriend. He had a quick, nice conversation with her and then ended the conversation with an "I love you." He sighed just after he hung up, but not in a light-hearted way. I then asked him a leading question, "That sigh didn't sound happy. Is there something wrong between you and Amber (his girlfriend)?" This is when his verbal dam broke and he let out everything. He went on and on for 15 minutes. I was listening intently, using my best listening skills. After the 15 minutes of solid, unfaltering narration where he explained what was wrong, I led him to keep talking by saying, "So all of this is making you feel differently toward Amber?" That was enough to keep him going for another 20 minutes. He only stopped when we arrived at the concert. I said, "Why don't we just wait to go in? I want to know more." He continued and about 20 minutes later he had let everything out and he felt great. He gave me a hug and thanked me for listening and reassured me that his brother is the only one out there who he knows really cares and will really listen.

Why I Consider This a Success: My new listening skills reminded me to create the airspace for my brother to talk himself through his issues with his girlfriend. It took a load off of his shoulders that I could actually see had been lifted. He later told me that his relationship is stronger now that he has gotten his insecurities on the surface for himself and now he knows what he needs to share with Amber.

Plans for the Future: I want to maintain the conversation style with my brother because he is more or less my best friend and I love having the ability to talk about anything with him.

Success Script—Listening for Connection

Title: Creating Space before a Discussion
Name: Laura
Date: ??

Background: *My stepfather and I engage in conflict a lot. With me still living at home, our different living styles cause stress on both of us.*

New Behavior: *When I came home from work at 10:30, Monday night, my stepfather started to lecture me about my laundry not being done.*

Usually in this situation, I would have started yelling that it is my laundry and I will do it when I have time. If that bothers him, he can do the laundry for me.

Tonight, however, as soon as I heard him say, "We need to talk about your laundry," I knew where this conversation was going. (My bedroom floor and futon were covered with clean and dirty clothes.) I stopped in the doorway, paused a moment and asked myself what was really bothering me. Was it that he was telling me to do the laundry or that I was tired and hungry? As soon as I realized that I was most aware of being tired and hungry, I responded, "Right now is not a good time for me to talk. I am hungry and really tired. I do know I need to do the laundry and I was wondering if we can talk about it in the morning." He said it was okay and made me some dinner.

Why I Consider This a Success: *I took a moment to breathe and think about my own needs and then to negotiate a better time to talk with him when I was ready to talk calmly and to think about both of our needs.*

Plans for the Future: *I intend to support myself better in conflict situations. I plan to really check in with myself and see what needs of mine are met or unmet.*

👍 Success Script—Listening for Connection

Title:
Date:

Optional: create a Mind Map, a doodle, or other visual aides

CHAPTER TEN

φ

Talking for Connection

Brad: *Last Friday night, Marie went to a party with some friends and then went clubbing. When she started to tell me about it the next day, I immediately began to get jealous, as I normally do when she does such things. Like always, I began to grill her with questions: "What did you wear? Who was there? Did you dance with any guys?" Regardless of her responses, I was getting more and more angry. I had an image in my head of what her experience was like, and I didn't want to hear or believe that it was any different than what I imagined.*

Right as my emotions were bubbling over and my voice started to rise, I stopped. It sounds incredible, but I actually remembered Rosenberg's lesson about being responsible for our feelings. It was not what Marie had done that was making me angry; it was my own insecurities. I promptly told Marie that I didn't want to fight, and instead wanted to take a little time to think about some things. I promised that I would call her later.

After hanging up the phone, I tried to pinpoint the source of my insecurities. After some soul-searching, I realized that it was because I couldn't be there with her to share in her experience that was creating my jealousy. I didn't like that she was partying with other guys, not because I didn't trust her, but because she was with them and not me. After realizing this, I began to feel much better.

That night, I called Marie back. I explained my insecurities, and she appreciated my honesty. In fact, she told me that it was for the same reasons that she got jealous when I went out with my friends. We realized that we were missing each other and that was the source of our anger. This realization made us both feel a lot better, and best of all, we had saved ourselves a fight. By recognizing that I was responsible for my feelings, not for her feelings, I grew closer to her instead of alienating her.

I always thought talking was a bit selfish, that listening was more connecting.

They are two sides of a coin. If I don't talk, you have nothing to listen to! Well, not nothing, just a lot less. Others can often sense or read our feelings, energy, and body language, but without our words, they will have only a blurry picture of who we are and what we are experiencing. Some people deliberately reach out to others by their willingness to share what is inside them.

Let's see if we can find ways that make sense to you to expand your ability to connect with others through talking. As you might guess, I am going to suggest that when you are talking for connection, it will enhance your relationships if you frequently share your observations, feelings, needs, and requests.

OBSERVATION—REMEMBERING YOUR AUDIENCE AND BEING CHOICEFUL

Here are some considerations that could improve your ability to connect with your listeners. If we bring our options to awareness, we can act in ways that are more closely aligned with our values.

CHOICES FOR TALKING

> 1. **Be choiceful in stepping into and out of roles**
> 2. **Be choiceful in the setting and timing of speaking**
> 3. **Revisit a conversation you think did not go well—give it another chance**
> 4. **Speak to your loved ones as if you loved them**
> 5. **Plan a talk about talking**
> 6. **Practice a difficult scenario out loud before doing it for real**

1. Be choiceful in stepping into and out of roles

> **Rick:** *Honestly I can say I have two different sides—occupational and regular me. I will respond to different situations depending on what side I am showing. The occupational side has been trained not to show any emotion whatsoever. This side was formulated into a shell empty of emotion in order to combat the everyday stress of police work.*
>
> *But I soon saw myself changing. This occupational side started creeping into the rest of me. Like the old saying—leave your work at work; don't bring it home. I found myself the opposite. My work was starting to take over me, what I believed, and the way I acted. Honestly, by my actions now, you can easily tell what I do for an occupation.*

If you have a role of authority (such as a parent, social worker, medical doctor, airline pilot, or a member of the police department) society expects you to have a particular expertise and responsibility. Therefore, in prescribed situations, you need to communicate with your words, tone of voice, and body stance that you are in charge. The challenge is to empower yourself to use that authority wisely when it is appropriate, to remain professional, to not exceed the authority needed, and to let go of that role in other situations. It takes awareness to both claim authority and to relinquish it.

2. Be choiceful in the setting and timing of speaking

> **TJ:** *We have been taking turns taking our trash to the end of the driveway on Mondays for the trash company to collect. I wanted to change the system and get my roommate to take over the responsibility of dishes and I would deal with the trash. I thought I would get the better end of the deal, so I thought carefully how to present my request in a way that would address both his needs and mine.*
>
> *The problem was when I did not think about his state of mind. He had just gotten off the phone with his ex-girlfriend and he was pretty upset. Instead of negotiating a better arrangement, we got into a big argument over the trash.*

Ned: *In past relations of mine, I find that when the two of us can talk and actually listen to one another, things are okay, but if I see her at school with a bunch of her friends, I've learned to avoid trying to talk with her about serious things. She will be distracted and I know she won't listen to me.*

Communication coaches will tell you that neglecting to carefully pick a good time to bring up a matter is the number one cause of failure in resolving conflicts. Besides asking a person whether this is a good time for them to talk, one can also use some common sense. When a person is exhausted, drunk, or headed out for an exam or a job interview, it is not a useful time to talk. This may be obvious, but I confess that I sometimes get so focused on what I want to share and so excited about it, that I have been oblivious to whether the listener is really available to listen.

The rhythm of talking is also important. Talking too long invites the listener to disengage. For those of us who can go on for thirty minutes without coming up for air, it is consistently helpful to remember to stop every few minutes and connect with your listener. This gives the other person a chance to reflect, respond, grunt at you, smile at you, whatever. This is a good time to ask, "Still interested?" "Up for hearing some more?" Most listeners do not feel comfortable interrupting with, "Wait, I am losing you here." The more customary response is to tune you out or fall asleep.

Talking in bite-size chunks helps you and your listener stay in closer connection. It gives you, the speaker, a moment to re-gather perspective on what else you want to say. This improves personal relationships. It seems to improve sharing information also. I have been shortening the time I talk in class before I stop to get student input and have much better discussions.

3. Revisit a conversation that you think did not go well—give it another chance

Allyson: *Some of my friends still live at home with their parents, so they like to get out as much as possible. When they were looking for a party spot, they told me they wanted to use my house. I told them I had a big exam the next day, but they kept right on nagging and then acting like they assumed they would have the party at my house. I did not know what to do, but it seemed like it was worth a try to use the lessons from class. The next time I saw them and they started asking what time they should tell people to come, I just said, "No, I am not having this party. You either need to find another location or skip it." They finally got it that I was serious. I can see how I waste a lot of time trying to avoid conflict.*

Janet: *My son, Jon, told me he was talking with a realtor about getting a place of his own. Before he could elaborate any more, I blurted out "Your credit is bad—the bank won't give you a loan." Later I realized my words were belittling, judging and insulting. I did better when I returned to the conversation.*

Only on TV do people always say it the way they wanted to the first time. And that just means the scriptwriters wrote and rewrote the lines before the show. In real life, we often do not speak clearly; the other person does not understand what we meant; or something is just "off" in any particular conversation. Notice when the memory of a conversation does not sit well and try again. If you miss it the first time around, give it another try, as soon as you can. You usually have the option of blowing it, thinking about it, and then returning to a conversation and cleaning it up.

4. Speak to your loved ones as if you loved them

> **Suzanne:** *I have been known to say to my boyfriend, "God, stop bothering me," when all I really wanted was for him to give me a few minutes to read something. He got mad, I got upset and then a big fight followed. What I could have said instead is "I need a minute to read this article. It is important. Is that okay with you?" I'm sure he would have understood and given the time I asked for. This could eliminate a lot of silly fights.*

This reminder about how we speak to our loved ones calls many people up short. Perhaps we have lapsed into old habits and respond to feeling any kind of relational distress by complaining and blaming. Even if this blame is not spoken, but sits unresolved in our minds, it may well come out in our tone of voice and in our choice of actions.

As we relax with loved ones, we are inclined to get sloppy about the energy we bring them. In his book on communication skills for developing more loving relationships, author Randy Fujishin, Gifts from the Heart, reminds us that a relationship needs to be fed and nurtured regularly, like a growing tree. We need quality time together, not just the leftover time. Using life-alienating language and sharing only surface stuff instead of the underlying feelings and concerns slowly deadens a relationship.

How alive are your relationships? Have you stopped talking about things that are important?

5. Plan a talk about talking

> **Jana:** *My boyfriend and I have been dating for about 4 years. During the first year, when our trust was developing between each other, we always fought over what we now consider to be stupid things. After we almost broke up one day, I realized that all of our arguments seemed to include one of us saying something like, "You aren't even listening to me!" and the accused person getting even more angry.*
>
> *So I asked my boyfriend to sit down with me and talk about our arguments and how we could change things between us so that we could both be happy in our relationship. He agreed that when we were upset it seemed the other person was not listening. When we could acknowledge this pattern together, we could see why things were getting messy. We decided we needed to slow down and let the other person know we were listening and understood what they were saying before telling our side of the disagreement. It worked. For the past three years, we have gotten through our arguments more effectively and solved problems more efficiently. The disagreements are now small and we can move on after a disagreement and not dwell on it forever. We have had a more pleasant, exciting and fun relationship.*
>
> **John:** *I see I am task-oriented and my girlfriend often tells me "the story of her life" before asking me for even the simplest things. I cannot stay focused and I slip out of listening. To help with this problem, we talked about it and have agreed that she shall try to get to the point directly on simple matters and I shall try to remind her gently, if she forgets. Also I have promised to try to stay focused and listen carefully for more important items, like how she is feeling or how her day went.*

The fancy name for this is *metacommunication* or communication about communication. Many find it useful with friends or partners to choose a quiet time to talk about how it is when things are tense between you. You might say something like, "I notice that sometimes I fly off the handle and say things I don't mean. I want to change that. Here is what I am considering. I want to stop talking before I mouth off next time and go for a walk. I promise I will initiate picking up the conversation again within a few hours or at least tell you that I have not forgotten my promise, but that I need more time to sort myself out. How does that sound to you?"

In Sleeping with Bread: Holding What Gives You Life, Dennis, Sheila, and Matthew Linn write about the benefits of asking yourself at the end of each day, "For what moment today am I most grateful? For what moment today am I least grateful?" This practice increases awareness of what brings you aliveness. It is also a nourishing bond for relationships. Some couples make it a daily or weekly practice to talk together about the "ups" and "downs" specifically between them.

6. Practice a difficult scenario out loud before doing it for real

> **Ryan:** *I learned some important tools in class to help me with feelings of anger. The first is to identify scenarios that could result in feelings of anger, and then to practice in my head how I want to act before those scenarios happen. Then I will be better prepared to deal with them when they actually happen.*

One more suggestion: identify conversations that might be difficult for you or wherein you frequently lose your connection to self and others. Get a friend to role-play with you. You could ask:

- *When I try to ask someone out, I shut down and get tongue-tied. Would you be willing to help me figure out what to say and then to practice it with me?*

- *Every time my father wants to talk about my future, I get furious with him. Would you be willing to play his role, so I can practice what I want to say until it comes out the way I want it to?*

THINK ABOUT ONE IMPORTANT RELATIONSHIP: Consider each of the above suggestions (1-6). Identify two that might contribute to your communication. Comment.

FIND AND SOMETIMES SHARE YOUR FEELINGS & NEEDS—BEING AWARE

> **Jeff:** *I got into an argument with my cousin over my puppy. He bought the puppy for me and she lived with him for the first week. One morning he called and asked to take the dog with him to the shore. I said "no," but he came over and tried to take her anyway. We got into a yelling match and a little scrap. At the time I thought I won because the dog did not go with him, but my cousin and I did not resolve the issue for days.*
>
> *After I thought about it, I saw that I was feeling guilty that I was not giving the dog proper training, and afraid that the dog might have liked him more than me. I also realized that I was probably going to sleep all day and it would be good for the dog to get some exercise. When I finally did talk with my cousin, I shared what was under my anger. He said he just missed the dog and wanted to spend some time with her. It could have been resolved in minutes if I had shared where I was coming from and listened to him.* [feeling = regret or concern; guilty = an evaluation mixed in with the feeling]

All right. So how do you find your needs?

Well, you will recall the three stages of becoming assertive we looked at in Chapter Three:

1. **PASSIVE** "I have no needs and if I had some, they are not important."

2. **AGGRESSIVE** "It is very important that I meet my needs, regardless of how that affects you."

3. **ASSERTIVE** "We both have needs and all of our needs are important."

I was brought up to believe that taking care of other people was more virtuous than taking care of my own needs. Even though in some areas of my life I operate comfortably out of the third stage, there are also areas wherein my thinking seems currently to still come from the first stage. That makes it a struggle to even notice my needs and hard to see them as a gift when I do find them. Let me share my personal process in this. Perhaps others will find parts of it familiar and helpful.

I know that some people find their first clue to an unmet need in their feelings such as tension, fear, discomfort, sadness. It is a body sensation for them. My first clue that I have an unmet need is usually when I notice I am thinking a criticism or judgment of the other person, sometimes quite harshly, such as: "She is rude." "He is such a pain." "That person is so inconsiderate." "I cannot believe that person is so immature." "What a jerk!"

(You will recognize that this is an example of what Rosenberg calls life-alienating language.)

A familiar judgment is "They are not acting right." In my mind there still lurks an elaborate system of right-wrong behavior and the assumption that if everyone "acted right," everyone would be kind and happy and all of my needs would be met and I would never have to ask. People would just sense what I wanted and do it joyfully! It is a rule-based system, not a person-based system. I have come to realize that holding this fantasy of a right-wrong system is quite costly to me. It keeps me from seeing clearly how people are unique and that the particular needs most alive for them at the moment are unknowable. I cannot possibly guess their needs accurately nor can they guess mine. And even our constructed ideas of a right-wrong system are different!

When I hear myself making these criticisms, I next judge myself as "unloving," "hateful," and "petty," so I am tempted to escape my "negative thinking" quickly. A counseling friend once reflected that people often want to clean up their act before they even know what their act is!

That's me. So, I remind myself to stop and breathe. The starting point of getting unstuck and going forward is to recognize exactly where I am in my thoughts, feelings, evaluations, and actions and then to accept myself in that exact place. Often I journal. Sometimes I talk to a good friend with whom I can share my scariest thoughts and deepest fears and she listens with all the skills we talked about in the previous chapter. Eventually I get through the places where I am scaring myself about my worth as a person and then I can see my need. Journaling and talking are strategies that help me to claim myself exactly where I am.

After I have waded through whatever and actually found a need, it is really important for me to sit with the need and value it. I remind myself that having an unmet need is not a failing on my part, nor is it a sign of weakness, an inconvenience, a limitation, nor a moment of selfishness.

Hey! You talked about finding, but not about sharing your feelings and needs.

> **John:** *I want to remember to explain my no's. It is like showing your cards in a card game. When you show the other person what intentions you have, it is then easier to come up with win-win solutions. My girlfriend and I were out shopping and she wanted to take the bus to another shopping center. I said, "No, I don't want to because I am hungry." Instead of fighting over whether we should go home or to the other shopping center, we came up with the solution of going to the other center and finding a restaurant there.*

Oops! I fairly regularly notice my feelings, and often find related needs. I still frequently forget about sharing them in give-and-take conversations. I tend to share thoughts instead. Focusing on noticing feelings and needs and then sharing them is a perspective often not taught in our culture. If your life experience is similar to mine and you think this is valuable, it may take some practice.

VALUE OF SHARING FEELINGS AND NEEDS

1. **Increases your self-understanding and aids in re-centering in challenging times**
2. **Gives people information about how they can enrich your life**
3. **Creates a successful path through conflict with a friend or partner**
4. **Honors the world by sharing an authentic voice**

1. Increases your self-understanding and aids in re-centering in challenging times

Some people discover their own thinking, feelings, and needs by talking out loud. One way to get your feet back under you when you feel distressed is to go to a friend who can listen to your critical statements about both yourself and the other person, without getting lost in your volcano and forgetting that you will get through the issue in your own timing. They don't fuel your fire by agreeing with your complaints nor do they pour water on it by telling you to get over it. They just listen.

2. Gives people information about how they can enrich your life

> **Kelly:** *This is my third year in college. I am becoming more and more stressed with everything I need to do: studies, time to work so I can pay for college, and a social life. I know I am not getting enough sleep. I am also really shy and hate to talk about my problems. I thought if I just worked harder, I could do it all. It was registration time for classes and time to meet with my advisor. I decided to talk to her about the amount of stress I have had lately and my fears for my health.*
>
> *Because I shared my experience of this semester, she helped me come up with other options. Summer classes were something that stuck out for me because that would give me a lighter load during the semester.*

When you could use help and you try to tough it out, you miss the possibility of getting help. You also deny other people the opportunity to give to you. Rosenberg reminds us that it is human nature to experience deep satisfaction when one is able to give something meaningful to another person. Of course, if you demand help or expect that it will be given, you spoil their pleasure.

I GET BY WITH A LITTLE HELP FROM MY FRIENDS: Identify three possible requests you could make of friends or family members.

Ask yourself if you are willing to actually request any of these things. Comment.

---

3. Creates a successful path through conflict with a friend or partner

For a solid relationship, you do not need one without conflict. Instead, you need one wherein the two of you create a sure path through the conflict. This is usually based on sharing what is inside—your thoughts, feelings, and needs—and then listening carefully to the other person. The following is the beginning of a fictitious conversation based on real ones I have had with friends.

> **Barry:** *Got a couple of minutes? I want to check something out with you.*
>
> **Naomi:** *Yeah. Go for it.*
>
> **Barry:** *OK. I am telling myself you think I'm stupid because I broke the faucet this morning and that you are angry. Is that accurate or just my story?*
>
> **Naomi:** *I don't think you are stupid, and I am rather angry. Do you want to hear my thoughts on the matter?*

Barry: *Yes. That's what I want to know.*

Naomi: *It seems to me that you frequently break things and it bugs me because it seems to me you don't care. Do you share that perception?*

Barry: *That I break things—yes. That I don't care—no. I feel very discouraged about it.*

Naomi: *Hmmm. It seems to me that you usually make a joke about how you cannot get quality things from the hardware store these days. Do you agree with me about that?*

Barry: *I hadn't thought about it. Yeah, I do joke. Just like my father, I guess. It doesn't express my feelings very directly, does it?*

Naomi: No. *What are your feelings?*

Barry: *Well, most of the time when I start a project, I feel a little fear that I am going to goof it up and that you are going to get angry.*

Naomi: *Wow! That sounds uncomfortable. Hmm. Does it seem to you that I often get angry?*

Barry: *Nooooo, I guess not. Think I am still tensing myself over my older brother's criticism. For me, the sun rose and set around him and I could never make him happy.*

Naomi: *Umm. That sounds frustrating.*

Barry: *Yah. I want to think about that one. I know I can do better than I've been doing.*

Naomi: *Thanks for bringing that up and letting me know what is going on for you. I was aware of the tension around home repairs, but I couldn't figure out what was happening. I have a better understanding now.*

Barry: *Thank you for looking at with me. I'm glad I brought it up. I was getting aware of your discomfort as well as my own, but I hadn't really explored where it was coming from.*

Maybe you wonder how Barry could so calmly share with Naomi his inner dialogue.

The prequel to this conversation that you don't see is that when Barry noticed he was irritated with Naomi around repairs, he went to his friend Oliver, who could listen and help him get under his complaints. This brought to light for him his feelings of hurt and fear. From there he was able to identify his next step—to ask her what was happening instead acting on the story he had created.

When you have heavy relationship issues, you might want to recall this prequel—to give yourself a break and cultivate a friend outside the relationship to listen and help you translate your complaints into requests, before you discuss them with the person involved. Your goal is to get beyond your complaints and your criticism about the other person and to observe yourself. I hope you will work with your friend until you at least get through your blaming voices before initiating a conversation about a tense matter. (If you do not have such a friend, a counselor could help.)

If the conversation could still be difficult to hear, it is considerate to prepare your listener and give them a "heads up."

Here is an image that helps me. I picture placing the difficult, tender conversation in a gift box. Next I talk about the gift, not the content, so that the other person has an initial awareness and choice about receiving the upcoming conversation at this time. "I have a potentially difficult matter to discuss with you. Is this a good time for you?" "I've been thinking about our conversation yesterday and I would like to hear again several things I think you said. Ok?" Or, "I know I am somewhat jumbled here. Can you hear this as my stuff and not take it personally?"

When I unwrap and share my gift, I bracket my statements frequently with reminders to the listener to stay centered, to keep in mind that I am offering my truth rather than THE TRUTH. "I am telling myself . . ." Or, "Here is my story on this." Or, "My memory of that event may be totally distorted. Do you share my perception on this?" "As I recall . . ." "It seems to me . . ."

4. Honor the world by sharing an authentic voice

Here is a conversation between my student, Jay, and myself. His authentic complaint was valuable.

> **Jay:** *Judging people won't get you anywhere—I actually felt judged today when you joked that I am handing in only one of every three papers. I believe I have handed in 5 out of 7. Your comment didn't make me want to do any more work for your class right away even though that would only hurt me. The message I received from you during this comment was that I didn't care about your class. This made me feel angry and one positive thing that I could use this anger for was a wake up call.*
>
> *After the anger subsided I realized that I needed to do well in this class—for the remainder of the semester—for me to feel positive about my experience in the class and for me to feel happy instead of angry. Also, so I wouldn't receive any more negative comments from you.*
>
> **Bonnie:** *Thank you for the courage to tell me directly what reaction my statement evoked. Your feedback brought to my attention that making a flip comment to you did not communicate my concern. I feel sad. I am guessing you are not the first student I have insulted unintentionally. Your honesty helped me become more aware. That was a gift.*

Fritz Perls, a philosopher and founder of Gestalt Therapy, says that the greatest gift we can give anyone is to share the inner workings of an authentic and real human being. (I trust that taking you through the personal journey of how I get from criticism to awareness of needs will be helpful to some of you, my readers, in considering how you move from one to the other.)

To be where you are and to share that gives others more permission to be where they are. It also gives people another model of how the world really looks to someone else. When we try to construct our understanding of how life really is, it is easy to get confused and compare our inner experience with the apparently happy and successful outer image of another person.

I hope you notice that the reason this book sings is because so many students were willing to share their authentic voices of successes, failures, frustrations, questions, insights, self-doubt, and celebration, with each other and future readers. I am so grateful for their most generous offering.

REQUESTS—ASK FOR THE KIND OF LISTENING YOU WOULD LIKE

> **Dan:** *I was dating this girl, Sally. We were in a long distance relationship. She was in Connecticut and I was up here in Vermont and we talked on the phone all the time. One night she was venting to me about something and I kept throwing in my two cents about how to make her life easier for her.*
>
> *To my great surprise, she started yelling at me that I always had to give advice, and that I could never just plain listen when she was venting. She told me off in pretty colorful terms and then hung up the phone. I found out the hard way. When you give advice and someone does not want it, all it does is cause problems in the conversation.*

This is a clear example of a typical interaction. Not getting what she hungered for, Sally yelled at Dan for not listening. Two possible conversations could have happened that would have kept them in connection. Before talking about her issue, Sally could have said, "I want an ear to hear me and maybe a shoulder to cry on, but no advice at this time. Are you OK with that?" Or Dan could have asked, "Are you wanting any thoughts from me or do you just want me to listen for now?"

We are often not clear what we even want from our listener when we talk to them. It is useful to think about that before we begin talking and then to clue our potential listener in to exactly what it is we believe would best suit us at the moment. (To clarify what you want from your listeners before you speak in a meeting and to get others to do the same, will save hours of time!)

As we have already noticed, it is not helpful to expect someone to mind read and guess our needs. Even when our needs seem perfectly obvious to us, they may not be to the other person. If the person does not seem to be responding to the obvious, it would be helpful to request exactly what we want. When you want a specific kind of listening, use your knowledge of good listening skills and your assertiveness skills to make a specific request. This will improve communication all around. Most people, most of the time, enjoy being able to give to someone exactly what they want, if it is a free gift and not an expectation.

We looked in the previous chapter at the components of mindful listening. Some friends, having gotten peaceful about the possibility that the answer could be "No," always open a conversation with the question, "Is this a good time to talk?" They want to know whether the other person has any listening energy or listening time at the moment.

When you are the one talking, you have the opportunity to let the other person know what specific kind of listening you would enjoy. Remember to ask for what you do want, and not to waste time focusing on what you don't want. Then make your request for time-specific, concrete, and doable actions. Next ask if a person is willing to do a specific action.

Students always reflect that using good communication skills is much easier when both parties know them. Some even want to give up and say they will use them only with someone who also knows them. I counter, "I agree it is easier and I do hope you will learn skills that are so solid that you are able to communicate well even with people who do not use good communication skills." NVC was set out by Rosenberg to be effective whether the other person uses it or not. Also, if you are steady with it, eventually many of the people around you will learn better skills.

SOME SAMPLE REQUESTS FOR THE KIND OF LISTENING YOU WANT

- *Would you be willing to tell me how you feel when I share this information with you?*
- *Would it fit for you to let me rant and rave for awhile? Can you stay centered?*
- *I want some feedback on how I could organize my thoughts for a speech. OK?*
- *Are you up for letting me know when you are tired of listening to my stuff tonight?*
- *OK with you to just listen for now and hold any advice you might have?*
- *I want to think aloud on this paper. Would you be willing to just sit with me and smile?*
- *Will you let me know where you think my plan will run into problems?*
- *I am ragged out. Can you give me a shoulder to cry on?*
- *I am so lost. Will you help me sort this mess out and give me some suggestions?*
- *I want you to notice and tell me the two parts of my paper you enjoyed the most. OK?*
- *Are you up for telling me what you just heard? I am not at all sure I was clear.*
- *Are you willing to set aside your video game and listen to me for maybe ten minutes?*
- *I would like to hear your feelings about this project. Want to share them?*
- *Ready to brainstorm options that might work for both of us?*
- *Cool with you to join me in listening to music?*
- *I had a dream about you last night. Can you listen without analyzing it?*
- *I would like you to interrupt me if you are confused at any point in my explanation. Are you up for that?*
- *Trust your gut—if you get uncomfortable with anything I am saying, tell me to stop, even if you don't know why. OK?*
- *Then let me know if you are up for looking at the point of discomfort. Does that sound like a workable plan to you?*

LISTEN TO ME: Create two imaginary requests related to listening that you might make.

AND AN ATTITUDE—INVESTING MORE EFFORT IN ONE RELATIONSHIP

First, choose a relationship that is important to you. Then consider doing any of the following:

- If you seldom speak your requests directly, encourage yourself to make a little request.

- Deliberately listen twice as long as usual.

- If you had a difficult encounter, go back and think about it. Take it apart in your mind or in your journal in order to get beyond who's-right-who's-wrong, and the blame-self-and-blame-other thoughts. Find a non-critical understanding of everything both of you did. Try to see clearly the good motives you both had, underneath the problem.

- When you make a mistake, own it as soon as you can.

- Forgive the other person once in a while even if they really blew it big time. (Once in a while for the big stuff, not every day.)

- Build trust by keeping promises. Be on time for appointments.

- Bring flowers for no reason at all. Do the dishes occasionally when it is not your turn.

- Catch the other person doing something you appreciate every day. Tell them about it.

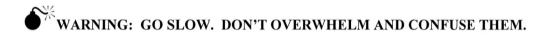 **WARNING: GO SLOW. DON'T OVERWHELM AND CONFUSE THEM.**

MAKE A CONSCIOUS EFFORT TO DEEPEN ONE PARTICULAR RELATIONSHIP
Identify one relationship you would like to strengthen.
What are two specific ways you could bring conscious effort to this relationship?
What hesitation do you have about doing so?
Can you think of a strategy that honors both your hunger to connect better and your hesitation to act on that?
Is there one action you are willing to commit to do at this time?

Success Script—Talking for Connection

Title: People Are Not Mind Readers
Name: Jana
Date: 9/29/06

Background: *My parents have been going out to run errands and leaving me at home to keep an eye on my four siblings, ages 8-17, without checking with me about it.*

Since I transferred to Champlain College last spring I have been living at home to save money. Whenever I am home, my parents seem to assume that I don't have any plans and just take off, leaving me as the person in charge. They never ask if it is okay with me and never turn on their cell phones so I can make sure that it's fine with them to leave the high school age siblings in charge. Quite often, I do indeed have plans and want to head out to meet up with my friends. This leaves me in a bind between keeping my plans and being loyal and helpful to my family, which makes me really frustrated. Now that I think about it though, I never really spoke up to my parents about this situation and the frustration it causes me.

New Behavior: *Last night, before my parents took off, I spoke with them about my frustrations. I said I would really appreciate it if they would check with me and see what I may have planned before assuming that I am game to baby-sit all the time. My parents and I agreed that from now on, they will make sure that I am okay with accepting the responsibility for watching my siblings, before they run errands or go out to dinner with friends.*

Why I Consider This a Success: *Both my parents are happy with this decision. They know I am open and willing to watch my siblings, but also that I do have a life outside the house. I also now understand that they were not trying to "use" me, but never really knew how I felt because I never spoke up about it. I now feel more valued.*

Intention for the Future: *In the past I have been very passive about doing stuff for people. I just wanted to please everyone. I told myself I was being used. I am now trying to use my skills in making effective requests in more situations. It will probably make my life less stressful and more enjoyable.*

Success Script—Talking for Connection

Title:
Date:

Optional: create a Mind Map, a doodle, or other visual aides

CHAPTER ELEVEN

φ

Dealing with Anger in a Connecting Way

Brady: *I am a pretty laid back guy, so I don't get angry that often. But recently my dad was pushing me to try for a job that he thought would be great, but that I did not want to do. I got really angry and made a lot of judgments about him. "He thinks he knows everything and that his way is the one and only way to go." When I remembered to listen to my feelings, I realized that I don't really know what I will do for the summer and it feels stressful to me. I saw that I was really angry at myself for not having a plan of what to do and not really at my dad for trying to give me some direction.*

Sam: *One example of masking feelings happened for me last week when I invited friends to go to my family's lake house in Maine. I got a very lukewarm response considering how much fun they said they had last summer. I got angry. Underneath that was a feeling of hurt and uncertainty about the friendships. When I calmed down, I realized that I was asking my friends to make plans months in advance, not their style.*

OBSERVATION—LOOKING INTO THE HEART OF YOUR ANGER

Both anger and conflict are valuable parts of our lives! Anger is an alarm clock that tells us to wake up and pay attention. Don't push anger away until it has given you some insight into where you are hurting and what you are deeply wanting at that moment. And, if anger is your best strategy for protection from being abused, <u>don't let go of your anger until you have worked out better ways of protecting yourself and expressing your needs.</u>

The first challenge is to quickly notice your anger and refrain from speaking or acting on it, i.e. contain it. Be with your feelings, re-center yourself, find the needs related to your anger, and then choose your response. Your goal is to act thoughtfully, even powerfully, rather than react. Clearly, it is to your advantage to build both personal and professional relationships wherein people feel confident of your ability to remain respectful even when you are tense or angry. Understanding your own anger will add to your ability to respond in a connecting way to someone else's anger.

We usually think of anger as loud, even explosive. I have recently begun to see another set of behaviors as also expressing anger, a quieter type of anger in which a person lets it leak out in little ways. I had prided myself in how seldom I explode. Seeing the anger I have expressed in some quieter ways was quite stretching and humbling for me. When a person has not yet found skills to notice their needs and is instead focused on "being nice," they are prone to quiet anger. Other contributors to quiet anger are resentment, bitterness, hopelessness, and despair around chronically unmet needs. Quiet anger releases the internal pressure a little at a time and brings some relief. Unfortunately these actions are at least as harmful to a relationship as explosions of anger and perhaps more so because they are somewhat less likely to be noticed.

Emily: *I never considered my irritated tone of voice, sarcasm and trying to be right all the time, as expressions of anger and therefore violent communication! The day I read this, I was having a difficult time while walking the kids home from school. It was 6 pm by the time we got to the front door. The sun had already set and we were all very hungry, tired and ready for a rest. I heard myself saying sarcastically to Aiden, "Would it be too much to ask for you to just walk down the hall to the door without me having to carry you?"*

Then, I realized what I had just said. I stopped, took a breath, apologized to Aiden and gave him a hug. I know I am not up to the noticing-the-needs-under-the-anger stage yet, but being in the phase of observing my behaviors is good enough for me now. I celebrate my small achievements.

QUIET ANGER IS OFTEN EXPRESSED BY

- Sarcasm

- Passive-aggressive behaviors such as being late regularly or forgetting commitments

- Putting the other person down, especially in public

- Making it a point to prove that you are right and the other person is wrong

- Smugness or self-righteousness, expressed in attitude, comments, or tone of voice

- Habitual crabbiness or bitchiness to a person or in a particular situation (a job?)

- Frequent complaints about small matters

- Minor punitive, vengeful actions

- Harsh tone of voice and non-verbal signs of irritation at the person

What needs are under these actions? When I have expressed myself in some of these ways, it was my best effort to request connection, appreciation, and support. You can guess that people around me often missed the message! So, if you find yourself expressing your anger in quiet ways, I hope you will be gentle with yourself and listen for the underlying needs, perhaps ones that have been unmet for a long time. Then you can find more accurate ways of reaching out for what you want.

How do you experience anger? Let's start by capturing some real examples, so you can study the components, see what is happening inside, and put them into a different perspective.

CLAIMING YOUR ANGER: Identify two situations in which you expressed anger explosively or quietly. If you did not express it, can you recall situations when you felt anger?

I feel powerful when I am angry.

> **Eric:** *Reading the chapter on expressing anger fully was actually kinda helpful for me because when I get mad, I really get mad. I can say the most hurtful, degrading things to people when they make me mad and in the past I usually would feel a sense of satisfaction doing this because I am rather quick with my words and can easily overpower someone in a confrontation. But recently I have been trying to stop doing this not only because I really don't get the pleasure I used to out of it anymore, I also am a little more mature now and can see that I am really not helping anything by doing this.*

Exploding at someone can temporarily feel satisfying. We may even get a positive reinforcement for explosions as people often jump to do what we want when our demand is attached to a strong expression of anger. Regular experiences of anger—expressed or unexpressed—frequently results in health problems. It also consistently causes relationship problems in the long run and may eventually cost the relationship itself.

Jorge Rubio, an NVC teacher, points out that the thought that one is powerful when one vents explosive anger is an illusion. The reality is that one is instead deeply vulnerable at that moment. This is a cry for help in a language that few will hear accurately (NYIRT, Binghamton, NY, 2009).

SELF—ASSESSMENT: How are you doing with your anger these days?
How did you react the last time something irritated you?
How often were you angry last week?
How do you evaluate your skills in getting through a situation when you are angry?

Wait a minute! What if I do not want to back away from my anger? There are many good reasons to get angry about social injustice in the world today.

The anger is a useful alarm, but it is counterproductive when it dictates our reaction. When we let the anger lead us immediately to an action instead to introspection, we waste precious information about what is going on inside us. I prefer paying close attention to my anger, feeling it, honoring my passion, taking it apart to gain the valuable information within it. When I am distressed by anyone's words or behavior, I return to the basic NVC exercise of staying with the blame other-blame self thoughts and feelings until I can reach underneath my judgments to clarify my deep hunger for justice and fairness, my pain at the unmet needs in the world, my concerns, my hopes.

Then and only then, do I want to expand my vision to focus on seeing the feelings and needs of all people involved. I recall that everyone is trying to meet the same universal human needs. When I see the needs a person is trying to meet by the actions that I do not like, it expands my options of response. Perhaps I can show them more effective, less costly strategies to meet their needs. Even if I decide that my next action is one of saying, "No! You may not continue this behavior," I believe lasting change depends on seeing everyone's humanity and aiming to meet all needs.

FEELINGS AND NEEDS—MANAGING YOUR ANGER IN DAILY ENCOUNTERS

Stevie: *Studying this book actually helped me this weekend when I flew to Colorado to look at schools and visit my friend. My friend had a party. As everyone started drinking more and more, people got intoxicated. I was sitting outside chilling with some kids I met and this really hammered kid comes up the stairs and rubs my hat like I was 4 and he was my uncle. Then he knocked off my hat and said—"Oh, I'm sorry man, lemme get that for you." He picked up my hat, put it on my head and tried to pull the front down over my eyes.*

Since I read this on the flight over I simply counted to 10 and then realized that I didn't need to get mad over this. The kid was clearly drunk and being a buffoon. Maybe his need was to make friends. My need that was unmet was for mutual respect. So, I just looked at him and gave him a smile and continued on like nothing happened. If I had not read this stuff, I might have been prone to fight or do something stupid, but since I was actively thinking about my nonviolent communication, I let it slide off my shoulder.

Jeff: *According to Rosenberg, the first step to fully expressing anger in nonviolent communication is to separate the other person from any responsibility for our anger. This made me recall one violent incident in my life. My girlfriend in high school cheated on me. I ran into the other kid at a party, and after talking for several minutes, I decided he deserved to be punished, and I hit him. This only caused more problems, including hospital bills and a lawsuit. On top of that, it resolved nothing.*

I wish I had used Rosenberg's four steps to express anger. 1. Stop and breathe. 2. Identify my judgmental thoughts: "This kid was a scumbag who thought he could do whatever he wanted." 3. Connect with my needs: mainly an honest relationship with my girlfriend. 4. Express my feelings and unmet needs: I could have told him how hurt I was that she had cheated on me and that he had participated, knowing we were together. If I had used these 4 steps, I could have realized that he was not the focal point of my anger, avoided thousands of dollars in lawyer bills, and been able to move on with my life a lot easier.

ROSENBERG'S FOUR-STEP RESPONSE TO ANGER

1. **Stop. Breathe.**
2. **Identify our judgmental thoughts.**
3. **Connect with our needs.**
4. **Express our feelings and unmet needs.**

1. Stop. Breathe.

Lucy: *When I am upset, annoyed or mad, I tend to say mean things. I am currently in a long distance relationship. At the beginning of the year I used to fight with my boyfriend over the telephone all the time. We finally decided that any time either one of us is mad with the other to just end the conversation right there. We take a step back and come back to the conversation when we have both calmed down and had time to think about what went wrong. So far it has worked very effectively.*

Nick: *Thanksgiving at my home is often very overwhelming for me. This time there were 3 sets of grandparents, 10 cousins, 7 uncles, and 6 aunts. They repeatedly kept coming up to me asking the same questions as the last person did. I felt as if my brain was going to explode, but this time I did not.*

I took deep breaths whenever I noticed my temper beginning to creep in. I also did a lot of listening without jumping in with my thoughts. I even sat down with my really old grandfather to hear what was on his mind. Without breathing and listening more deliberately, I am sure I would have lost my cool as usual. I learned some new things about my relatives and had a good time!

Stop. Shut your mouth. Breathe. Jorge Rubio offered the colorful image of wishing for magnets in his lips that would automatically slam shut whenever he started to speak from anger! Be with your feelings until you are ready to move to the next step (NYIRT, Binghamton, NY, 2009).

2. Identify our judgmental thoughts.

Jan: *It has become clear to me that I have an attitude problem. When I look negatively at a person before even beginning a conversation, that influences the way I respond to them. I am very good at having an evaluation ready for people before I talk to them.*

Last weekend I was meeting my friend at Brooks. I parked in front of him and then got on the phone. All of a sudden I look in my mirror and see him driving away. I got really mad, jumping to the conclusion that he left because I wasn't giving him any attention. I followed him to our next location and jumped down his throat and he started yelling back at me, big time. When we actually talked, I found out he did not even see me in the parking lot, so he assumed I'd meet him at the next spot.

Rosenberg says judgmental thoughts will be found in some form underlying all anger. I think this applies to quiet as well as explosive anger. When you are able, gently notice the blaming thoughts you are having about the other: "They should...." "She deserves...." If you are really steamed up, you probably also have some critical thoughts of yourself under all of your storm.

Are you crazy? Of course I think "they should." They <u>should</u> stop killing, they <u>should</u> stop telling lies, and even they <u>should</u> be respectful to me.

I understand that you strongly object to some behaviors and would like to see the person change them. I have similar thoughts. The invitation here is to notice those thoughts and move away from this system of thinking in order to express your deep hunger for someone to change their behaviors in ways that are more likely to produce the results you want to see.

A judgment always implies that there is a rulebook somewhere, that these people are violating a rule, and that it would help them improve their behavior if we informed them of the rule or punished them for failing to follow it. Unfortunately, when you start a conversation about the "wrongness" of another person, they have a strong invitation to shut out everything you say, and become defensive and hostile. There are more connecting ways to share your values.

3. Connect with our needs.

> **Kate:** *In class, we worked on a time when we became angry at someone's comment. I chose when someone told me I was a shallow person. I kept thinking, "He doesn't even know me." As I told my small group and they kept listening, I made the realization how hungry I was to be understood for who I am. I began to feel the tension I had been holding about the situation release from my body. I am impressed with the difference it made to express my anger in that process rather than to suppress it and let it eat away at me.*

> **Tom:** *I am working on stepping back and refocusing on what are the feelings underneath the anger, so I can get a better understanding of the situation. I observe that often times I have trouble admitting when I'm wrong so even if someone is talking to me with no anger involved about how they disagree with me, I might get angry because I'm embarrassed at the possibility of being wrong. I want to change that.*

What feelings are under your anger? What needs? Some people prefer to look for feelings first and then find needs. Others reverse that. Some find judgments after this process rather than before. All help us clarify needs. Once we understand these needs, our perspective shifts.

I am angry that you aren't here.		I am furious because you invited those noisy kids.
↓ *becomes* ↓		↓ *becomes* ↓
I am lonely and I want comfort.		I am afraid that my need for a quiet time will not be met.

4. Express our feelings and unmet needs. Hmmm. Rosenberg adds "You may need to offer empathy first." My summary of all this = Make a decision whether to express our needs, listen to the other person first, or withdraw from the conversation.

> **Topher:** *I work at a gas station. I am a fairly confident worker and tend to take my work and reputation seriously. On Easter Sunday I showed up 15 minutes late to work and got told off in front of the whole store by the girl I was replacing. At first I was pissed off and frustrated by the incident. Although the other employee and I had never really gotten along with each other, I tried to put myself in her shoes. She had a kid and she had to work 10—5 on Easter. Me being late was that much longer her kid had to spend it without her. Seeing this I realized I understood. The next week I approached her and told her that I recognized her position and why she got mad. I also told her I did not agree with how she talked to me about it and requested more respect in the future. After that conversation we have gotten along much better.*

> **Sharaz:** *Last Sunday, I attended a wedding reception in a small town near Burlington. Everyone got along, but as I drove home, a truck was tailgating my girlfriend and me. I came to a Yield sign and the individuals in the truck pulled aside my car and shouted, "Hey, nigger, get out of our town." After driving away, I stopped to breathe and give my girlfriend a hug. I identified my judgments (internal cursing) and reminded myself they are young and probably not educated enough to understand racism. I knew my need was for safety and to be heard and comforted, which my girlfriend did. I don't think of any way I could have handled it better.*

If you have gathered yourself by this point, decide whether it is time to share your feelings and needs, to listen for theirs, or to withdraw from the conflict. If you guess that the other person is not yet able to listen, do not start by sharing your feelings and needs. When your intention is to connect with the person who stimulated / invited—not caused—the anger, you will probably choose to listen to them for a while until they feel heard and calm down.

Remember that if their mouth is full of words, their ears are not working well, especially if you shout! When no one is listening, there is little point in talking and a lot of reasons for silence.

After their tension lessens, they may be ready to listen. At that point, it may be connecting to tell them about your experience <u>focusing on your underlying feelings and needs</u> (not on your smog of judgments.) There will also be situations when your best option is to withdraw. Some people stay in relationships wherein they are abused or in danger because they keep trying to explain to the other person why they want to / will / might leave and then wait for the other person to understand!

ANGER WORKSHEET: Refer briefly to the two situations you described earlier in the chapter or describe two more situations that invite your anger.
Situation in which I got angry (Use observations, not evaluations)
a. *The woman in the office locked the exercise room without giving a reason*
b.
c.
My blaming statements about the other person (enemy images)
a. *She is a dip, she is stupid, she is rigid*
b.
c.
My underlying feelings and unmet needs
a. *Fear and frustration; ease in getting to exercise; autonomy—do not enjoy extra rules*
b.
c.
What I did in this situation
a. *I was quite sarcastic with her*
b.
c.
What I would I like to say or do in a similar encounter in the future (request of myself)
a. *I would like to ask for more information and to share my concerns respectfully*
b.
c.

REQUEST OF YOURSELF—DIFFERENTIATE BETWEEN STIMULUS AND CAUSE

Sarah: *I never give myself a minute to take in information and reflect on what I want to say. Unfortunately, I usually end up regretting the things I say. I have spent a lot of time reflecting on how I can slow down my reactions. I am going to try really hard to stop and think before saying something back. I could even walk away and tell the person I need a few minutes before continuing the conversation.*

TJ: *When we talked about anger in class, I volunteered that slow drivers make me furious. It was a great experience when I grew up and learned to drive. I felt in control of my car. I finally realized that I was angering myself. The stimulus was slow drivers when I had a need to go fast. The problem is you cannot hold random people accountable for your needs. Only you can prevent your anger.* [need = adventure; strategy = driving fast]

One major confusion around anger is the failure to notice the difference between stimulus and cause. It is easy to forget and to believe that someone else caused your anger. This could lead you to think they deserved punishment, lecturing, or other education about their faults. Of the options available for responding, these are fairly ineffective in changing the behavior that you do not like.

Someone else can be the stimulus, the trigger, the spark, the invitation, but not the cause. Perhaps you recall our class lesson discussed earlier on lighting matches by dragging a matchbox against them. Those matches without a head did not light, no matter what the stimulus, whereas those with a match head did. (See page 29.)

If you can get a firm hold on the fact that the other person does not cause your anger, you will improve your ability to interrupt your habitual response of getting angry when someone invites you to do so. This will take practice. I do know that I cause my own anger. I also forget it repeatedly, but I stay stuck in that illusion a much shorter time than I used to. When I become angry, I am quicker to step back from it and consider what is really going on.

So, if I cause my own anger, why am I doing it?

Phil: *Anger is an important issue to me—a dominant aspect of my life.*

Over break my girlfriend was staying at my apartment. You need a parking permit, but my girlfriend does not live with me, so obviously she does not have a permit. At 8 am one morning, I heard the sound of a truck outside. Sure enough, my girlfriend's car was chained up and about to be towed. I ran over and asked the man if I could just move the car. He replied by telling me that once the chains are hooked up, you have to pay $50 to get it back.

Before I reacted harshly, I remembered that the man was simply doing his job and it was not anything personal toward me—he did not know me or my girlfriend. I paid the $50 and got the car back. I was obviously upset about the fine, but I was glad that I was able to handle the situation civilly and peacefully. In the past, I would have blown up and yelled at the guy. I was proud of myself. So was my girlfriend!

Your anger is a telegram from you to you. Your body and brain are offering you important information about yourself and possibly about the situation. Anger telegrams state loudly, "Pay attention to what is happening here. I do not like it." Perhaps you are not meeting your needs for safety in this situation. Perhaps you have a deep concern for someone else's wellbeing. Perhaps it appears to you that some other need will not be met. Perhaps you have a hurt from long ago in this area that has not been healed and makes you vulnerable to overreacting when someone's words land in that tender place. It may just mean you are exhausted and need rest. It may be some combination of these. When you get underneath the anger, you can find out.

> **Tristan:** *Rosenberg goes on to speak about how anger is not an undesirable emotion, and that it does serve a purpose. By using anger as a "wake-up call," we are able to hear anger as being an alarm telling us that a need is dangerously not being met. However, when we apply judgment and violence (emotional or physical) to our anger, we use anger unconstructively—by diverting it toward punitive actions. These callous actions of violence also stem from believing that anger is the result of external causation, not the result of our interpretation of stimuli.*

Meanwhile, the more you can become familiar with the statements and actions that tend to trigger you, the easier you will find it is to recover from them, to regain your centeredness. Of course, the calmer you are to start with, the less distance you have to go to return to that calmness.

I DON'T LIKE THEM: What actions invite your judgments? Identify two and write down your critical inner dialogue about people who do these actions, then your feelings and needs.
I don't like people who
a. *Tell boring stories*
b.
c.
They should
a. *Notice whether their listeners are really interested*
b.
c.
My feelings
a. *Impatience, frustration*
b.
c.
My needs that are not met or that I fear will not be met
a. *Autonomy—control over my own time*
b.
c.

AND AN ATTITUDE—ANGER IS CONTAGIOUS; SO IS COMPASSION

> **David:** *When I was a teenager, I used to drive fast through the neighborhood. One lady called me up and verbally attacked me, yelling, even swearing. I told her I was not speeding, but whenever I saw her I would speed up because I was angry at her. Later, another neighbor called. He said, "I know you have a little niece and two nephews and you love them and want them to be safe." I agreed. He said, "That is all I want for my kids. Can you and your friends driving on the street slow down, please?" I said, "I see where you are coming from. I would never want anything to happen to any of the kids." I slowed down and told my friends to slow down too.*

Aren't you going to tell us how to deal with <u>other</u> people's anger?

OK. Start with your attitude. Recall that an angry person has some reason for their anger and look for their unmet need. People who feel threatened protect themselves. If you can remember that this person is always trying to get needs met, you will approach them with a different energy.

Anger is contagious; so is compassion. Without noticing it, you often absorb and respond in kind to the feelings of people around you. (This is called "emotional mirroring.") You are often unaware of how your feelings and words influence the behavior of others. Much of the work in this chapter is focused on turning down the invitation to join another person in being angry, and instead becoming the one who sets the energy tone. When it becomes habitual for you to look for the needs that underlie all actions, you can issue others a strong counter-invitation.

When a person is angry, even threatening, listening carefully and respectfully can be a useful, calming action. Listen, reflect minimally, and then listen some more. Remember that when someone's mouth is full of words, they cannot hear you. Can you bring yourself to a solid listening mode? Our attitude offers a strong invitation to the angry person to regain their composure.

What if they are angry at you specifically?

Listen. Get your best translating skills out and hear through any criticism or judgments they put out. Focus on their feelings, needs, and requests. Ask for specific observations with a non-defensive attitude. "When you say I am being unfair, can you help me understand exactly what you mean? What do I do that you see as unfair?" If the other person can't or won't give specifics, guess and check it out with them. Your willingness to try hard to understand their complaint opens a door for resolving an issue. It does not mean you share their point of view. But it further tangles a situation when you disagree before you even know what it is they are angry about and what it is they are requesting be changed. Remember to not counterattack, and to not change the subject.

Agree with any part of what they say that is true. Start by agreeing with the facts, "You are right, I did get pretty sarcastic." "Yes, I am an hour late." When you let go of your desire to appear perfect at all times, you will find more ease in admitting your behavior that you do not particularly respect. If it is unclear, ask what it is they would like to see happen in the future and promise to think on it. You likely have reasons you were sarcastic or late. Save the surrounding facts that may justify or mitigate your behavior for a second conversation.

LISTENING CAN SAVE THE DAY

Alexandra: *This past summer I was living in NYC. I had been cast in a film and since the city fulfills my needs for enjoyment and energy, I decided to spend a month there after the shoot was complete. I had intended to go alone, but a friend wanted to join me. He had just graduated from college and wanted some excitement. One night, he came home severely intoxicated or drugged or both. He pulled me from my bed and proceeded to physically assault me, for whatever reason, I don't think I will ever know. At first I was just really scared. I could not get out of his grip. I screamed for help and struggled, which made me tense and hoarse and clearly infuriated him.*

Suddenly a calm came over me and I was able to remember he was my friend and that although I was in trouble, he was too. Instinctively, I began to ask him questions, quietly and carefully, and then repeated back what he was saying, as a question. He began crying realizing what he was doing. When he released me from his grip, I stifled my urge to get revenge. Instead I distracted him long enough to escape to safety at a friend's home.

Ryan: *In the fifth grade, I could finally walk home by myself. One afternoon, the class bully followed me home. He had been making threats all week to beat me up and I knew this was exactly what he intended to do. I was frightened and tried to ignore him hoping he would think I wasn't scared and leave me alone. This strategy did not work. About 500 meters from my home, he pounced. He tackled me to the ground and began to hit me. My first reaction was to hit him back and yell at him. This only made matters worse. As his punches kept coming, I realized that I wasn't going to get anywhere by hitting him back, since he was much bigger than me.*

So, I asked him, "Why are you hitting me?"

"Because I don't like you," he retorted.

"Why don't you like me?" I asked.

"Because!" he shouted, hitting me again.

"Did I do something to you?" I asked.

"Yes," he said. "You think you are so smart by always answering the teacher's question. And all the girls like you."

"So, you're angry with me because I answer the teacher's questions and I'm popular?"

"Yes!" he hollered, as he hit me again.

"What can I do to make you less angry?" I asked.

That startled him. He got up, looked at me, and walked away. Apparently I had struck a nerve. He never threatened or hurt me again.

Anger is contagious; so is compassion. Perhaps it would bring you deep satisfaction to start an epidemic of compassion going. In the movie, <u>Pay It Forward</u>, the main character deliberately sets off a chain reaction of doing unexpected kind deeds with the request to pay it forward, rather than to pay it back. Another such effort is the bumper sticker: "Practice random acts of kindness."

CONTAGIOUS COMPASSION: Describe a time you have offered, experienced, or seen an unexpected act of kindness that moved others.

⬇ ⬇ ⬇ **DELVING DEEPER: BOWS, ARROWS, AND TARGETS** ⬇ ⬇ ⬇

Laurie: *Early this semester, I was clashing regularly with my mother. It was awful. We went to a few therapy sessions together. We both felt the other was not hearing us. I honestly thought that she did not care for me, that she wanted me to feel hurt. Boy, was I wrong—she really does love me! We just have different styles of communicating. I am an emotional person who can become explosive when I am upset and she is the opposite.*

I finally saw that when I communicated with explosions, she felt as though she was walking into a lion's den and immediately shut down. I want to remember that blaming her for my feelings and yelling at her is a big waste of energy. When I stay in my anger, I am disconnected from myself, my mother, and my life.

Recently I read a treatise of instructions for dealing with anger. It was written in the eleventh century by a Tibetan Buddhist teacher in the Kadampa tradition to his students studying to become Buddhist monks. (No, I did not read the original! I found a translation in <u>The Places That Scare You</u> by Pema Chodron, a contemporary Buddhist.)

The first instruction is to avoid setting up the target for the arrow. The more we launch our anger and aggression into the world, the more we set ourselves up as a target for arrows of anger to come our way. In modern terms, we invite blowback. (The Wiki definition of blowback is "negative effect suffered from one's own weapons.")

In what ways do you set yourself up as a target for other's arrows?

This teaching goes on to recall that even if we feel fear in the face of another person's anger, we can still reach for that place inside ourselves that sees the other person's action as a cry for help.

**Avoid setting up a target
for the arrow.**

Success Script—Dealing with Anger in a Connecting Way

Title: From Complaints to Solution
Name: Sarah Beth
Date: ??

Background: *For the past two years I have been attending Champlain College. My family was a huge part of my life. Now I rarely get to see them because it is such a long drive home. My 19-year old sister, who was once one of my best friends, has taken it upon herself to lecture me about never making time to go home. It makes me feel guilty when she accuses me of abandoning her and my other siblings. I usually get angry with my sister and shut her out instead of listening to what she is saying.*

New Behavior: *When I went home over Thanksgiving break, my sister started in on me again. She told me that it really hurt her feelings that we had grown so far apart. She then continued to talk about all the times she had needed me when I wasn't there. I really wanted to yell at her and tell her to deal with her own problems and that I didn't need to be there for her to succeed in life.*

Before I replied this time, I tried to put myself in her shoes. I realized she must have felt really bad about having no control over a person in her life who had always been there for her. I also tried to figure out why it made me feel so guilty and what needs of mine were not being met. The next day, I tried to use my Conflict Management skills. I told her I also wanted to stay close to her and was sad I did not see her more often. We decided that she would try to come up and visit me as often I go to visit her. We will try this solution and see if it works.

Why I Consider This a Success: *I feel like both of our needs for connection were met. I see that my needs really matter to her and she knows that her needs really matter to me. It was great to finally get it off my chest. I was proud of myself for listening to her needs instead of reacting to her complaints.* [I think *that both of our needs for connection were met.*]

Intention for the Future: *I plan to stick with the solution we came up with. I hope to see my sister more, which will meet both of our needs to be part of each other's lives. If this solution doesn't work, I guess we'll have to figure out something else to help us stay in touch.*

Success Script—Dealing with Anger in a Connecting Way

Title: Lessons from my Father
Name: Daniel
Date: ??

Background: I was raised to never assume anything about someone simply based on the actions you can see, because if you do that you can get caught off guard very easily. This came from my father and his experience of being a police officer. However, this applies to any real life situation in relation to making a neutral observation rather than an assumption.

In another class, a partner and I have to post and edit each other's writing on the Internet by a specific time and date. We are graded both by content and by posting them on time. Lucille is my partner. It was the first assignment and I had posted by the due date, but Lucille had not. Then the date came when we were supposed to edit each other's papers. She had not edited mine and still had not posted her paper.

Instead of yelling at her and telling her she was lazy and did not care about the class and was screwing me over, I simply asked if everything was all right because she had not posted anything yet. This is when she told me about the major crisis going on with her mother and how all of her class work had been put on the back burner for a little while. I was grateful that I had not made any assumptions.

New Behavior: This experience definitely reminded me why it is a bad idea to make assumptions about motives behind other people's actions.

Why I Consider This a Success: I did not assume anything. I did not make things harder for Lucille by accusing her falsely. Avoiding evaluations and asking for additional information makes things run more smoothly in life.

Intention for the Future: I intend to use neutral observations when faced with actions of others that puzzle me. Unless you are a psychic, you never really know why exactly people do things they do. If I start to jump to conclusions in the future, Lucille will definitely pop into my mind.

Success Script—Dealing with Anger in a Connecting Way

Title:
Date:

Optional: create a Mind Map, a doodle, or other visual aides

Part Four: Moving Into Action

Alexandra: *My boyfriend and I were in the middle of a conflict situation and having trouble reaching each other and making a connection. It appeared he believed I meant one thing when I was saying another and, of course, I thought I was being perfectly clear! I remembered to not label this as a problem, but to see it as an opportunity to get to know the person he is better through this conversation. That shifted my energy and then we were able to work together again.*

Kiki: *My paycheck had not arrived and the bills were about to be overdue. I asked my father to help me out. He automatically said "no." We began to argue—I was explaining how much I needed the money and he was trying to explain to me that I was irresponsible with money. I finally stepped back and thought a moment about his needs. I asked, "What can I do that would prove to you I am responsible?" He thought a minute and suggested a budget. We agreed that if I could come up with a budget and live within it, he would feel comfortable lending me money in tight spots.*

If you notice tension, you have choices in how you can proceed. When you bring options to your awareness, you can make a more deliberate choice.

Choices? What kind of options do we have in tense situations involving others?

CHOICES TO GET YOU MOVING THROUGH TENSE SITUATIONS

1. **Change your own actions and thinking**
2. **Change your environment**
3. **Ignore the tension and hope it goes away**
4. **Bring your concern up to the other person**

1. Change your own actions and thinking

Doma: *Sometimes we are having a difficult time. At that time we might be looking for a person who will help us. Who is that person? It might be anyone, but first take a look within yourself. In any situation, when you are dealing with a conflict, you have to take care of yourself, which means to solve a problem from the root; you have to take care of yourself and to make yourself calm down.*

Look at your actions. In what ways are you doing your part in the dance? One of the lessons offered by 12-Step programs, like AA and Al-Anon, is how to bring your own behavior in line with your values. Participants learn to regain control in their lives by focusing on their own actions and making choices that enhance their lives, rather than letting their behavior be determined by those around them. As a student put it in the previous chapter, learn to become active rather than reactive. If you change your part, the resulting dance will have to shift.

Step back and carefully consider the tense interaction. Look at your "they should" stories. Then consider your feelings and needs. When you can see the situation more clearly, you may discover that the tension is about some story you were believing and not even about the outer situation.

2. Change your environment

It is a reasonable option to decide to change external factors when you believe this will contribute to better meeting your needs in the situation. You may decide that leaving the scene is the most satisfactory change, especially if you are relatively certain that it won't help to bring the matter up. And just because you now have some skills in conflict resolution does not mean you have to use them every time!

3. Ignore the tension and hope it goes away

Strategically ignoring a problem for a short time can be useful. Sometimes, external or internal factors do shift and the problem indeed goes away. If it is not major or threatening, you may wish to see if it recurs. (Some actions are so important that a single incident is enough to inspire you to take action to see that it does not recur.) Ignoring a problem for a long time is usually problematic.

Professionally, ongoing problems not dealt with in the workplace can sap the energy. At a personal level, to avoid noticing and talking about difficult patterns of interaction, frequently results in relationships that feel increasingly dead and inauthentic. The initial feelings of love can get buried beneath politeness, tolerance, habits, and a desire to not rock the boat. This often fuels an unexpected explosion or acting out later on. It also invites people to leave relationships.

4. Bring your concern up to the other person

Resolving conflict is not about surrounding ourselves with compatible people. It is about finding a sure path through the conflict. Relationships, whether personal or professional, are always between two people who have different life experiences, different values, and different temperaments.

Tense situations are opportunities for finding solutions that more fully meet the needs of both parties. Resolving conflicts builds strong relationships and more self-confidence. Therefore, you might want to cultivate an attitude of welcoming differences and staying with the dialogue even through the difficult parts.

In order to become effective in conflict resolution, everything you have learned to date will be called upon, plus a few new skills. Let's start by working our way through an elaborate model for assertively resolving conflict. I recommend you practice using all 17 of these steps—first in a hypothetical situation and then with small issues. This will allow you to become familiar with these skills, so they will be available in times of actual crisis when you have a need to assertively resolve conflict. Any specific conflict situation might call for a shorter version of this sequence.

Practice, of course, will improve your comfort level.

I am worried about my own ability to resolve conflict because I think you have to pay attention to both people's needs. I still do not do that regularly.

That is useful self-awareness. And, yes, assertive conflict resolution does indeed depend on paying attention to two sets of needs. Let's review the three stages of finding and asserting your needs.

1. **PASSIVE** "I have no needs and if I had some, they are not important."

2. **AGGRESSIVE** "It is very important that I meet my needs, regardless of how that affects you."

3. **ASSERTIVE** "We both have needs and all of our needs are important."

Here are some suggestions to help you move yourself toward an assertive stance for the purpose of a successful resolution of conflict.

Start with your intention to take seriously your needs and the other person's needs. (Just saying the right words generally won't get you through a problem to a reconnection.) Becky Bailey, a leading educator on parent-child communication, says: 55% of communication is non-verbal—physical body-language, stance; 38% of communication is tone of voice; and only 7% of communication is in the actual words. Your intention will shine through all of these.

> **Allyson:** *I started this class with the mindset that it is better to avoid conflict than manage it. In the past I would have rather made up a crazy story to tell someone to avoid them being angry at me. This was causing me problems. I now see that conflict is unavoidable. I need to learn to support myself and not back down for fear of other's reactions.*

If you tend to be passive, like Allyson, you will make the conflict resolution process more productive if you make several commitments to yourself.

- *I will not abandon myself in times of conflict.*
- *I absolutely will pay attention to my own feelings and needs.*
- *I will give myself the time, space, and safety I need to stay centered.*

> **Jaycee:** *What I learned is that when you have a conflict to solve, you need to think about the other person also. You are not just the only one that has needs to be met. Before this class I would go into conflict very angry at the other person, thinking I was the only one who was right. I would have just started yelling at them. Now I know this does not help.*

If you tend to be aggressive, like Jaycee, make these helpful commitments to yourself.

- *I will focus on the long-term benefits to me of maintaining this relationship.*
- *I will recall my intention to understand and equally value the other person's needs.*
- *I will give myself the time, space, and safety I need to stay centered.*

The upcoming chapter will give you a model for walking through conflict to a resolution.

Pay attention to your intention to connect.

If you have the intention to connect,

make your words and actions

congruent with your intention.

φ

Resolving Conflict Assertively

PREPARE

1. Become aware of tension and discomfort.
2. Breathe and get grounded.
3. Listen to yourself. Find underlying feelings and needs.
4. Check your attitude.

INITIATE

5. Share topic and intention. Agree upon time and place.

DIALOGUE

6. Sit down, get present, and repeat your intention.
7. State concisely your concern and invite their response.
8. Listen—seek to understand before seeking to be understood.
9. Listen—get all of their feelings, needs, and concerns on the table.
10. Breathe, slow down, and check your attitude.
11. Speak—get all of your feelings, needs, and concerns on the table.

RESOLVE

12. Summarize the needs of both parties and write them down.
13. Brainstorm possible strategies and write them down.
14. If it is major, give it time. Wait for further inspiration.
15. Decide on individual and joint next steps. Write them down.
16. Try them out. Check back on how it is working.

UPGRADE

17. Start over again if it does not work the first time.

PREPARE

Preparation is essential. Henry Kissinger, a Secretary of State under several presidents, won a Nobel Peace Prize for his work in resolving conflict between nations. He claimed that 50% of the total time on any negotiation process was best spent in preparation and planning.

1. Become aware of tension and discomfort.

> **Julia:** *This week I heard myself say to my boyfriend, "Don't put the dirty socks on the table." Then I realized what I had learned the day before—that this was not how a good request should be. So I thought for a while and tried again. "I see dirty socks on the table and that takes away my appetite when I think of eating on that table. I need to have a hygienic dining table where I could lay my sandwich without wondering if someone had laid dirty socks there before. Would you be willing to take your dirty socks and put them in a laundry basket now?"*

Ask yourself whether you are enjoying life. If not, in what areas do you find stress? What is happening in your relationships? What seems easy? Where are problem areas? Notice tension. Is there a problem in the work setting that is lessening productivity? The first part of problem-solving is to become more deliberately aware, and to be open to noticing discomfort. If you notice problems when they are small, you can handle them when they are small. If you are the one to initiate a discussion of a tense issue, you have the opportunity to get ready and prepare for the encounter. Most people find that the sooner they can prepare for and bring up a problem, the easier it is to resolve and the more trust it builds in a relationship.

The New York City fire department decided several years ago to focus on preventing fires rather than just being effective in responding to fires. They put more effort into figuring out and fixing the persistent causes of fires with better building codes and public awareness. Soon, they had fewer fires and smaller ones. Police departments often look at neighborhoods that produce more than an average amount of problems and then try to address the underlying causes. Recreation programs are a typical response to channel youth boredom and energy into productive outlets.

Do you have conflicts with specific people that are recurring? Do you have patterns of conflict in your life which occur again and again? Can you think of possible underlying causes? What needs are unmet for each of you? Is there an underlying conflict on which this one rests?

RECURRING CONFLICTS OR TENSION: Think about your life and identify two situations wherein you can see some tension or conflict.		
Person and/or Situation	**My unmet needs**	**Their unmet needs—a guess**

2. Breathe and get grounded.

> **Charlie:** *We have to start with ourselves. Even though the conflict usually involves another person, in order to resolve it, the first step is always inward. We can't help others until we have heard our own voice.*

Create time to prepare yourself for major encounters. You have some important internal work to do. Get a good night's sleep. Eat sensibly. Drink a glass of water. Do you have other calming practices—such as yoga, exercise, music, prayer, meditation? This is a perfect time to use these aides. Withdraw. Breathe and consciously relax to center yourself.

3. Listen to yourself. Find underlying feelings and needs.

> **Phil:** *Sometimes if I am trying to do school work and become confused or frustrated that it is not going the way I want it to, I become very angry. I want to notice my feelings and calm myself down, instead of taking it out on others who clearly don't deserve my anger.*

<u>Start exactly where you are, not where you think you should be or wish you were.</u> This is the only authentic, alive starting point. Ask yourself, "What evaluations and distressed feelings do I have? What blame-self thoughts am I having? What blame-other thoughts am I having?" Take some time to really listen to yourself. Do not rush yourself through this stage. Be open to the possibility that your perception of the situation may change as you sit with it. Then ask yourself, "What unmet needs are activating my strong feelings? What fears and hopes do I have?" You may want to write things down in a journal or talk to a friend.

4. Check your attitude.

> **Daphne:** *I noticed I was very angry with my mother. She planned our vacation, but hadn't included me in the planning because I was away at school. I had to sit down and decide how I wanted to confront my mother about this. I knew that if I swore at her or put her down, it would not help the situation at all. So, I figured out my feelings and needs and got ready to listen, then the talk went well.*

Let go of enemy images. Think about the qualities you appreciate in this person. It will improve your attitude if you have these things firmly in mind. You will lower the tension in the conflict if you can share with the other person something you value about them that is relevant and sincere. Do <u>not</u> just say a compliment to make it easier, if it is not heartfelt. Empty praise is deadly.

Get ready to listen to the other person. Can you recall a conflict with someone, when one or both of you were saying, "Would you just be quiet and listen to me a minute?" Now is the time to gather your strength to be ready to assume the role of the first listener—the listener who can hold their own thoughts until they have listened thoroughly to the other person and who listens so well they translate any complaints they hear into requests.

Imagine what the other person's feelings and needs might be. Work through any evaluations this brings up for you. Recall your intention to allow the conflict to increase connection between you.

It will help your attitude to brainstorm multiple strategies because thinking of only one strategy, may tempt you to assume that your needs will not be met unless the other person cooperates with you in meeting that one strategy. That assumption could invite you to get desperate and pushy. The purpose of this exercise is to loosen your thinking. When you brainstorm again with the other person, you will undoubtedly find even more strategies. Eventually you may come to habitually assume there are always additional options, even if you cannot see them. Knowing there are many options will help you let go of your favored strategy and focus on underlying feelings and needs.

YOUR SIX STRATEGIES	
Situation: *My boyfriend wants the house cleaner than I do. I hate doing housework.*	
Two ways x could change their actions / attitudes to meet my needs	*He could clean it to his standards.*
	He could lighten up on his standards.
Two ways I could change my actions / attitudes to meet my needs	*I could work on my resistance to housework.*
	I could pay someone to do my half.
Two ways another person could meet these needs	*My mother could do all of the house cleaning.*
	We could get someone to live in the spare bedroom in exchange for housecleaning.

YOUR SIX STRATEGIES	
Situation	
Two ways x could change their actions / attitudes to meet my needs	
Two ways I could change my actions / attitudes to meet my needs	
Two ways another person could meet these needs	

INITIATE

5. Share topic and intention. Agree upon time and place.

> **Abby:** *Lately there has been a lot of tension between my roommates and me, so I left the room and hung out with other people. This weekend while I was home I thought a lot about how to fix my living situation. What I was doing made it worse because it probably looked like I didn't care or was doing something bad.*
>
> *I decided to go to the store, get cards for each of my roommates, and write each a note on the line of "I would really like it if we could talk. I don't like all the tension in the room." This opened the door to a private conversation with each of them, which cleared away a lot of the tension. I was able to save the friendships that I have made in the last two years. I do think I will choose to be friends, but not roommates, next year.*

This is a crucial step—give it adequate attention. You are setting the stage and you want to do everything you can to get it off on the right foot. You are inviting the other person to join you as a participant in problem-solving. You want a colleague who will work with you in facing a shared and difficult task, not an opponent. I am repeating this visual reminder for you.

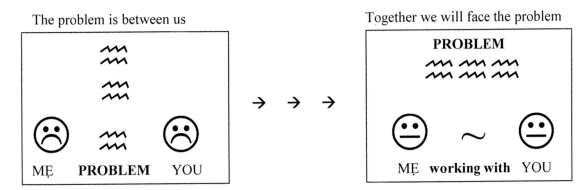

It is important to briefly name the topic when you first bring it up. Confrontation is often frightening for people, especially when a relationship is new. When you bring up a concern, the other person's inner voice may set off alarms: "Oh, no! This is the beginning of the end. Everything is falling apart. I remember how conflict preceded my last breakup. This is terrible."

You recall that when a person becomes this frightened, their brain will likely overload on emotion and "become stupid." It will help both of you if you are able to limit the problem so that the other party can see the boundaries of the trouble and not fear for the relationship. Of course, if the relationship is indeed in jeopardy, you need to find the integrity to say so—without blame.

Before you start the encounter, think about the best time to talk. Poor timing is the cause of many failed efforts at conflict resolution. <u>An error that many people make is to try to resolve issues as soon as they arise without doing the preparation.</u> It will benefit you to return to the matter soon, but your preparation time is essential.

There are other considerations around the timing. Resolving a conflict is much easier with mutual respect, thus you need to pick a time that works for the other person as well as yourself. Some people will have trouble waiting to discuss something later. Others will use the intervening time to think over their preferences. If you know that a friend does not wait well, bring it up when you have time to talk and you guess that they have time to talk. Here are some times to avoid: when someone is about to take an exam, has not had their morning cup of coffee, is walking out the door, is exhausted, or has had even a few drinks. You want them at their best in this encounter, too.

Many people experience it as a violation of trust to spring a discussion of a problem on them without any warning. Your friend or lover might find it jarring if your actions have just indicated things are fine between you, for example, sending a love letter and then bringing up a major problem. Asking when other people are around is also not appreciated. However, if you have any concern that you or the other person might become explosive or violent, it is helpful to plan a conversation in a public place like a restaurant where the environment will support you in being civil to each other.

If you want to talk with your parents about a later curfew, you will have a better shot at convincing them of your increased responsibility if you bring it up long before you go out instead of after you have come home late.

If all times are bad times, pick the best of the bad times. For example, if your roommate has been depressed for two months, don't postpone indefinitely talking to them about something important to you. Figure out whether morning or evening is likely to be better and go for it.

When initiating the conversation, it is helpful to briefly identify the issue, to emphasize your intention that both people's needs be considered and to ask if they are willing to look at this with you. Here are some examples for requests to talk.

- *We are going to share this apartment. I want it to work really well for both of us. Ok with you for planning how we divvy up the chores this evening? We could clear away supper dishes and then talk at the table?*

- *I would like to talk with you about my curfew and see if we can come up with a change that works for both of us. Is now a good time to talk?*

- *I recently became aware that I get tense whenever we talk about your mother. Can I come to your place this afternoon, around 5:00, so we can explore that together and see if we can get the matter to a more peaceful place?*

- *There seems to be a lot of tension between us about the upcoming vacation time. Can we talk about our ideas and plan a vacation we could equally enjoy? I would like to go to Denny's, so that the place helps me remember to keep my cool. Would Saturday afternoon around 4:00 work for you?*

- *This relationship works for me in so many ways that I am eager to pay attention to and clear up any tension spots. I have noticed that several times lately we have gotten into arguments after going out to parties. Would you be willing to explore with me what that is all about so we can figure out how to not have any more fights after parties? And is now a good time for us to talk or would later today be a better time? Or even tomorrow?*

INITIATING CONFLICT RESOLUTION: Create three requests, including a brief statement of topic, a solid intention of meeting both sets of needs, and a suggested time and place.

And if the other person says they do not want to talk?

Breathe. Ask why they do not want to have a conversation. Listen and reflect their thoughts to be sure you understand their perspective. <u>Do not argue</u>. Thank them for answering your question. Stop talking and return to your planning stage with this additional information. You may need to consider some other strategies to meet their needs—perhaps to involve another person.

Example: *No, these kinds of discussions go on forever and both people end up feeling worse.*

After reflecting on their statement and underlying needs, make a new request, such as:

- *Would you agree for us to talk for one hour and then decide whether it is worth meeting again?*

- *Is there some structure or format that you can recommend that you think would be helpful for us to go through to resolve this issue?*

- *Would you be willing to write down three ways you picture we could resolve this and to read three ideas I write down?*

- *Do you think it might work for Claudia to sit with us and keep the discussion on track?*

- *I understand you do not trust that talking will help. Would it work for you to write down your strategies for us to get through this and give it to me next Saturday?*

HEARING A "NO" AND RE-REQUESTING: Create a refusal and new request.
Refusal:
New request:

DIALOGUE

6. Sit down, get present, and repeat your intention.

Prepare physically right before important encounters. Get a good night's sleep. Drink a glass of water. Eat sensibly. Take time for any of your other calming practices.

Create a space where you won't be interrupted. Turn off cell phones and the TV. Then sit down together, take another deep breath, and repeat your intention that you want that everyone is listened to and is satisfied with any solutions, that everyone's needs matter. Again, set the stage for a successful negotiation by first reflecting the importance of the relationship to you or the value to you of finding a solution that really works for everyone.

7. State concisely your concern and invite their response.

Put your topic on the table simply, without extended logic and justifications. And immediately ask them for a response. Here are two examples:

- *I have had success in the past with roommates by creating a chore chart. I like to be able to plan ahead when I have household responsibilities. What kind of planning works best for you? How do you see us managing this?*

- *I take full responsibility for myself at school. I would like the freedom to not have a curfew here at home. What would you need to be comfortable with this?*

Be prepared to stop talking
even before you get your brief message out.

8. Listen. Seek to understand before seeking to be understood.

> **Peggy:** *Just the other night my boyfriend and I had a fight that could have been avoided if I had communicated a little better. It was dinnertime and I was hungry. We talked about getting some food, however he fell asleep on the sofa. I waited awhile, but was getting really anxious and really hungry. I was on my way out the door to get something from the car when he awoke and asked if I was leaving. I said, "I am not leaving, but if you are going to continue to sleep, I am going to go get some food." He responded in a very snippy way, "Fine, then eat without me."*
>
> *If I had stopped right then and asked, "What did you hear me say?" we could have avoided an upsetting fight, because he thought I didn't want to eat with him.*

If they show verbal or non-verbal clues of distress or disagreement even before you finish your initial summary of concern, stop talking and listen if they spontaneously talk and reflect their feelings and thoughts. (They are not hearing well at that moment, even if you raise your voice.) The best first response is to listen and give empathy for their pain whether or not it was based on an accurate understanding of what you remember you said.

You have taken the time to get yourself well-listened to in your preparation time. Now is the time to see that they are also well-listened to. Bring out your best listening skills. Use regular reflections and check for their accuracy. When you ask for feedback often, you will be amazed at how often the message sent was not the message received. Try it and see for yourself.

If there has been any misunderstanding, next focus on getting the message you intended across— not on whether your mouth or their ears were at fault. When what they heard was not what you meant to convey, be careful not to focus on the rightness / wrongness of their words and blurt out, "No, no, that is not what I said." Remember to say in some form, "Thank you for letting me know what you heard. I see that I did not communicate what I was trying to say. Let me try again."

FOR INCOMING COMPLAINTS, START HERE

Jenny: *The new thing I learned this week, was that when someone is complaining, they are inviting you to hear them. The conversation can begin with the complaint.*

If you have not noticed there is tension or a problem and therefore have not done your careful preparation and then initiated a discussion, a person approaching you with a complaint or a judgment may catch you off guard. This is a much more challenging place to begin resolving the conflict.

So you have two choices—start listening and asking questions to understand their perspective or find a way to postpone the discussion. The emergency exit lines we looked on pages 88-89 could be useful at this moment.

Reminder:
Hear only the feelings, needs, and requests that are under complaints and judgments.

You want to help the other person get their words out and calm their emotions so they can again listen to your initial statement. You are also starting the journey into their world, so that you see how the situation looks from their frame of reference.

Listening when you have differences of opinion can be challenging, but the rewards are impressive in your increased ability to handle conflict productively. In Seven Habits of Highly Effective People, Stephen Covey (rephrasing St. Francis of Assisi) challenges us to seek to understand before seeking to be understood. That goal becomes increasingly important to me. I think the key is in being solid in my attitude of appreciation for both myself and the other person.

9. Listen. Get all of their feelings, needs, and concerns on the table.

> **Ned:** *When you are carefully listening to people, it decreases the chance of conflict. We all love it when someone listens to us.*

> **Jeff:** *My girlfriend in Massachusetts called and I was at a party having fun. We got into a big fight because I thought I was doing nothing wrong and she thought I should give her more attention.*

> *I did not understand until the roles were reversed. At first I felt angry, then I thought about what was under the anger. I felt lonely. I was missing her and wanted her to be missing me. I felt inadequate that she did not need me and afraid she might find someone more fun to be with. Now if she calls when I am at a party, I go to a quiet room to take the call. I don't talk to other people in the middle of the call and I assure her that even though I am having a great time, it would be even better if she were here with me. It has improved the trust level in our relationship.*

Listen until you fully grasp the other person's reality. Go slow. Offer regular paraphrasing to see that you understand. In a situation when you want something from the other person, your listening is to find out their perspective and their needs in the current situation, so that you can aim for solutions that meet both sets of needs.

Whether personally or professionally, it is always helpful to find out how the matter looks to the other person. I like it when I remember to be curious about differences instead of irritated.

Recently I was riding on the Burlington city bus and I asked the bus driver if he would make a stop near my home. He said that the rules said he could only stop at designated stops. I could have argued with him that many times drivers stop anyway. (On the other hand, I have seen others argue about extra stops with other drivers and I never observed that challenging the driver got them anywhere with a driver who felt inclined to only stop at designated stops.) Instead, I reflected, "Yes, I understand there are a number of rules that bus drivers need to follow." Then we made small talk about other matters. Without any further conversation on designated stops, he silently made the extra stop for me. I was grateful as it was raining hard.

Your ability to listen carefully until you really see their point of view will go a long way toward resolving the conflict smoothly. As you are listening, reflecting, asking questions, and listening some more, ask yourself, "What are they observing?" "How does it appear to them?" "What are they needing / wanting / hoping for?" If they are complaining, even judging you, translate their complaints in your mind to feelings, needs and requests. What would they like to have happen? Reflect that. It does not mean you are going to do it. It does mean you understand them.

Notice that this emphasis on listening is a definite change in the usual pattern of response while in conflict. When the other person expresses any opinion that disagrees with our own, we have a cultural habit of responding with the good reasons why they should agree with us. An argument often follows in which no one is doing much listening nor changing their minds.

It may help you to recall that most opinions were not formed by logic and few are changed that way. When a person feels attacked, they tend to cling harder to their opinions!

All of this listening stuff—it is impossible to do all this in a conflict.

Maybe you are right. I certainly do not do all of these things all of the time. On the other hand, by considering these various strategies, I have slowly become more proficient in careful listening during conflict. So, I invite you to consider all these, practice all of them so you are familiar with them, and pick just a few that might be helpful for you to recall the next time you are in a conflict.

LISTENING POSSIBILITIES: Review the various suggestions for better listening to the other person during conflict. Pick three ideas you would like to remember during a conflict.
Of these suggestions for listening, which, if any, is your next focus? If there is one, ✔ it.

10. Breath, slow down, and check your attitude.

> **Nate**: *My younger brother had to get his passport photo faxed up to a job he just got. He was really kind of blowing it off and I wanted to make sure he followed through because I wanted him to keep the job. When we were talking on the phone, I told him, "Get off your lazy ass and get on it." As could be predicted, he hung up on me. Later on that day, I was talking to his roommate. I said I needed to get a hold of my dad and get the passport. The roommate commented, "Ted is a big boy—I think he can take care of himself." I got extremely angry.*
>
> *Before I burst out and yelled at him, I thought about the reading and asked myself what was really going on that I was so angry and what reason could the roommate have to make that comment. I realized that when my brother hung up on me earlier, he probably was ranting about me trying to take care of him and his roommate just heard his side of the story. His roommate was trying to support Ted's cause with me. That really helped me because it allowed me to cool down and not get super angry.*

When you are in dialogue, it is another level of challenge to return to self-awareness frequently—to attend to what is outside and then attend to what is inside—outside—inside—outside—inside. If it remains peaceful inside, you can give more attention to the other person, but it is still valuable to check yourself once in awhile or keep an ear open for inner activity. Are you still present?

You are carrying a heavy load here. I have boldly challenged you to hold your own issue, to listen to the other person even when their perspective may by quite different, and to listen under any complaints and evaluations they have of you to hear their feelings and needs. This may take serious translation skills to find the needs and ignore the rest. How is your attitude?

Breathe and go slow—it will help. Drink another glass of water!

11. Speak. Get all of your feelings, needs, and concerns on the table.

> **Ayme:** *Recently, I was feeling really suffocated by my boyfriend. I was not meeting my needs for time by myself or time with my friends because every time I wanted to spend time with someone else, it turned into a huge fight. Instead of just yelling at him as usual, I decided to stop, breathe and look at what the situation actually was. I told him we both needed time to think it through. I lay down on my bed and put on some good classic rock tunes and reflected on the situation. When I was cool and collected, I called him and asked if it was a good time to talk. Then I told him how I thought. I think he seriously recognized my needs that have to be met if we are going to stay together and that it would benefit him too. We are still working on it.*

> **Brian:** *A couple of weeks ago I was trying to register for classes. Like normal I was having a very hard time doing the whole process. In previous years it was a piece of paper that you had to fill out. This year it was a stupidly confusing online process. I am not very computer savvy and I couldn't even find the courses I needed. This year the college has also set a $200 late fee for anyone not finishing the registration process by a certain date. I needed help with the whole process so I went down to the registration offices and tried to get them to help me.*

> *The woman's first response was that I needed to wait for my advisor. I politely listened and then explained that my advisor was out of town for the next five days and I needed to get this done before then. She obviously didn't have time to help me, but it was absolutely imperative to me that I finish it that day. I persisted with listening to her and holding on to my needs, explaining to her that I had been trying and I needed her help to finish this. Eventually she helped me with the process and showed me how to do it. When I finally understood I picked my courses and got the dean to sign my papers instead of my advisor. The only reason I was able to get help was because I tried to use some of the concepts from this class. I have learned how to be better assertive with my needs.*

After you understand where the other person is coming from, return to speaking about your perspective, your needs, and your concerns. Because you started out preparing for the encounter, you probably took at least several hours and maybe several days or weeks seeing that you got the careful listening you needed to clarify your own thoughts. This work will lessen the amount of time and effort needed during the conflict for you to find what you most deeply want to see happen in this situation.

Remember that your needs are valuable and that you are giving others a gift when you share them honestly. Give as much careful attention to seeing that all of your needs get on the table as you gave to the other person to help them get their needs on the table. Recall that this was your promise to yourself. I hope you will honor your commitment to yourself.

Do not consider the conversation over until you both have been fully heard, even if it takes more than one encounter.

RESOLVE

12. Summarize the needs of both parties and write them down.

> **Kelly**: *Last week I got angry at my boss for telling me how to open the restaurant. As a five-year employee, I think I am capable of opening the restaurant. I snapped at him and told him to stop looking over my shoulder all the time. When I wrote down my feelings and needs later, I saw that I felt hurt and ashamed and needed to be recognized for my contributions at work. I then thought about my boss's needs. I realized he wanted to be able to make suggestions without me flying off.*
>
> *I decided to ask if there was anything I was doing wrong and to tell him that I got myself very distressed when he barked orders at me. We had a good conversation. I see that practicing these communication skills is like developing a muscle.*

List all the needs, concerns, and hopes, as you understand them. It is very important to make this list focus on underlying needs, dreams, and interests, not on strategies.

Have one person write them all down and then check with the other person that they have accurately reflected their thinking. Notice the dreams you hold in common. (*"We both want to take a vacation this summer and we both prefer that we take that time together."*)

13. Brainstorm possible strategies and write them down.

By this time, both parties can clearly articulate the needs of the other party. As you recall everyone's intention to connect, the problem is already nine-tenths solved. Notice the rich amount of material you have to work with here.

Next, move to identifying strategies to meet the needs. Anchor this in a future perspective. Where do we want to go? What do we want to have happen? If there is no obvious strategy that meets everyone's needs fully, take the time to brainstorm new strategies. Review your written list summarizing all of needs you are trying to meet before starting the brainstorming process.

Remember that brainstorming is a time for listing creative, even wild ideas that will in any way contribute to satisfying any needs of either or both parties. It is crucial that there be no evaluation of any ideas, at this point. This process will not get off the ground if anyone makes negative or positive evaluative comments or even non-verbal expressions of judgments as people are suggesting ideas. It is a deliberate effort to activate dreams and possibilities. It is not uncommon for a suggestion that might seem silly to inspire another even more off the wall and that one to inspire a suggestion that is exactly what would move the situation forward.

To brainstorm, write all ideas for solutions down. When you run out of strategies, review the list of needs and dreams, and write down any additional strategies that emerge. After you have produced a written list of possible strategies, move to the stage of thinking together. As you slowly read each suggestion out loud, it is time to see if there is a single option or several options that you can agree might work for both of you.

14. If it is major, give it time. Wait for further inspiration.

Here is some wisdom I learned while counseling with couples. I have also read of similar results in negotiations between countries. After listing possibilities, wait a few days or even a week or two, and let new answers percolate up.

As both parties sit with an awareness of all the dreams and hopes involved, a remembrance of why they are working on the issue in the first place, and an intention to hold all needs as valuable, new solutions that had not been noticed before often emerge. It seems like magic, but it happens repeatedly. Try this out for yourself.

15. Decide on individual and joint next steps. Write them down.

> **Dorrie:** *My boyfriend lives an hour away and since I don't have a car, he ends up coming over often. My room has become his room and his socks and clothes and dirty plates are everywhere. I realized I needed my personal space back. I assured him I did enjoy his visits and company. I realized he needs some definite space in my house too.*
>
> *We agreed that he could have the large chair and a small table to claim as his own and to put all his over night things there. I am so happy I shared my needs and listened to his. We'll see how this works for both of us.*

Talk together and select the strategies that seem most promising to both of you. This will lead to a joint decision for action by each individual and by the two of you together. Write down who is going to do what and by when. It will be helpful to remember that each person is just agreeing to what seems best at the time. Because sometimes people do not know themselves well and because we cannot predict future circumstances, this is just a best guess.

<u>Do not make or expect a promise or commitment.</u> I hope you will resist the temptation to make a right-wrong rule that you can nail yourself or the other person on; and remember to aspire to let go of the false certainty of commitments and promises. Just agree to try out your newly devised strategy or strategies. Set another specific date to get back together and to hear from each party how well the planned strategy is working out for them.

What??? No commitments? No promises??

No. Not. Remember that you were just in disagreement about this issue. Let your new strategy settle in for awhile. Eventually you might want to say, "As far as I can see this is working very well for me. I imagine it will continue to do so. I promise I will do my best to bring it back up for discussion, if that ever changes."

16. Try them out. Check back on how it is working.

Each person involved needs to speak about their experiences with the chosen strategies. Of course, it is also time to tweak the plan, if you can now see together a better way of doing things.

UPGRADE

17. Start over again if it does not work the first time.

This is pretty fancy—let's get practical. What do you recommend when my roommate blows it off? We went through this whole process—my nights to do dishes are Tuesdays and Wednesdays and his are Mondays and Thursdays. In two weeks, he has done them once. Now what?

You start over! It probably did not work because your roommate did not identify accurately his needs the first time, or the situation has changed in some way. Create some more planning time for yourself. Give yourself empathy for the frustration of not getting your need for ease met. You then say to yourself, "Oh, marvelous—we now have more information. Let's try again to find a plan that really works well for all of us."

When a college builds sidewalks, they will notice soon that students are making their own paths elsewhere. At this point they can put up signs and exert effort to get everyone back on the sidewalks or they can grouse or they can say, "Oh, marvelous—we now have more information. Let's try again to place the sidewalks where they will be most useful." You have that same choices. You can exert major energy to get your roommate to follow through on their agreement, i.e. to stay on the sidewalk, or you can grouse about it or you can earnestly try to find a plan that matches needs so well that it just flows.

If you get beyond your right-wrong thinking about your roommate's choices and instead focus on his actions and the underlying needs met by whatever he did instead of the dishes, you can try again to devise a plan that meets everyone's needs. Let go of your judgment that "he blew it off" and say instead "that he did something other than the dishes." When you are able to move beyond your blaming thoughts, you will find yourself in a more creative and alive space. A commitment to truly honor both sets of needs is an electric energy. New strategies may well emerge.

Take a minute to imagine how <u>you</u> would feel if you were inaccurate in guessing your own needs and your roommate, friend, or parents responded with the belief that you still had an honorable reason for your every action and that a way to meet everyone's needs does exist and they were willing to re-engage in planning. Here are some examples of what might have happened.

- He may have been doing some other chore he saw as an equal substitute.
- He may have wanted to say "Yes" when a friend called at the last minute to go somewhere.
- He may have decided you dirtied up too many pans while cooking for someone else.
- He may have decided that it was not fair when you had a friend help you on your dishes.
- He may have decided his grades were falling behind and he needed to hit the books sooner.
- He may have planned to do them after his TV show and he just forgot.
- He may have planned to do them after his TV show and found you had already done them.

How might that look in action?

Arlene: *This morning my boyfriend, Russ, told me he liked my hair better when I straighten it rather than leave it wavy like it is today. I flipped out on him and told him he was rude and insensitive and how mad I was. He reacted defensively by yelling back at me and said I was over-reacting.*

Now that I am home, I realize that I had lots of other emotions beside anger. I am frustrated because it takes me an hour to straighten my hair and I don't always have time to do it. I felt hurt because I wanted Russ to like me no matter how my hair looks. I feel sad because I want him to think my hair looks nice.

When we considered this situation in class, we had a very lively discussion—from the analysis that Russ was trying to offer a compliment and the judgment that Arlene was acting like a crazy female (from a male who admitted he had had a similar experience), to a label that Russ was a control freak and an assessment that Arlene was willingly giving up her right to self-presentation. It took awhile to get beyond the easily accessible judgments and labels to try to find the needs that Arlene and Russ might have in this situation. Therefore I am guessing that this is a good example for us to work on here. Let's take the real conversation above and play it out several ways.

The following scenarios about Arlene and Russ are entirely fictitious.

Scenario One

Arlene has been studying diligently in this class and has started asking herself regularly, "Am I enjoying myself?" She is also doing yoga twice a week, and had a good night's sleep when Russ makes his first comment.

Arlene therefore notices her tension, manages to get her mouth shut. She picks up the coffee cups and walks to the kitchen where she first turns inside to give herself some empathy. She rages inside for a minute, expressing her "blame him—blame herself" voices.

That idiot! He is so insensitive and rude. He only sees me as a body, not a person. What a jerk! He makes me so furious. After all I do for him he only notices my hair. Well, Arlene, you know that he likes your hair fixed up—would that have been such a big deal for you to get up an hour earlier to fix your hair?

Fortunately, Arlene has worked with her blaming voices enough that she remembers to not scold herself for having these voices. She reminds herself to breathe. She next remembers that Russ cannot cause her feelings. She breathes again and becomes aware of the part of herself calmly watching the anger show put on by another part of herself.

Hmm, Arlene, I notice you are generating a lot of emotion here—it must be for some very good reason. I wonder what honorable needs you have here that are not being met or you fear will not be met and what feelings are below the anger.

Needing? Oh, I really want to be seen as a whole person. And I so want be to acknowledged for all the effort I put into this relationship. I would like it if he thought I was the most beautiful girl around, but I guess that is not really a need.

Okay. Need—what is the need under that thought? I would like to be more trusting of our connection, maybe a need for a shared reality that our relationship is the primary relationship for both of us.

No, that's not quite right. I do know that this relationship is primary for both of us. I want to relax in knowing our connection is strong.

I want my inner beauty to be acknowledged.

And what are you feeling?

Lonely—I want to be seen accurately. Even afraid. I guess I am also needing to know that I am loved no matter how I look. No, that's a strategy to support my need for esteem. Sad because I want a better connection between us, more ease in the relationship.

Arlene then becomes curious about what's alive inside Russ—what feelings and needs he has that prompted his statement about her hair. She wonders briefly if he is angry because he wants more time with her, but she reminds herself that she is not a mind reader and, fortunately, does not need to be. At that point she feels calm, curious, and ready to resume conversation with Russ.

Arlene fills the coffee cups and returns to the table.

She wants to look at him before making a guess whether it would be more effective to aim at starting the conversation by listening or by expressing her thoughts. (If he seemed stressed, aggravated, she would choose to listen first.)

She finds him watching the bird feeder out the window. He seems oblivious to her distress. Arlene is tempted for a minute to drop the whole matter, but she recalls that her needs matter and that she wants a better connection.

Arlene: (setting his coffee down in front of him) *I see the redwing blackbirds are hungry this morning.*

Russ: *Yah. Great birds.*

Arlene: *Russ, can I talk with you a minute?*

Russ: *Sure. What's up?*

Arlene: *When you commented a few minutes ago about preferring my hair to be straight, I made myself really crazy for a bit. I was telling myself . . .*

Russ: (interrupting) *Yeah, well, you over-react.*

Arlene: (deciding to find the 1% she agrees with and to agree with it 100% and to switch to listening) *That's true—sometimes I do over-react. Are you wishing I would be calmer?*

Russ: *I don't know—you keep my life interesting.*

Arlene sees that he does not seem to have much frustration about her emotional side at this moment. She also notices that this is another part of herself that has been seen and accepted by Russ, one of her hungers. She returns to wanting to share her experience with him.

Arlene: *So may I tell you about what I noticed happening inside me?*

Russ: *Sure. What's up?*

Arlene: (speaking slowly, sharing a valuable piece of her inner world) *When you commented on my hair, I told myself that my appearance was the only thing about me important to you.*

Russ: (with feeling) *That's not true.*

Arlene: *Yes, I know. I am sad that I still trip into that way of thinking so easily. It has gotten better now that I can talk about it.*

Russ: *Anything I could do to help you right now?*

Arlene: *Would you be willing to tell me three things you appreciate?*

Russ: *OK. You drive out here to see me all the time even when you are busy with school. You are trying to improve us understanding each other with your conflict class. And you bake the best biscuits in the world. Are we good now?*

Arlene: *Thanks for answering my question. I have one more request. I want to understand better where you were coming from when you said you liked my hair straight.*

Russ: *I don't know. I was just thinking about last weekend and how sexy you looked when we went out to dinner.*

Arlene: *So you were recalling last weekend.*

Russ: (smiling at her because he is learning her language) *When you dolled up, you met my need for beauty in my life.*

Arlene: *Thanks for explaining. I missed that entirely. I was telling myself that you thought I should have gotten up an hour earlier this morning to fix my hair.*

Russ: *(*change of mood*) I did not mean to hurt your feelings. Guess it was a dumb thing to say this morning.*

Arlene: *I am the one who made myself crazy, not you. And now that I understand the context, I am not doing that to myself. Do you want more coffee?*

Scenario Two

Take two. Return to the script where she emerges from the kitchen with coffee, connected to herself. This time she senses that although he is watching the birds, Russ is tense. Arlene takes another deep breath and remembers her desire to renew the connection.

Arlene: (setting his coffee down in front of him) *I see the redwing blackbirds are hungry this morning.*

Russ: *Yah. Great birds.*

Arlene: *Russ, can we talk for a few minutes?*

Russ: *Sure. What's up?*

Arlene: *I may be mistaken, but it appears to me that your jaw is clenched and your eyes kind of all scowl-ly. Are wishing for more ease between us?*

Russ: *All right, yes, I am tense. I make a simple comment and you run off to the kitchen. I can't say anything around here.*

Arlene: (deciding <u>not</u> to reflect the logic that running to the kitchen is a world better than getting into a big fight, she makes a guess about his needs.) *Are you wishing there was more peace in the house?*

Russ: *You over-react all the time.*

Arlene: (ignoring the barb and curious about his feelings and needs, questions him) *Are you wanting more acceptance for being just the way you are?*

Russ: *Well, I do not want to start World War III every time I make a comment.*

Arlene: *Aaah—you would really like a calm response?*

Russ: *Yes, that would be nice. I could drink my coffee and wake up in peace.*

Arlene: (helping him form a request, says thoughtfully) *Hmmm - more space to wake up slowly and not need to watch your words.*

Russ: *Yes, exactly. Can you do that?*

Arlene: *I don't know. I could try. It would be easier for me to stay calm if you did not make comments about my hair. Is that possible?*

Russ: *I will try.*

Arlene: *Thanks. Me, too.*

Arlene is feeling good about their connection. She checks with herself. Does she currently feel a need to share more about what her fixing or not fixing her hair means to her? She sees that she is really centered in listening and ready to listen more, so she follows that hunger. (She knows that she can and will bring up the hair discussion again, if and when it again becomes active to her.)

Arlene: *Is there anything else you want me to know?*

Russ: *Well, actually, yes. You have not been spending much time with me lately and I don't like it.*

Arlene: (translating his complaint to a positive request) *So you wish that we were spending more time together like we used to?*

Russ: *Yah, I miss you. The house is empty.*

Arlene: *Umm—a bummer, being alone so much.*

Russ: (as he is well-heard, he can move on to exploring other feelings) *Yes, but I am also proud of you for all the work you do as a student and the good grades you are getting.*

Arlene: *Oh, mixed feelings—both missing me and pride in my work.*

Russ: *Yeah, that's it in a nutshell.*

Arlene: *Thanks for helping me understand where you are.*

Russ: *Thanks for listening without blowing up. I notice you have been doing that more often.*

Arlene: *Thanks for noticing. I am pretty pleased about that, too.*

<u>CUT!!</u>

Let's reflect a minute on this extensive conversation. First, in written form, this dialogue can seem totally hokey. The music that makes it hang together is missing. You will recall that less than 10% of communication is in the actual words. I have tried to capture some of Arlene's thoughts, but the medium is limited. Second, it could have taken longer. This imagined version of a connecting conversation is probably shorter than a real life version.

Third, notice the important role that listening for connection plays. Taking the time to listen carefully is the basis for effective problem-solving. Given this space, the person being listened to will often find their way to any tender places they are ready to explore.

I observed this happen at a weeklong training in NVC that I went to several summers ago (NYIRT, NYC, July 2005). A woman shared that she was trying this kind of listening with her husband. She could not see his need, so she just guessed, "Are you tense because you are wanting more support?" He responded, "No, I am tense because I am afraid I am going blind." This was a total surprise to both the wife and the husband. He had not brought that information to his thinking mind yet and she had no clue of his fear either.

In the fictitious script above, Arlene did not need to guess about Russ' hunger for more together time. If she is able to be present in a non-demanding way, he will bring up whatever is alive for him. Recall in the first scenario, that Arlene's emotional responses were not much of an issue, at that time, for Russ. So she let it go too and stayed with his energy, his agenda.

Third, have they solved the deep issues that are stirred in both of them about how she fixes her hair? No, not directly. It is also unlikely that a discussion of the importance of aesthetics or the rights to self-presentation would have moved them much closer to resolution. The messages that they have each gathered over a lifetime about the significance of how she does her hair were not arrived at logically nor will they likely be changed logically. This is also true of most other issues we each carry—not all, but most. When I finally got a hold on this fact, I managed to usually stop wasting energy arguing issues that will seldom be resolved by any amount of logical argument and supporting evidence.

Nonviolent Communication focuses on establishing connections whereby people find joy in celebrating their own needs and in meeting each other's needs. As Arlene and Russ continue to connect—both in conversations about hair and other daily matters—it is likely that their opinions about her hair will shift until it is no longer an issue that distresses either of them. They will find some peaceful resolution.

The Arlene and Russ dialogue above is fiction. Here are three true stories from students on their path to successful conflict resolution.

Nesreen: *Recently I got into a bad argument with a close friend of mine, who is also my supervisor at work. She took me to her office and explained I was being too bossy. I was annoyed, but luckily had time during my lunch break to think about it. I knew I have the tendency to demand instead of ask, so I admitted to myself I was wrong. The problem was when she continued telling me that everything I was doing was wrong. I became angrier and angrier and made a lot of judgments in my head about how heartless she was and how she must be trying to hurt me. I did remember not to blow up at her at work.*

When I got home, I talked to my mother, who did not listen as well as I had hoped, but I did release some tension.

I worked on it for four weeks, using everything I learned in class, before I confronted my friend. I saw that I had not had much sleep the night before our initial blowup and had not even been able to get substantial food. I was hurt because I wanted my friend to think better of me and I was frustrated with how busy I was at work. With some perspective I saw I did not know her motives. Even though I wanted to ignore it, I saw that our friendship had gone downhill and I knew I needed to confront her.

I expected it to be a scary situation. I found it to be freeing. I first asked her if it would be okay if I talked for awhile and got everything out on the table. I told her everything and then made a request. If in the future I am doing a lot of things wrong, I requested she would give me only three problems at a time and three compliments as well. When she spoke, it completely amazed me. I thought she would become angry, but she understood and promised to do better. Then she added she wanted us to talk about these things more!

Akimi: *I was angry at my friend because I could not get in touch with him when we were supposed to hang out that night. "What a jerk!" I kept saying in my head. My roommate asked me if I was ok, so I started talking to her about how I was feeling. When I heard myself say, "Only thing I want is a little more attention from him" I experienced a shift in my perspective. I saw that what he wanted from our relationship was very different from what I want from it. My anger was replaced with sadness because I noticed that my needs were not going to be met in this relationship.*

After I came in touch with my emotions I considered the two choices I had; one was to communicate my feelings and needs to him, and the other was to keep my thoughts to myself and withdraw from the relationship. I was afraid to talk about my real feelings and pulled myself away from him without telling him what was going on. He got confused and withdrew too. We saw each other a week later at a bar when I was with our common friends; it was so awkward I decided to communicate with him after all.

When we sat down to talk, he was upset and blamed me for the way I acted. I listened; then I told him how I felt and what I wanted. We wanted different things from the relationship and decided it was not going to work out. However, because we talked, we also understood that we both wished to remain friends. If I had avoided communicating, I would have lost a friend and probably put our common friends in an awkward position.

Ned: *I came home from work late on a Sunday night after working twenty hours all weekend. I walked in to see a dirty house, no clean dishes, and my roommate lying on the couch still in his snowboarding pants doing nothing. Immediately I felt frustrated. Instead of getting mad and yelling at him, I decided to stop and breathe. I walked right past him to my room and sat at my computer. I saw I was judging my roommate as lazy and not caring about the house being dirty at all because he would rather relax himself and do things he enjoys like snowboarding and drinking beer.*

By writing out my judgments, I could see my needs. I wish that I could have been snowboarding all day and I shared the need to relax after a long day of work. My unmet need was that the kitchen was such a mess; I would have had to wash some dishes and clean off a counter before I could cook something for myself. [unmet needs = ease and consideration; strategy = clean kitchen]

To resolve the matter, I went back to the living room, sat on the couch next to my roommate, cracked a beer for myself, and asked how his weekend had gone. I met my first need to relax and I also expressed the fact it would be appreciated if he kept up on the house chores a lot more, especially on the weekend when everyone else is at work.

I have worked hard on the way I handle my anger this semester. Last year this same roommate and I have yelled at each other over an hour on several occasions. I have found that talking calmly to the other person and not letting these thoughts and feelings get backed up in your body is good. When anger builds up, it will erupt and you will not present your thoughts and feelings to the people around you in an appropriate manner.

FOUR STEPS AND AN ATTITUDE

OBSERVATIONS
Increase the accuracy
of how you see, think, and talk about any situation.

FEELINGS
Notice the flow of your feelings
for additional information.

NEEDS
Identify which basic human needs
are most alive for you today.

Actively consider which basic needs
are priorities for others around you.

REQUESTS
Value yourself enough
to let others know what you would like.

Value others enough
to make requests, not demands.

AND AN ATTITUDE
Realize the deep satisfaction
of connecting with yourself and others.

Intentionally reach for that connection.

LOOK AT ALL YOU HAVE DONE WITH THESE BASIC TOOLS!!!

Optional: Write a Success Script, Mind Map, or other response

CHAPTER THIRTEEN

φ

What's Next?

First, where are you now? It is time to sit back and look at the big picture. What have you learned about yourself? I hope you will take time to notice and enjoy your gains. It will energize you.

Nesreen: *Before taking this class, anger was just an emotion I felt. I either blew up at a person or held it all in and never talked about it. I was trying to fit in, but ended up losing relationships using either strategy. This class has aided me in understanding my anger and making a choice of how to deal with it.*

Shanelle: *I have begun to evaluate myself and my current situation more often to see if my life is making me happy. I have started eliminating some activities and people who were emotionally draining to me. And I have a better connection with the remaining friends. Even my parents have noticed I am happier.*

Jeff: *I used to try to win arguments simply for the sake of winning. Sometime I lost track of the point of the argument and just focused on winning. I remember pushing my roommate to do his share of the house cleaning. I brought up the past, called him names, and yelled at him. Now, I try to focus on respecting the other person and his/her side of the argument, even though I may not agree with it. I remember to find the one part I do agree with and to agree with it 100%, like we discussed in class. I also am better about keeping in mind my goal of putting the relationship first. I want to keep on doing this stuff.*

Jenny: *I'm more conscious that when I'm very stressed up, I become easily irritated at things and people that disturb me. Knowing this has made a huge difference in helping me see the cause behind my irritation or the quarrel.*

Ryan: *The third most important thing I learned from Nonviolent Communication is to connect compassionately with myself. As Rosenberg states, "when we are internally violent toward ourselves, it is difficult to be genuinely compassionate toward others." Statements such as "I should have known better!" or "I shouldn't have done that!" prevent me from learning because "should" implies that there was no choice. I am forever "shoulding" myself. When I make a mistake, I am really hard on myself afterward. Sometimes I'll even beat myself up months later.*

By forgiving myself, I connect with the need I was trying to meet when I made the action, which I now regret. By connecting with the unmet needs that existed when I made my mistake, I can liberate myself from depression. Although I haven't quite mastered this yet, it has helped me to not be so hard on myself. By recognizing the existence of choice in all my actions, I can focus on what I want rather than what is wrong with myself. This has helped me create a slightly more peaceful state of mind.

Stevie: *I know that this class has impacted me personally because even my friends tell me that I react differently to situations. My friend Eddy went as far as to tell me that he likes the new Stevie, not getting belligerent and starting fights.*

Now I steer clear of confrontation and if it arises I am quick to seek a resolution. My friend Shawn was drunk at a party the other day and was trying to get me to fight with him against some other kid who wanted nothing to do with it. I talked to Shawn on what it was about. After he talked to me he was cooled down. I like not having to worry about myself getting into a stupid situation that I never would have meant to get into in the first place.

Laurel: *The area I feel I have improved most on is to stand back and do some self-checks on myself, to be the observer, to create more awareness within myself. Go ahead and praise your accomplishments and laugh at your mistakes. I don't dwell on my mistakes as much. I now look at these "problems" as learning opportunities.*

Meg: *I have been one of those people that say something and hope it will happen without asking anything to be done. When I say, "I'm cold" and then get mad when my boyfriend does not shut the window, it's not fair. I never said to him that I wanted him to shut the window because I was cold, so it's unfair for me to get mad at him. I wasn't clear with my needs.*

I am now seeing that this doesn't work and that it does exactly the opposite of what I want to happen. I am going to try to change this. I noticed just last night and I stopped myself (after I said something, though) and thought of a better way to share my need. At least I knew enough to restate my need in a more effective way!

Allyson: *I think the biggest thing I learned about managing conflict is that my trying to avoid it only causes more conflict, which in turn leaves multiple loose ends. Just knowing that conflict is healthy and natural is a nice thing to know when my whole life I have been doing everything possible to avoid it. I have learned instead to allow myself to be angry and find out what is underneath it before expressing it.*

Matt: *I think the most important skill I am taking from this class, is to notice when you are upset, and step back, breathe, and try to figure out what the reason is for the distress. This will lead to more fulfilling relationships, fewer disagreements, and fewer fights.*

Jan: *Most of us are using all of our energy and feelings on past experiences that have stayed with us. I do that a lot. We need to understand ourselves, forgive ourselves of these past grievances and move on. Make room for more happy memories and material worth our brain space.*

Two things you have learned about yourself in this book or class

WHAT'S NEXT FOR YOU?

Maybe you see the benefit of more exercise in your life. Or maybe the need that is most alive at this time is to slow down. Perhaps this book or course has stimulated a hunger to learn more about communicating in these ways. What's next for you? And how important is it to you?

> **Sarah:** *I made three goals for myself. The first is to take at least half an hour for myself each day (even if it's simply doing yoga.) The second is to not offer to do something for someone if I am going to resent it. And third, if I find I don't want to do something after I volunteered, I want to sit down and be honest with the person, even if I know they'll be disappointed. I want to quit things with notice instead of simply not getting back to people.*

> **Megan:** *I want to continue to commit deliberate acts of self-care, whether they are big or small. I will also remember that I have control over my choices.*

> **Nick:** *When we looked at the girl and her boyfriend fighting over how she fixed her hair, I learned a lot. I saw that the needs of the girl were just as important as the guy's. Once you can see the needs of all the people involved, it makes trying to figure out what you can do differently next time much easier.*

> *Out of all this, I wish I was able to think this way more, especially during a conflict, rather than three hours after the conflict and damages are done.*

> **Amy:** *I am ready to discontinue making harmful diagnoses and assumptions so that I can give myself and others the opportunity to define feelings/needs and carry out the requests made by me and of me.*

> **James:** *I have come to realize that I have some work to do in the recognizing and meeting needs category. I also want to improve on my ability to give genuine comments that are actually meaningful to me and the other person.*

> **Abby:** *I learned in class that I could look at my issues rather than blow up at another person because of my own insecurities.*

WHAT'S NEXT?
The three most important things you want to do next.
And what request of yourself are you ready to make at this time to move in this direction?

Congratulations! You are off on your next adventure.

Closing Suggestions for Continued Improvement

- Ask yourself about the timing: "Is this the time in my life to put more energy into communication?" Find your answer from a hunger to meet your need, not from any "should."

- When you know your next step, remind yourself of your intention in some concrete way such as writing a plan or a request to yourself or a memo to put on the frig or drawing a picture.

- Inner work—become more aware of your inner voices by talking to yourself or journaling. Remember your goal is to witness with compassion, not to change anything. Ask yourself, "Am I enjoying myself?" Figure out your needs met and unmet. Give yourself empathy every time you find you are distressed.

- Outer work—some very organized people make little charts for themselves to remind themselves to practice this daily. "How many times did I really listen today?" Others make a heart commitment: "I have deep hunger to incorporate this into my life. I will remember that hunger, that vision, and act on it."

- If you are going to try to use these skills more often, you might wish to practice them with less important relationships and about minor situations, with less resting on the outcome; and then move to significant relationships and major situations. If you never try to use them until the crisis comes along, it is probable these ideas won't be very available for you to use.

- Don't worry about blowing it—regularly. Get up and take another step forward.

- It may be useful to have a conversation with close friends to give them a brief overview of what you are aspiring to do before initiating changes in your ways of interacting.

- Skill-building workshops and study-practice groups are invaluable. To move the ideas from theory to practice usually takes some work with others. Check out the website for the Center for Nonviolent Communication (www.cnvc.org) for more information about NVC and about ways you could connect for more learning—both local study groups and regional workshops.

- NVC is not your only source of information. If you go to a different training on communication skills, you will hear many overlapping ideas.

- If you are interested in how to use these skills in social action, you will find many different groups have explored making non-violence their core approach to change. Google it.

- Laugh a lot—it will help you regain your center more easily.

☺ ☺ ☺ ☺ ☺ ☺

DELVING DEEPER: ONE LAST INVITATION

↑ ↑ ↑   ↑ ↑ ↑

Recommended Books and Other Sources of Information

Bailey, Becky A. Easy to Love, Difficult to Discipline: The 7 Basic Skills for Turning Conflict into Cooperation. New York: HarperCollins, 2000.

Belgrave, Bridget and Gina Lawrie. The NVC Dance Floors. Oxford, England: Life Resources, 2003.

Bolton, Robert. People Skills: How to Assert Yourself, Listen to Others, and Resolve Conflicts. New York: Touchstone Book; Simon & Schuster, 1979.

Bryson, Kelly. Don't Be Nice, Be Real: Balancing Passion for Self with Compassion for Others. Santa Rosa, CA: Elite Books, 2004.

Chodron, Pema. The Places That Scare You: A Guide to Fearlessness in Difficult Times. Boston: Shambhala Publications, 2002.

Connor, Jane Marantz and Dian Killian. Connecting Across Differences: An Introduction to Compassionate, Nonviolent Communication. New York: Hungry Duck Press, 2004.

Covey, Stephen. The Seven Habits of Highly Effective People. Salt Lake City: Franklin Covey Co, 1989.

DeVito, Joseph A. The Interpersonal Communication Book. 12th ed. Boston: Allyn & Bacon, 2008.

Ellis, Albert. Handbook of Rational-Emotive Therapy. New York: Springer Publishing Company. 1977.

Fisher, Roger and Scott Brown. Getting Together: Building Relationships As We Negotiate. New York: Penguin Books, 1989.

Fisher, Roger and William Ury. Getting To Yes: Negotiating Agreement Without Giving In. New York: Penguin Books, 1991.

Fujishin, Randy. Gifts from the Heart: Ten Ways to Build more Loving Relationships 2nd ed. Lanham, MD: Rowman & Littlefield Publishers, 2003.

Gilbert, Daniel. (2006, July 24). He who cast the first stone, probably didn't. New York Times.

Gendlin, Eugene. Focusing. New York: Bantam Books, 1981.

Hammarskjöld, Dag. Markings. New York: Alfred A. Knopf, 1964.

Katie, Byron. Who Would You Be Without Your Story? New York: Hay House, Inc., 2008.

Killian, Dian (author) and Mark Badger (illustrator). <u>Urban Empathy: True Life Adventures of Compassion on the Streets of New York</u>. New York: Hungry Duck Press, 2008.

Leu, Lucy. <u>Nonviolent Communication: Companion Workbook</u>. Del Mar, CA: Puddle Dancer Press, 2003.

Linn, Dennis, Sheila Linn, and Matthew Linn. <u>Don't Forgive Too Soon</u>. New York: Paulist Press, 1997.

---. <u>Sleeping with Bread: Holding What Gives You Life</u>. New York: Paulist Press, 1995.

McLaglen, Mary et al (producers), and Mimi Leder (director). (2000). <u>Pay It Forward</u> [Motion picture]. United States: Warner Bros.

Maslow, Abraham. <u>Toward a Psychology of Being</u>. 1962. New York: John Wiley & Sons, 1998.

Max-Neef, Manfred A. <u>Human Scale Development</u>. New York: The Apex Press, 1991.

Mellody, Pia. <u>Facing Codependence</u>. New York: Harper & Row, 1989.

Moore, Kristin Anderson and Laura H. Lippman, eds. <u>What Do Children Need to Flourish? The Search Institute Series on Developmentally Attentive Community and Society</u>. New York: Springer Publishing Company, 2005.

Myers, Wayland. <u>Nonviolent Communication: The Basics As I Know and Use Them</u>. Del Mar, CA: Puddle Dancer Press, 2002.

Nelson, G. Lynn. <u>Writing and Being: Embracing Your Life through Creative Journaling</u>. 2nd ed. Makawao, Maui, HI: Inner Ocean Publishing, Inc, 2004.

Peacock, Fletcher. <u>Water the Flowers, Not the Weeds</u>. Montreal: Open Heart Publishing, 1999.

Perls, Fritz. <u>In and Out the Garbage Pail</u>. New York: Bantam, 1972.

Rivers, Dennis. <u>The Seven Challenges Workbook: A Guide to Cooperative Communication Skills</u>. Open Source material—see website www.newconversations.net

Rogers, Carl R. <u>On Becoming a Person</u>. Boston: Houghton Mifflin Company, 1961.

Rosenberg, Marshall B. <u>Nonviolent Communication: A Language of Life</u>. 2nd ed. Encinitas, CA: Puddle Dancer Press, 2003.

---. <u>The Nonviolent Communication Training Course</u>. (9 CDs) Boulder, CO: Sounds True, 2006.

---. <u>Speak Peace in a World of Conflict</u>. Encinitas, CA: Puddle Dancer Press, 2005.

Tannen, Deborah. <u>You Just Don't Understand: Women and Men in Conversation</u>. New York: Ballantine Books, 1990.

Some Universal Feelings

Feelings When Needs are Met

Affectionate	Ardent
Alert	Animated
Alive	Amazed
Appreciative	Carefree
Creative	Compassionate
Confident	Comfortable
Curious	Dazzled
Delighted	Eager
Engrossed	Energetic
Enchanted	Enthusiastic
Encouraged	Engaged
Excited	Exuberant
Friendly	Fascinated
Grateful	Giddy
Intrigued	Interested
Joyful	Jubilant
Peaceful	Passionate
Proud	Safe
Rested	Surprised
Stimulated	Tender
Thankful	Touched
Vibrant	Warm

Feelings When Needs are Unmet

Apprehensive	Afraid
Aggravated	Agitated
Alarmed	Annoyed
Anxious	Ashamed
Bitter	Burnt out
Blue	Baffled
Brokenhearted	Bored
Confused	Cranky
Crabby	Cross
Disturbed	Distressed
Depressed	Detached
Disappointed	Devastated
Disgusted	Despair
Embarrassed	Enraged
Exhausted	Fragile
Furious	Hurt
Heartbroken	Lazy
Lonely	Miserable
Nervous	Overwhelmed
Reluctant	Regretful
Sorry	Stressed out
Worried	Yearning

Universal Needs, described by Maslow and Rosenberg

ABRAHAM MASLOW: HIERARCHY OF HUMAN NEEDS

Physical Needs—air, food, water

Safety Needs—shelter, safety from environment and other humans

Belonging Needs—affiliation, connection with others—particular ones and community

Esteem Needs—achievement, competence, self-esteem, recognition by others

Cognitive Needs—understanding of a subject, exploration of an unknown

Aesthetic Needs—symmetry, order, beauty

Self-Actualization Needs—realization of one's potential, comfortable acceptance of oneself and the world, identification of that which one most deeply hungers to do and be doing it

Self-Transcendent Needs—connection to something beyond oneself, helping others find self-fulfillment or realization of their potential

MARSHALL ROSENBERG: SOME UNIVERSAL NEEDS

Physical Well-being Needs—air, food, water, shelter, rest, movement, touch, sexual expression

Autonomy Needs—choice of dreams / goals / values, choice in plans for fulfilling them

Integrity Needs—authenticity, meaning, purpose, self worth, way to contribute to life

Celebration Needs—honoring small successes and big successes, mourning losses of loved ones and dreams

Interdependence / Connection Needs—acceptance, appreciation, consideration, community, emotional safety, honesty, love, respect, reassurance, support, trust, understanding

Recreation / Play Needs –creativity, fun, laughter, relaxing activities

Spiritual Needs—beauty, harmony, inspiration, order, peace

Resolving Conflict Assertively

PREPARE

1. Become aware of tension and discomfort.
2. Breathe and get grounded.
3. Listen to yourself. Find underlying feelings and needs.
4. Check your attitude.

INITIATE

5. Share topic and intention. Agree upon time and place.

DIALOGUE

6. Sit down, get present, and repeat your intention.
7. State concisely your concern and invite their response.
8. Listen—seek to understand before seeking to be understood.
9. Listen—get all of their feelings, needs, and concerns on the table.
10. Breathe, slow down, and check your attitude.
11. Speak—get all of your feelings, needs, and concerns on the table.

RESOLVE
12. Summarize the needs of both parties and write them down.
13. Brainstorm possible strategies and write them down.
14. If it is major, give it time. Wait for further inspiration.
15. Decide on individual and joint next steps. Try them out.
16. Check back on how it is working.

UPGRADE

17. Start over again if it does not work the first time.

Acknowledgements

My first note of gratitude goes to Marshall Rosenberg for his vision and to the many Nonviolent Communication trainers who have given time and passion sharing this message with me and many others around the world.

Bonnie Patricia Peplow has been my editor, collaborator, and consultant throughout the entire writing, rethinking, and rewriting process. If I had given her more time to work with the final edition, she would have caught all the errors and made clear every sentence. I did not. (There are even a few paragraphs in the book that I re-vamped after she read them meticulously, line by line!) You would be safe to assume that any errors are mine.

Additional editing help has come from many sources. Using their knowledge of NVC, Ishana Ingerman and her daughter, Mika, offered many helpful comments, words, and phrases that captured my thoughts with more precise language. Maggie Randolph and Carolyn Stevens read carefully for errors and found a number when I was still innocent enough to believe that I could and had (!) caught all the mistakes. Glo Daley reflected, from her Buddhist perspective, that to ask, "How could you make your life more wonderful?" implied that life as it is day-to-day is somehow not wonderful. Substituting other words for "wonderful" has improved of the book. Jason Kelly showed me how to interrupt and stay connected. Numerous students over the years took the time to let me know some exercises were "really dumb" and often reminded me "real people do not talk like that." They then helped me find better exercises and language that made more sense to them.

The cover art was inspired by a Celtic Knot tied for me by Richard Dahl in 1980. Without this, I could never have made the one on the cover. David Hamblin, a skilled photographer, graciously agreed to forgo gardening one afternoon to make the cover picture accented by long shadows. Rick Jasany took the following photo in a Burlington garden. Emily Merrill has patiently organized the permission forms from the students. Steph Victoria looked with an artist's eye at my original layout and gently helped me upgrade from homespun to stylish, like adding the graphic doodad at the beginning of each chapter. (Steph: *"The graphic is how a visual reader knows that a new chapter has started."* Bon: *"It says Chapter Two, in great big letters. That isn't clear enough?"* Steph: *"No."* Bon: *"Oh."*) Several artistic friends agreed. I yielded the point that some music is out of my range of hearing.

My website was created by the joyful Pan Vera. Pan@i-commercesolutions.com

The less direct emotional support was equally vital. All of the above mentioned are friends and have provided emotional support as well. Jonathan McCandless gives me Quaker inspiration and keeps me up on local politics. Cheryl Burghdurf reminds me to take time for tea and laughter. Nik Gruswitz gives the most wonderful hello hugs and his sweater always smells of his Chinese herbs. Melinda Lee is an NVC buddy who encourages me to turn awareness of needs into requests. Sophie Quest has shared her delightful campsite by the lake and thoughtful discussions. Zed Zabski comes through when you need a favor. Bill Kilgour holds the reality that life changes depending on how you see it and he chooses to see goodness in everyone. My cat, Klara, has given up some of her daily brushing for the excitement of watching pages zoom out of the printer.

And a daily gratitude for the many blessings from the Universe.

About the Author

Bonnie Fraser grew up in the mountains of Colorado, and studied history and English at Maryville College, Maryville, Tennessee. She next did a variety of interesting jobs—from teaching literacy in Liberia, West Africa, and teaching junior high English in Wisconsin, to being a dorm mother at the Pennsylvania School for the Deaf, and working in residential centers for juvenile delinquents. In 1983, Bonnie got a Masters in Counseling degree from Arizona State University, Tempe, Arizona, with additional training in Gestalt Counseling and Inner Child Work. As a counselor, she has helped couples and families struggling with communication issues, people in addiction recovery, and housewives returning to the work force. In Arizona, she also taught classes in several community colleges. Recently she taught at Champlain College in Burlington, Vermont, from 1996 until she retired in 2007.

She values self-awareness and lifetime learning and can often be found in bookstores or on the internet. Bonnie is active with the Quakers. She is a contributor to Manpollo, an online group encouraging people to recognize and deal with the potential of global climate chaos.

Studying NVC has greatly enriched Bonnie's life. She frequently goes to trainings and workshops in order to enhance her own growth. She also leads NVC workshops and study groups and uses NVC in her consulting with individuals and organizations. It has brought Bonnie greater depth and ease in communicating in connecting ways.

She splits her time between Burlington, Vermont, and Scottsdale, Arizona, loving Vermont's mountains, green trees, falling snow, rainy days, and the Dobra Teahouse; and Arizona's solemn cactus, flamboyant bougainvillea, the majestic Grand Canyon, and Changing Hands Bookstore.

For questions, suggestions, or comments, e-mail Bonnie: bonnie@connectionselfcare.com or see the website, www.connectionselfcare.com or call her at 480-278-3702.